FIELD & STREAM
THE TOTAL
GUN
MANUAL

FIELD & STREAM

THE TOTAL GUN MANUAL

David E. Petzal &
Phil Bourjaily
THE GUN NUTS

weldon**owen**

CONTENTS

SHOTGUNS

DEAR READER

Sitting down in David E. Petzal's office on my first day as a junior editor at *Field & Stream* 14 years ago was a lot like shooting a gun for the first time—thrilling and terrifying.

There I was, about to work with a man whose stories I'd been devouring regularly for years (it's not hyperbole to call him a personal hero of mine), and the only thought pulsing through my brain was, *Don't screw up!*

Of course, I did so immediately by being overly eager to impress Petzal with my firearms knowledge. When it comes to guns, I had what you might call a typical rural boyhood. I lived in a house where seeing guns was as natural as seeing the lawn mower, and how you handled them—and how you did not—was pressed into my consciousness seamlessly and continuously. There were mornings spent following my father and brothers on hunts before I was old enough to get a license, afternoons out shooting milk jugs in the pasture. When I was 11 years old, I got—wrapped up under the Christmas tree with the socks and the books—my first centerfire rifle, a Model 700 in .270 Win.

But talking to Petzal, and later to Shotguns Editor Phil Bourjaily, it became very clear how much I did not know. With their typical grace and good humor, these world-class firearms and shooting experts showed me that not only was there no shame in admitting what you don't know, but that it's actually one of the most crucial steps toward becoming an expert shooter.

The world of guns and shooting is infected by the embarrassing and anachronistic idea that a lack of knowledge or experience is a direct reflection on your manhood. That attitude will only hold you back and make you look like a fool.

Both Petzal and Bourjaily have long maintained that their favorite people to teach are rank beginners who have no preconceived notions or anything to prove. Even with experienced shooters, the ones who become the most skilled, develop the deepest understanding of guns, and have the most fun are the ones who come to the task with an open mind. (Many experts believe that women, who are unconcerned with proving their manhood, are by and large better students and shooters than guys.)

My shooting improved considerably and the world of firearms became much more interesting to me when I admitted how much I had to learn. Here are just a few of the things I didn't know.

GUN SAFETY SHOULD BE SECOND NATURE, BUT YOU SHOULDN'T ACT LIKE IT IS. Do I have to tell you that if you mishandle a firearm you can kill yourself or, worse, someone else? Surely you know the rules of gun safety (they're item #1 in the book—go ahead, read them again right now). But that doesn't mean you don't have to always be vigilant. Petzal, just a few years ago, told me with horror and humility that he was chided for just once letting his muzzle stray somewhere it shouldn't have during a rifle course at Gun Site Academy. There is such a thing as getting too comfortable with firearms.

EVERYONE NEEDS INSTRUCTION. Wait, why was Petzal—a former Army Drill Sergeant, a shooter of vast experience, and one of the world's leading firearms experts—taking a riflery class anyway? He was doing it for same reason PGA pros hire a swing coach and a Major League ballplayer at the top of his form gets instruction at every game. Good shooters become great through continual instruction and endless practice. This is a lifelong process.

A LOT OF IMPORTANT TOPICS DON'T MATTER VERY MUCH. Hunters and shooters, not to mention gun writers, expel a lot of hot air debating things like ideal cartridges and best guns. There is a fair amount of this kind of thing in the pages of this book as well. That's okay. It's good fun and gives shooters something to talk about and the gun industry something to do. In the world of guns, there are so many fascinating topics to explore—ballistics, products, history—that it can keep you busy for a lifetime. Go for it. That's what being a gun nut is all about. Just don't confuse the fun stuff with what truly matters. Can you put the bullet where you want it? Everything else is secondary.

THIS ISN'T HEART SURGERY. It should be a given that much about guns and gun safety is deadly serious, but beyond that you might want to lighten up. Remember, this is supposed to be fun. Cursing every missed clay and pouting because your friend has a tighter group than you will screw with your head and turn you into a worse shot— and make you the most unpopular person at the gun club and hunting camp. Chill out before you're forced to do something drastic, like sell your guns and take up golf.

I was lucky to learn these lessons and many more from Petzal and Bourjaily, and you can too. What you hold in your hand is the distillation of more than 70 combined years of experience, delivered in the sensible, no BS style that

these two writers bring to everything they do for *Field & Stream*, whether it's a magazine story, an online blog, or a television show. We've also enlisted a small army of photographers, illustrators, designers, and editors to put together what we think is one of the most complete—and fun—books on guns and shooting ever published.

The last bit of advice Petzal gave me that day in his office was to emulate the legendary Warren Page, one of *Field & Stream*'s greatest shooting editors. Page, who actually interviewed for the Fishing Editor position but turned himself into one of the country's leading rifles expert, once told Petzal that an important part of the process involved "falling asleep every night with a gun book on my chest." Petzal gave me a reading list and advised me to do the same. I only wish that *The Total Gun Manual* had been around at the time.

ANTHONY LICATA
Editor-in-Chief
Field & Stream

THE GUN NUTS CODE

The best smell in the world is smoke curling out of a just-fired paper hull. • THERE ARE ONLY TWO THINGS THAT ARE MORE FUN THAN A GOOD ARGUMENT ABOUT CARTRIDGES, AND THEY ARE NOT LEGAL. • WHEN YOU GO TO A GUN SHOW, YOU'RE AFRAID YOU'LL SEE ONE OF YOUR OLD RIFLES AND BURST INTO TEARS. • The three men whose hands you would most like to shake, but cannot, are *John Wayne, Charlton Heston,* and *Gunnery Sgt. Carlos Hathcock.* • You measure your past life in terms of hunts you've been on: Your daughter got divorced the year you went on your first elk hunt. Otherwise you'd forget. • *You never criticize another hunter's dog, even if the owner is a good friend. You can make fun of his gun, though.* • WHEN SOMEONE TELLS YOU WHERE YOU'RE MISSING A TARGET, YOU NOD POLITELY AND IGNORE THEM. IF THEY CAN TELL YOU WHY YOU'RE MISSING, YOU LISTEN CAREFULLY. • YOU LEAVE THE CANDY BIRD FOR SOMEONE ELSE TO SHOOT. • When a gun writer says something unflattering about a rifle or cartridge you favor, you wonder whether you could take him in a fight. • HULLS AND BRASS ON THE GROUND AREN'T LITTER TO YOU. THEY ARE FOUND MONEY. • You wonder who will get your rifles after you're gone and if they'll take care of them the way you do. • *When someone mentions Africa, you wonder: How would I do in a Cape buffalo charge?* • Your all-time favorite movies are *Jeremiah Johnson* and *Quigley Down Under.* • YOU WONDER WHY THERE IS NO ONE LIKE ELMER KEITH ANYMORE. • When you have to move, your first concern is that there is a shooting range near where you're going to live. • Used guns are fine things: They have a past, they are often good deals, and the previous owner has spared you the trauma of putting the first scratch on a new gunstock. • You wonder why women outshoot you. • *If you are a woman, it's perfectly obvious why you outshoot men.* • IF YOU'VE OWNED DOGS, YOU MISS THE DEPARTED ONES MORE THAN MOST OF THE PEOPLE YOU'VE LOST. • Long ago you gave up hope that any news reporter would learn anything about guns. • YOU ARE NOT A GUN SNOB, BUT YOU BELIEVE IN DRESSING UP FOR UPLAND HUNTING. THAT MEANS NO SYNTHETIC STOCKS, NO CAMO. • If you're old enough, you're aware that our country was safer when kids could bring guns to school than it is now when kids are sent to the principal's office for wearing T-shirts with pictures of guns on them. • GUNS CAN'T LOVE YOU BACK. ON THE OTHER HAND, THEY DON'T DIE.

DAVE PETZAL

I started reading gun books at age 15 and felt bad about it because I was supposed to be studying for college. I still have a number of books from those days, and they are without exception worn, smudged, torn, and dog-eared. I've read them over and over and over because they were valuable. But they were not the only source of learning I found. Hunters, competition shooters, handloaders, and the rest of our fraternity are the greatest resource of all.

It's one thing to read how a Mauser action works and quite another to see it demonstrated by a gunsmith who works on Mauser actions. It's one thing to read how to shoot and quite another to see someone who can really shoot working his art.

This is a very good book; in fact, it's a terrific book, but it's not the be-all and end-all of firearms knowledge. It should spur you on to seek out people who can teach you. Shooters are the most generous people in the world when it comes to sharing information. You may learn so much that, someday, you can write your own book.

PHIL BOURJAILY

Converts make the most committed adherents. I grew up never wanting to shoot anything other than the occasional tin can. It wasn't until I was a senior in college, home and bored on Christmas break, that I finally went hunting with my father and one of his friends. There were a lot of birds that year, and the three of us shot and shot—and missed them all.

At the end of the hunt, a pheasant crossed in front of me, left to right, at 35 yards, a much more difficult shot than the ones I had missed all day. When I pulled the trigger, it cartwheeled into the long grass. From that moment on, I didn't want to do anything but hunt. Thirty years later, I have been lucky enough that my job is writing about shotguns for *Field & Stream*.

That's me. Now, about this book:

Recently I took a class to become a certified National Sporting Clays Association Instructor. Our teacher told us he divided students into two categories: "splitters" and "lumpers." The splitters, he said, want to you to break shooting down for them and tell them how it works. Lumpers don't care how it works as long as it works. I'll confess to being a splitter myself, but a book like this one comprises a pile of tips. Some are for splitters, some for lumpers, and some are just for pure entertainment. I hope you enjoy it.

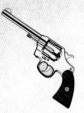

A BRIEF HISTORY OF FIREARMS

9th Century | Gunpowder
Invented in China

10th Century | Fire Lance
A bamboo tube that used gunpowder to fire a projectile is first used in China.

1360 First firing of guns from shoulder in Europe.

1475 | The Matchlock
The first gun to use a trigger, which brought a burning match into contact with the powder.

1498 The principle of rifling is invented in Germany, although it will not be used effectively until the next century.

1509 | The Wheel Lock
A spring-driven, wind-up action created a spark, which was much more efficient than the matchlock, which required a constantly-burning match.

1836 | The Pinfire
French gunsmith Casimir Lefaucheux invents the pinfire, an early modern-cased cartridge.

1836 | The Colt Revolver
Samuel Colt invents and patents the Paterson Colt revolver, powered by a percussion cap, and revolutionizes handguns.

1776 Kentucky frontiersmen coin the term "shotgun," as reported by James Fenimore Cooper.

1740s | The Pennsylvania Rifle
Created by German gunsmiths in the New World, this long rifle became an iconic hunting and military weapon in the colonies.

Late 1600s | Rifles, especially the German Jaeger flintlock rifle, become popular for hunting in Europe, especially for big game.

1630 | The Flintlock
With a more reliable ignition system and faster lock time, this gun made wingshooting feasible.

1857 | Smith & Wesson Revolver #1 Horace Smith and Daniel Wesson make the first Smith & Wesson revolver, chambered for the first .22 rimfire cartridge, the .22 short.

1874 | Winchester Rifle Model 1873 Rightly famous as "the gun that won the West."

1875 | Boxlock Action
Two British gunsmiths, Anson and Deeley, design a hammerless action for shotguns that is still in use in guns today.

1950 | Remington 870
This slide-action shotgun became the most popular gun ever made, selling more than 10,000,000 units over the years.

1880s Smokeless powder revolutionizes rifle ammunition, doubling the velocity of black-powder ammo. Smaller-diameter bullets are now practical, and ranges are dramatically increased.

1947 | AK 47
The Kalashnikov AK-47 is issued to the Soviet Army, and becomes the most popular and effective military rifle of all time.

1955 | AR 10
Invented by military arms designer Eugene Stoner, this gun was a precursor to the AR 15/M16, America's military rifle.

1882 | Pump-action Shotgun
Christopher Spencer, inventor of the Civil War–era Spencer repeating rifle, makes the first pump-action shotgun.

1887 | Mondragon Rifle
Mexican general Manuel Mondragon patents the first fully automatic rifle.

1936 | Winchester Model 70
This bolt-action sporting rifle is widely regarded as one of the best hunting guns ever made.

1956 | .44 Magnum
Smith & Wesson introduces the Model 29 revolver, chambered for the revolutionary .44 Magnum cartridge.

1898 / Mauser 1898
Peter Paul Mauser perfects his bolt-action Model 98; a military weapon for 50 years, it is still unsurpassed for sporting use.

1934 | The .357 Magnum
Developed as the first magnum handgun cartridge, the .357 was unsurpassed in power until the advent of the .44 magnum in 1955.

1963 | Remington Model 1100
The first reliable gas semiauto shotgun's soft recoil quickly makes it a favorite of hunters and target shooters alike.

1985 | Inline Muzzleloader
Missouri gunsmith Tony Knight's reliable, easy-to-maintain rifle attracts countless new blackpowder hunters.

1900 | Auto 5
Gun designer John Browning patents the first successful semiautomatic shotgun.

1990s Sabot slugs and rifled shotgun barrels begin a revolution in shotgun slug accuracy that continues today.

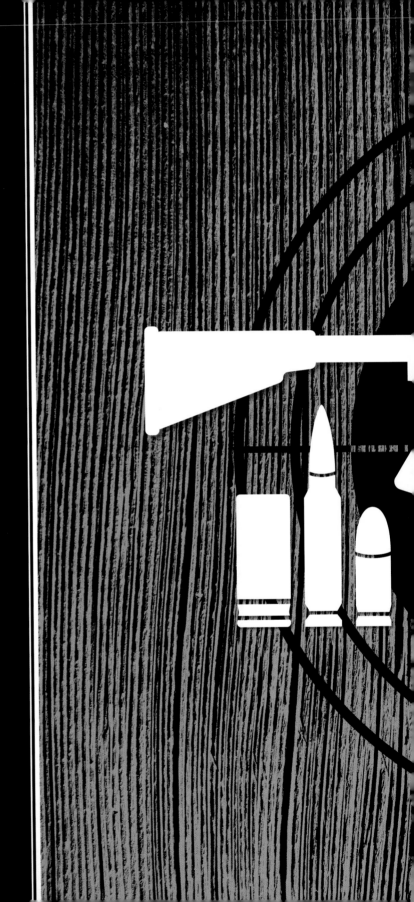

GUN BASICS

1 FOLLOW THE BASIC SAFETY RULES

If you've been shooting for any time at all and had any kind of proper education (by which we mean anything from a firearms certification class to a big brother who slapped you upside the head for acting stupid), you should know these rules. We're reminding you here because it never hurts to be reminded and because reading it together is a great starting point for a discussion about safety with a kid or any new shooter,.

ASSUME EVERY GUN IS LOADED Every time you see a gun, pick up a gun, or point a gun, always assume that it's loaded, and treat it accordingly.

CARRY SAFELY Make sure your safety is always on and that the barrel is pointing down when you are walking with or transporting your gun. The one exception is when you're hunting with a dog; see item 220.

BE SURE OF YOUR TARGET Be absolutely sure that you are shooting at an animal and not a human and that no people are anywhere near the animal you are shooting at. Never shoot at a sound or movement.

DRESS RIGHT Wear at least the required amount of orange so that you don't become another hunter's target.

CONFIRM YOUR KILL Make sure all animals are dead before you put them in or strap them onto your vehicle.

BE KID SMART Do not bring small children with you hunting. Wait until your kids are old enough to understand and follow all of these rules before you bring them hunting.

CLIMB CAREFULLY Do not climb up or down a tree or over a fence with a loaded gun.

KEEP YOUR FINGER CLEAR Make sure your finger stays off the trigger until you're ready to shoot.

SHOOT SOBER It's just plain common sense. Save those beers until the end of the day.

REMEMBER RANGE Look well beyond your target before you shoot. High-powered ammunition can travel up to three miles and still be deadly.

BUDDY UP Hunt with a buddy. If you can't, then at least make sure that someone knows where you will be and a time to expect you back.

STRAP IN If using a tree stand to hunt, don't forget to wear a safety belt. A lot of hunting injuries involve falling from a tree stand. And you don't want to have to tell the guys at work that's how you broke your arm.

CHECK IT OUT Before you begin the hunting season and before you use any new or borrowed equipment, make sure to go over everything and make sure that it is working properly. Make sure you know how everything operates before you attempt to use it while hunting.

STORE SAFE Store and transport ammunition separate from your guns. Keep everything under lock and key when it's not in use.

2 DON'T BE THAT GUY

You're ready to go, with the latest and greatest gear, you're carrying the latest and greatest rifle or shotgun, and you're off to hit the woods to give the game what for. Before you take one step onto the hunt, however, stop and make sure you aren't making a fool of yourself.

CHOOSE THE RIGHT CAMO We have camo up the kazoo, but it's all Southern—southern swamps, southern oaks, southern kudzu, and southern highway litter. You won't find Dismal Swamp in Wyoming. Wear it, and the animals will take off laughing.

KNOCK OFF THE SHINE When the whole world is brainwashed by camo, why do shiny rifles still sell? You might like shiny, but animals will see it and think, "Why die when I can run?"

FORGET "BREATHABLE" Those cool clothes are fine until you start to hustle. Then you'll be roasted in your own juices. Down, synthetic insulation, and oiled cotton are the clothing equivalent of a Dutch oven.

GET A WHIFF There are tons of ads for poly underwear "treated to resist odor-causing bacteria." Don't believe a word of it. And don't waste your money.

3 WALK LIKE AN ANIMAL

The sound of a human crashing through the brush silences the woods and spooks game. To see more, you must pay attention to your pace, your walking rhythm, and the placement of your feet.

SLOW DOWN Give yourself time to pick your route, step quietly, and notice what's going on around you. Slowing your pace allows you to hear more; your own footfalls can block out the sound of a squirrel cutting nuts or a gobbler drumming. Looking back from time to time also helps you find your way home at the end of the day.

VARY YOUR GAIT A steady drumbeat of steps signals *human* to any animal in the woods. Take a few steps and pause to look and listen. When you do stop for a moment, make sure you're near a wide tree trunk, a brushpile, or some other cover that provides concealment.

LOOK BEFORE STEPPING All animals, from chipmunks to whitetails, rustle leaves when they walk in the fall woods. Humans snap branches. Keep most of your weight on your back foot as you step forward and then set your foot down carefully, heel first.

GET ANOTHER WHIFF Deer scents may be the cat's meow for bowhunters who must work close in, but they're just silly for the rest of us.

TRUMP TECHNOLOGY WITH SKILL A hunter used to be a person who acquired a broad variety of skills by spending tons of time in the woods and working very hard at his craft. Now, the assumption is that you can bypass much of the process if you spend enough money. There's no substitute for know-how, so get out there and learn.

RESPECT THE GAME Killing is a part of hunting, but hunting is not simply killing. There is only one way to look at an animal you have just killed, and that is in sorrow. People who hate hunting will never believe or understand that, but who cares?—D.P.

TRACK AROUND OBSTACLES Follow the path of least resistance through the woods. Most hunters prefer to see where they're putting their feet, so they step onto and over blowdowns, especially in snake country. In truth, the best tack is to make a detour around obstacles whenever possible to save energy and to keep a lower profile.

Unless you're trying to flush rabbits or ruffed grouse, avoid thickets that may catch your clothing, making unnatural sounds. If you're walking with someone, go single file. Maintain an interval of several steps between the two of you so the person behind doesn't get swatted in the face with a branch.—P.B.

4 GET FIT FOR HUNTING SEASON

We've all listened to our pounding hearts during exercise since we were kids. We're so used to that sound, in fact, that it can be a surprise to wear a heart-rate monitor on a hunt. It doesn't take much effort to elevate your heart rate into the red, so make sure you exercise in those off months for better fitness on your hunt and a healthier life all around.

START WITH A STRESS TEST Treadmills and EKG monitors can reveal arrhythmias and arterial blockages that put you at risk for heart attack. If you are diagnosed with heart disease, your doctor can help you treat it properly and keep you able to hunt for years to come. As a precaution,

carry an uncoated aspirin in your pocket when you're in the field. There's no such thing as being overprepared.

GET WALKING Once you've got the green light from your doctor, get in shape with a sensible aerobic exercise routine. The fitter you are, the harder you can work your heart. Exercising as little as 20 minutes three days a week at 65 to 85 percent of your maximum heart rate can make a profound improvement in your overall fitness. It might not seem like much right now, but definitely you'll notice the improvement when you're packing out 60 pounds of elk meat. —D.P.

5 FIND A FRIEND

According to studies on primitive humans, a single man alone in the wilderness is lucky if he survives more than a year. Without help around, something will do him in. This same rule was echoed by a guide who operated out of Anchorage, Alaska: "Don't ever hunt alone in this state."

I once hunted caribou in northern Quebec with a tough 19-year-old guide. I had shot a caribou, and we were on our way back to the boat, him carrying a tumpline pack that probably weighed 150 pounds. Not far from the boat, he stepped into a bog hole and immediately sank up to his neck. He was in big trouble, and it took the two of us to wrestle him out of the pack and work him free. We were lucky. If he had been alone, he probably would have died.

Another incident involved a cowboy of considerable skill who ran a trapline during winter. One day, somehow, he lost his seat in the saddle. One foot hooked in a stirrup, and his horse walked 25 miles back to his ranch, dragging the man slowly to death. If there had been someone else around, he might have escaped with nothing more than some bruises and a headache. Pick your friends carefully. When you head into the field, take them along.—D.P.

6 DITCH BAD COMPANY FOR YOUR OWN GOOD

Some shooters and hunters are unsafe and will always be unsafe. It doesn't matter whether it's through stupidity, a short attention span, or an agitated disposition. If you find yourself in their presence, leave. Right away. You don't need to make excuses, although if you explain the reason for your departure it may do some good. Either way, just pick up and go elsewhere smartly, in a military manner.

I've done this at least four times. One was at a non-registered trapshoot where a brand-new shooter was put next to me on an experienced squad. He came unglued and sent a charge of shot into the ground a foot in front of me. I walked off the squad. The second time was at a quail hunt in South Texas where about a dozen hunters were shooting all at once and in all directions and very close together. Number three was on a nilgai hunt in South Texas where the halfwit outfitter ordered six of us hunters to stand in a mob and fire at a fleeing herd of the animals. There was a guy standing behind me shooting past my head. Four was on a whitetail drive in eastern Montana where one hunter's mindless offspring were racing around out of control.

In the best of all possible worlds, everyone who handles a gun would be safe, but this is not the best of all possible worlds. Leave. Now.—D.P.

BUY YOUR KID A RIFLE

Watch a kid play a video game, and it's easy to tell why my recommendation for his first gun is a single-shot .22. The majority of these rifles will be bolt actions, and they'll serve you and your offspring well. Here are some thing to consider.

STAY STEADY A rifle needs to be a lot more than just a way to make mountains of shell casings. The single-shot forces him to load one round at a time, which encourages him to not waste that round when sending it down range.

KNOW YOUR TARGET Show me a kid shooting a .22 with a larger-capacity magazine, and I'll show you a kid who'll use every one of those rounds to hit his target. There's no need to aim if he can just pour dozens of rounds in the general vicinity. Make him consider each shot.

SAVE YOUR MONEY A brick of .22 cartridges won't set you back terribly much. But the habits that kid forms with this first rifle will follow him the rest of his life. Teach him not to be wasteful.

RESPECT THE RIFLE It's not a toy, and it's your job to teach him that fact. There's no reset button on a rifle. A mistake here can kill someone.

DOUBLE DUTY The single-shot .22 will be great for learning range basics and plinking. And since most youngsters start off in the field hunting small game, the .22 is an obvious first choice.

GET JUNIOR A SHOTGUN

A 20 gauge is by far the best first gun for kids. The guns are light and slim, yet the ammunition packs enough shot that it's an easy gauge to hit with. The .410 can make hitting the target too hard, and the 28 is too expensive to shoot and limited in nontoxic choices.

THE CASE FOR A PUMP Inexpensive pumps are easy for small hands to operate; pulling the bolt handle of many autoloaders requires strength. Moreover, pumps are safer than autos or two-barreled guns once you begin loading more than one shell at a time, as you have to work the action to chamber a second round.

THE CASE FOR A SEMIAUTO Lightweight youth pumps kick. The recoil reduction of a gas semiauto makes it a better choice for kids who'll practice a lot. Loaded with one shell at a time, the semiauto is just as safe as a pump. You'll find that the first time you let kids load all three shells in a semiauto in the field, they'll empty it every time without hitting anything.

THE CASE FOR A DOUBLE Any break action has the advantage of safety. It's easy to see when a break action is open and completely incapable of shooting, and you can open it and peek down the bores to be sure they're unobstructed. That said, it also combines the disadvantages of a pump and a semiauto: it has the recoil of the pump and the instant follow-up/ammo-wasting capability of a semiautomatic. —P.B.

9 BUILD YOUR HOME GUN BENCH

While I leave major jobs to a gunsmith, I like to be able to take guns apart and put them back together, mount scopes, switch stock shims, and so on myself. My gun bench contains the following:

THE BASICS

- A gun cradle to hold guns so I can work on them with both hands
- A Phillips-head screwdriver for removing recoil pads
- A large flat screwdriver for removing stock bolts
- Mini versions of both flat and Phillips-head screwdrivers
- A socket wrench with extension for removing stock bolts that don't have slotted heads
- A spanner made for removing pump forearms
- A set of roll pin punches
- A set of gunsmithing screwdrivers with interchangeable heads so I don't mar any screws

- Loctite (blue) for scope mounting
- Scope levels
- Allen and Torx wrenches for scope mounting
- Brass/nylon hammer for tapping without denting
- A vise-grip pliers for grabbing things that are really stuck or for holding small parts while I butcher them. Also, good for pulling teeth.
- A set of jeweler's screwdrivers for very small screws.
- A Leatherman Wave multi-tool, mostly for its needle-nose pliers
- A complete set of hex wrenches
- A trigger-pull scale

ON MY WISH LIST:

- Brownell's padded magazine cap pliers
- A Hawkeye Bore Scope that connects with a TV screen so I can really get a good look inside a barrel.

I AM ALWAYS OUT OF:

- Spray cans of compressed air
- Birchwood Casey Gun Scrubber

CLEANING AND LUBRICATING SUPPLIES

- Cleaning rods with phosphor-bronze brushes and wool mops in all gauges (10-gauge brushes make good 12-gauge chamber brushes)
- Old toothbrush
- Round brushes
- Plastic pick (looks like a dental tool)
- Cotton patches
- Rags
- 0000 steel wool
- Shooter's Choice Grease for hinge pins and magazine cap threads

- Birchwood Casey Choke Tube grease
- Gun oil in spray cans and bottles (Not WD-40)
- Birchwood Casey Gun Scrubber or Liquid Wrench for thorough action cleanings
- Spray can of powder solvent for bore cleaning
- A box of Q-tips
- A can of lighter fluid for small degreasing jobs

- A bottle of lens cleaner for cleaning scope lenses. Also, lens tissue.
- A jar of Brownell's Action Lube (pretty much the same stuff as choke-tube grease)
- A bottle of clear nail polish for freezing trigger screws in place
- Many jars of J-B Non-Embedding Bore Cleaning Compound
- Shooter's Choice Powder Solvent

10 PROTECT YOUR HOME WITH A HANDGUN

Although handguns are by far the most popular home-defense firearms in America, they are also the most difficult to hit with. Just scoring well on a paper target is tough, but when your life is on the line? The New York City Police Department, which is allegedly trained in combat shooting, expends 74 rounds for each hit on human targets.

How about rifles? Poor choice. Their extreme range and tremendous penetration make them hazardous to other people besides bad guys, and they are only marginally easier to hit with than a handgun. Your best choice may well be a short-barrelled shotgun, as discussed in item 11. A charge of nine oo buckshot is the equivalent of that many 9mm bullets, and they will stop just about anyone. Shotguns are great intimidators, and may get you out of trouble without a shot being fired. Few people get brave looking down the muzzle of a shotgun.

If you're set on a handgun, here are some things to consider: For home use, as opposed to concealed carry, a long barrel (5 or 6 inches) is much easier to hit with than a short one. Revolvers are simpler to operate than automatics, but autos hold twice as many shots. If your handgun of choice doesn't have them, have luminous sights installed. The smallest usable caliber is .22 Long Rifle, and the largest is .45 ACP and .357 Magnum, both of which kick. The best choices are the .38 Special, 9mm, and .40 S&W.

Above all, remember that hitting with a handgun is a perishable skill. Practice as if your life depended on it. Because it does.—D.P.

11 USE A SHOTGUN FOR DEFENSE

Despite what you see in the movies, buckshot can't knock down walls or send people flying through the air. Nevertheless, shotguns make devastating close-range defense weapons. According to a recent Harris/National Shooting Sports Foundation poll, "home protection" is the leading reason Americans purchased their most recent firearm, so it's not surprising that Federal, Remington, and Winchester have developed new home-defense loads ranging from birdshot in .410 to oo buck over a slug in 12 gauge.

What makes a "home defense" load? Loads designed for indoor use have to pattern openly to hit a close-range target. They have to stop, incapacitate, or dissuade an attacker; ideally, pellets that don't hit the target won't pass through several walls to harm family members and neighbors. Most home-defense shootings occur at a range of 5 to 7 yards, so to test home-defense loads, I did my patterning at that distance, with a few longer 10- to 15-yard shots thrown in. Here's what I learned.

IT ALL GOES THROUGH WALLS Birdshot easily penetrates two thicknesses of wallboard; buck may shoot through half a dozen. Years ago I blasted a hole through the side of a chicken house with No. 7 ½ shot while trying to defend our flock from a weasel.

RIFLING AND BUCKSHOT DON'T MIX Rifling spins pellets in an expanding donut pattern. At seven steps, every single pellet of a oo buck load missed a 14x16-inch target—twice—from my Deerslayer.

SHOTGUNS ARE NOT AREA WEAPONS At typical five-to-seven-step home-defense range, even an open choke throws a pattern only 6 or 7 inches wide. That said, the advantage of shot over bullets is margin for aiming error. A 6-inch pattern 7 inches off center will still put some pellets into the vital zone.

PATTERN YOUR SHOTGUN An unchoked sawed-off shotgun is supposed to spray the widest patterns of all. Rather than put a hacksaw to my Benelli, I screwed in a pure Cylinder tube and tried both Federal 4 buck and a hunting load of ooo buck. Surprisingly, the Cylinder shot tight 3-inch clumps at 5 yards with each. With an Improved Cylinder choke, the patterns opened up to 6 inches. Based on my results, I would recommend Skeet or IC chokes. But before you trust your life to it, shouldn't you find out how it shoots?—P.B.

RIFLES

AND HANDGUNS

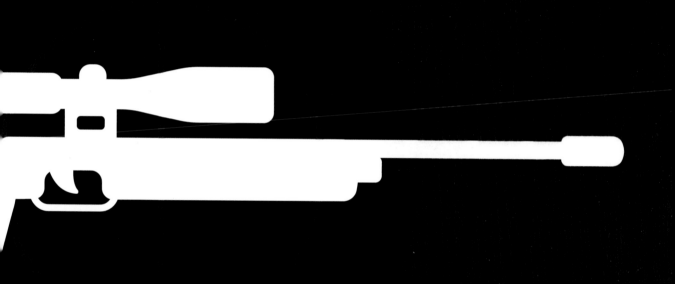

12 UNDERSTAND RIFLE ANATOMY

Rifles are exceedingly simple machines with very few parts. However, like computers or automobiles, they have their own jargon, which you must master if you are to learn about them. This is the basic nomenclature. Learn it, and the next time someone uses the phrase, "lock, stock, and barrel," you can explain its derivation. Isn't that worth the effort?

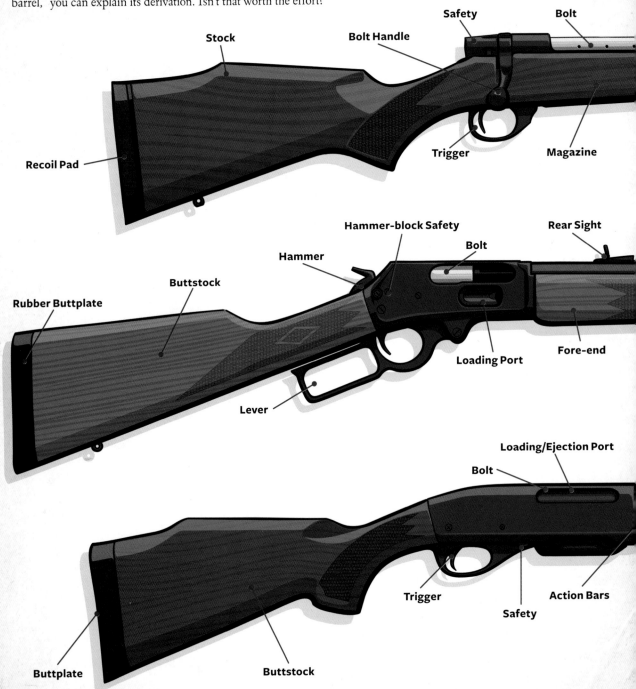

Stock

Safety

Bolt Handle

Bolt

Recoil Pad

Trigger

Magazine

Hammer-block Safety

Rear Sight

Hammer

Bolt

Buttstock

Rubber Buttplate

Loading Port

Fore-end

Lever

Loading/Ejection Port

Bolt

Trigger

Action Bars

Safety

Buttplate

Buttstock

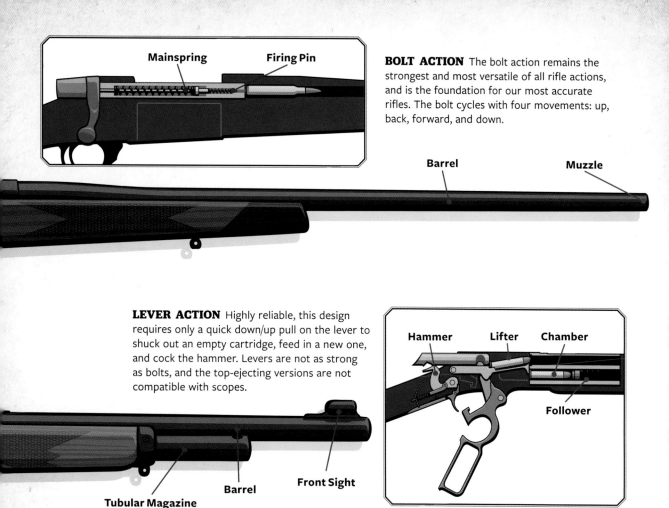

BOLT ACTION The bolt action remains the strongest and most versatile of all rifle actions, and is the foundation for our most accurate rifles. The bolt cycles with four movements: up, back, forward, and down.

Mainspring   Firing Pin

Barrel   Muzzle

LEVER ACTION Highly reliable, this design requires only a quick down/up pull on the lever to shuck out an empty cartridge, feed in a new one, and cock the hammer. Levers are not as strong as bolts, and the top-ejecting versions are not compatible with scopes.

Hammer   Lifter   Chamber

Follower

Tubular Magazine   Barrel   Front Sight

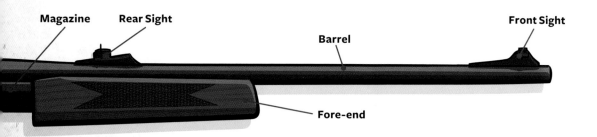

Magazine   Rear Sight   Barrel   Front Sight

Fore-end

PUMP ACTION The pump, or slide, action shares the speed and simplicity of the lever action, but is considerably stronger. In addition, it works well with modern cartridges and scope sights. To use, you just pull back on the fore-end and slam it forward and you're ready to shoot again.

13 SPEND YOUR MONEY WISELY

There are only three rational courses to pursue when buying a rifle:

ONE If all you can afford is a cheap gun, get a good cheap gun, get it a trigger job if it needs one, and let it alone.

TWO If you want something classy but don't have thousands of dollars to buy a true custom working rifle, save up your pennies until you have about half that amount and get a Kimber Model 84, or a Weatherby Mark V, or a Nosler Model 48 Trophy Grade, or a Sako Model 85, or three or four others that I can't call to mind right now. Are these rifles really worth twice as much as guns that cost, say, $800? Yes. Will you be tempted to "improve" them? Only if you're brain damaged.

THREE If you want to go whole hog and get a rifle from D'Arcy Achols, or New Ultra Light Arms, or the Remington Custom Shop, or Montana Rifles, or anyone in that exalted company, then you will want to think very long and hard before you even start saving. Much of what you are buying is intangible, and we will get into those details in another entry later on in this book.

14 TRY THE TRIGGER

Figuring out if you have a good trigger or a bad one is not rocket science. There are three important components to any trigger pull:

CREEP describes the movement of the trigger before it breaks and releases the sear, which releases the firing pin. Your trigger should have no creep at all: You pull and it should just go off.

WEIGHT OF PULL is the pounds and ounces of pressure it takes to make the trigger break.

OVERTRAVEL is the distance the trigger moves after it breaks. If there is excess overtravel, it will disturb your follow-through after you shoot.

15 KNOW WHY SHORTER IS BETTER

For a big-game rifle barrel, I think the most practical length is 22 inches. If you have a magnum, 24 is the most you want, and you can get away with 23 inches unless you're shooting something like a 7mm Shooting Times Westerner.

I've found that whatever small ballistic advantage you gain with a barrel over 24 inches is more than offset by the added weight and length. About a year ago, I grew fed up with the 26-inch barrel on a .338 Remington Ultra Magnum Model 700 and had it cut back to 23½ inches. Despite the huge charge of slow powder in this cartridge, I lost only 38 fps, and accuracy improved dramatically (which often happens, but not always, when you chop a barrel).

I have only two rifles with 26-inch barrels. One is a .220 Swift, where I want all the velocity I can get and other considerations come second. The other is a .300 Weatherby, which I reserve for situations where I know I'm going to take long shots or none at all, and I won't have to carry the thing around very much.

16 TAKE STOCK

When it comes to picking a stock, you have three basic choices. Here's how they stack up:

COMPOSITE Most composite stocks are made of fiberglass reinforced with other materials such as graphite and/or Kevlar. They tend to be expensive because they are built one at a time, by hand. But they are terrific stocks. A few composites are made of Kevlar and graphite; they are the lightest and strongest of all but are definitely going to be quite expensive.

FIBERGLASS Outmoded for fly rods but makes a terrific stock. Very strong, light, dead stable, and not as expensive as some other stock types. You can even get the paint "integral" with the fiberglass, which means you can polish out scratches with fine steel wool. Army and Marine sniper rifles employ fiberglass stocks.

LAMINATED WOOD Very strong and, if properly sealed, very stable as well. Laminated stocks can be made of one type of wood or of several types and left natural colored or stained. Some are quite good looking. This type of stock is often preferred by shooters who are looking for strength and stability but regard a "plastic" stock as they would a venomous reptile.

17 WEIGH YOUR OPTIONS

In rifle design, everything is a trade-off. When you remove weight, you make a rifle easier to carry, but you also make it harder to hold steady, and sometimes you need steady very badly. Years ago in Colorado, I was hunting elk at 8,000 feet and spotted a 5x5 bull uphill from me. The only way I could get a shot at the unfortunate ungulate was to sprint 40 yards nearly straight up to a little plateau.

Since sprinting 4 yards on the flat at sea level is an effort for me, I was on the verge of having a coronary by the time I got into shooting position, but I was nonetheless able to aim, courtesy of the 9¼-pound .338 I was carrying. It was no fun to lug around, but it was steady even when my chest was heaving like a bellows.

Recoil is also affected. A light rifle, chambered for a hard-kicking cartridge, will pummel you. The only way to avoid this is to use a muzzle brake, which creates problems of its own, including added length and weight and an inhuman ear-shattering muzzle blast.

Based on my own experience, here's a rough guide to what big-game rifles should weigh with scope aboard:

.243 up through .270: 6 ½ to 7 pounds

.30/06 through the .30 magnums: 7 ½ to 9 pounds

.338 Winchester, .338 Remington Ultra Magnum, .340 Weatherby, .375 Holland & Holland: 9 to 10 pounds

.416 Remington or larger: 9 ½ to 12 pounds

18 CHECK THE BASICS

Congratulations on your new rifle, and I wish you much joy in your future relationship. I trust that you haven't bought anything that is shiny, or too heavy, or too light, or that kicks more than you can handle. If all that is in good order, then your next step is to find out how well the thing actually shoots—or doesn't.

First, you want to weigh the trigger with a spring gauge, or ask your gunsmith to do it. It should break at not less than 3 pounds and no more than 4. Some very good modern factory triggers require no work at all, but there are also a lot of dogs. If yours barks, it's off to the gunsmith. There's no getting around this. A bad trigger on a rifle is like bad steering on a car.

At the range, load the magazine and see that the rifle feeds reliably. A surprising number don't, particularly those chambered for short, fat cartridges. If your gun is a bolt action, don't work the bolt timidly; slam it back and forth. That's the way they're designed to be used. It should go through chambering, firing, extracting, and ejecting without a hitch. If it doesn't, send it back to the factory or take it to a gunsmith. Or you can take it out hunting and hope that it will work.

Next, you're going to want to check for accuracy. Make sure that the scope-base and bedding screws are properly tightened. These are often installed by uncaring hourly-wage workers, and you can save yourself lots of grief with a few turns of a screwdriver.

Speaking of pain and woe, don't mount your scope unless you know how to do it correctly. This is so much of a problem that two gunmakers I know refuse to sell their rifles unless they perform this job. Have a gunsmith do it.

The more precisely you can aim, the more accurately you'll shoot. Generally, you want to have at least 8X available, but personally, I like 9X or 10X a lot better, and on varmint rifles I consider 20X the minimum. Make sure your scope actually works while you're at it.

More than once I've seen cases in which a gun seemed to just go haywire, but it was actually the scope that went weird. It's easy to spot one with loose adjustments or a busted reticle: The point of impact won't move up or down or right or left with any consistency, and the rifle it's mounted on won't group at all. Few guns, no matter how accuracy-impaired, won't give you some kind of a group if the scope is working.

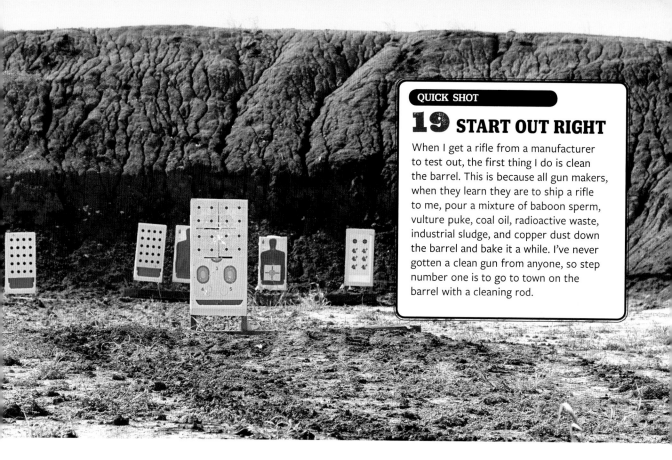

19 START OUT RIGHT

When I get a rifle from a manufacturer to test out, the first thing I do is clean the barrel. This is because all gun makers, when they learn they are to ship a rifle to me, pour a mixture of baboon sperm, vulture puke, coal oil, radioactive waste, industrial sludge, and copper dust down the barrel and bake it a while. I've never gotten a clean gun from anyone, so step number one is to go to town on the barrel with a cleaning rod.

20 TAKE IT FOR A TEST DRIVE

Once you know your rifle is basically sound, you'll want to pick your ammo. Let's say your new rifle is a .270. Choose from among 130-, 140-, or 150-grain bullets. What matters most is the type: Do you want tough, premium slugs for tough animals or the squishy, standard variety for squishy animals? When you decide, buy a box of each weight in the appropriate type and see which gives you the best groups.

You should do your shooting as early or as late in the day as possible. The more sun there is, the more mirage there is. Avoid wind. At 100 yards, anything short of a gale has little effect on big-game bullets, but strong air currents are fatal to rimfire accuracy and no help if you're trying for very small groups with a varmint rifle.

If you're shooting at a public range, pick a bench where you are not next to some dunce who thinks he is Rambo and is blasting away with a semiauto that spits empties at you. If this happens to me, I pin a tag that says "leprosy patient" on my shirt. People clear the area pretty quickly.

Don't let your barrel get so hot that you can't hold on to it. If an electrical outlet is handy, bring a fan along and stand the rifle in front of it for a few minutes. Or, find some shade and stand it butt down, barrel up. It'll cool faster. Clean the barrel every 20 rounds.

YOUR GOALS:
- Get at least three (or if you're of a suspicious nature, go for five) consecutive three-shot groups of 1½ inches or less for a big-game rifle, and five-shot groups of ½ inch or less for a varmint gun or a .22. Shoot at 100 yards, except for rimfires, which should be shot at 25 yards. Really good big-game rifles should print under an inch and varminters close to ¼ inch.
- There should be no flyers, which are errant shots not caused by shooter error.
- All the groups should be printing in the same place on the target.

That's it. If you want to sum up all of this advice in a single sentence, "Make sure the damn thing works" would do nicely. It's amazing how many people never take the trouble.

LEVER ACTION The familiar cowboy gun of the American West, the lever action is worked by pulling down on a lever located at the trigger and then returning it to a locked position. These guns are surging in popularity due to new cartridge designs that allow for aerodynamic polycarbonate-tip bullets to be used in the tubular magazines.

BOLT ACTION By far the most popular action among hunters, the bolt-action rifle is opened and closed manually by lifting and pulling a protruding handle that looks similar to a door bolt. Closing the bolt chambers a fresh round, which is lifted from a magazine located underneath the action. Strong and dependable, the bolt action is very accurate.

MODERN SPORTING RIFLE Built in the style of the M-16, the modern sporting rifle is essentially a semiautomatic firearm with an ergonomic stock and protruding magazine that has long defined military arms. Also called ARs (Armalite made the first models in the 1960s), these firearms are not fully automatic.

PUMP Pump rifles are operated by sliding the fore-end to the rear, which ejects the fired cartridge, and then sliding it forward, which chambers a new round. Not as popular as autoloading rifles, pump rifles do have a strong following, particularly in Pennsylvania, where hunting with an autoloading rifle is illegal.

SEMIAUTOMATIC Using a small part of the gas created by the combustion of a cartridge's powder, semiautomatic rifles automatically eject and chamber cartridges with each pull of the trigger. Also called "autoloaders," they offer quick follow-up shots that don't require the shooter to manipulate a bolt or lever.

SINGLE SHOT Single-shot rifles must be reloaded after every shot. Break-action single-shot rifles are opened at the breech for reloading. Other examples include the "falling block" single-shot action, in which the breech is opened by moving a lever on the underside of the gun. Single-shot rifles are very safe to operate, very accurate, and very strong.

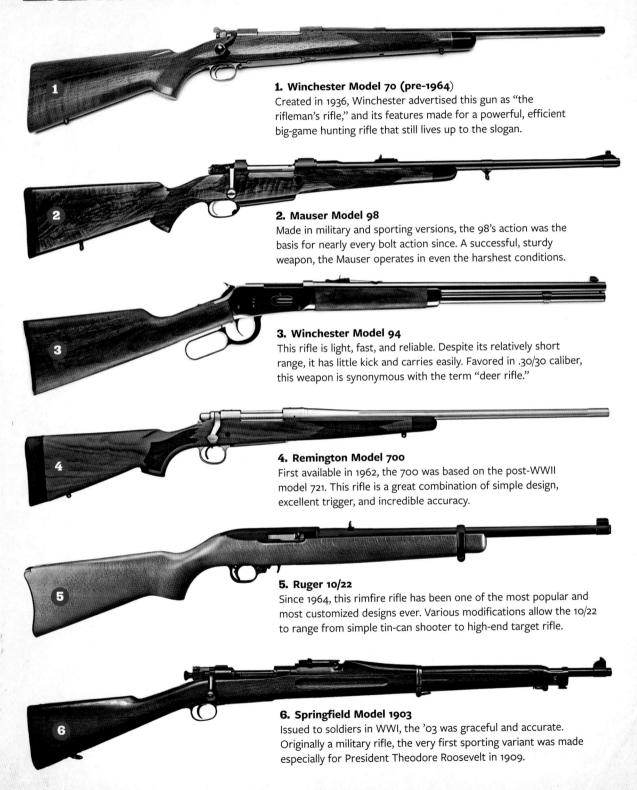

1. Winchester Model 70 (pre-1964)
Created in 1936, Winchester advertised this gun as "the rifleman's rifle," and its features made for a powerful, efficient big-game hunting rifle that still lives up to the slogan.

2. Mauser Model 98
Made in military and sporting versions, the 98's action was the basis for nearly every bolt action since. A successful, sturdy weapon, the Mauser operates in even the harshest conditions.

3. Winchester Model 94
This rifle is light, fast, and reliable. Despite its relatively short range, it has little kick and carries easily. Favored in .30/30 caliber, this weapon is synonymous with the term "deer rifle."

4. Remington Model 700
First available in 1962, the 700 was based on the post-WWII model 721. This rifle is a great combination of simple design, excellent trigger, and incredible accuracy.

5. Ruger 10/22
Since 1964, this rimfire rifle has been one of the most popular and most customized designs ever. Various modifications allow the 10/22 to range from simple tin-can shooter to high-end target rifle.

6. Springfield Model 1903
Issued to soldiers in WWI, the '03 was graceful and accurate. Originally a military rifle, the very first sporting variant was made especially for President Theodore Roosevelt in 1909.

7. Remington Nylon 66
First offered in 1959, this rifle had a stock that was made with a brand-new synthetic called Zytel. Light and accurate, the 66 paved the way for future synthetic stocks.

8. New Ultra Light Arms Model 20
With its 1-pound Kevlar stock, this .308 caliber rifle weighs a mere 5$\frac{1}{2}$ pounds with scope mounted and is just as accurate as much heavier guns.

9. Savage Model 110
Produced from 1958 onward, the first model 110s were unlovely, but they were inexpensive and accurate and are today offered in all manner of configurations.

10. Marlin Model 336
First sold in 1948, this is another great deer rifle like the Winchester 94—short, light, fast, reliable, and its side-ejection allows for a scope to be mounted as well.

11. Marlin Model 39A
This sublimely simple .22 rimfire has been in continuous production in one form or another since 1939, owned by almost every serious shooter.

12. Winchester Model 52 Sporter
The rimfire version of the unparalleled Model 70, this gun—produced between 1934 and 1958—was unrivaled for beauty and accuracy and remains so to this day.

13. Ruger Number One
This is the gun that single-handedly resurrected the single-shot rifle when it was introduced back in 1966.

14. Tar-Hunt RSG-12
Introduced in 1990 and still unrivaled, this rifled, bolt-action slug gun can shoot accurately at 100 yards.

15. Savage Model 99
The greatest lever-action ever made, in my opinion, and in production for nearly the entire 20th century, it takes so much hand labor that it is just too costly to mass-produce.

23 KNOW WHY SHORTER IS BETTER, PART TWO

I'm talking about rifle barrels. What the hell did you think I was talking about? Back when men smelled bad and carried Kentucky rifles, long barrels were just the ticket—44 inches was about standard. They decreased aiming error and having all that weight out there in front made offhand shooting that much easier.

This lasted until the Mountain Men (who smelled even worse) took over, and the Hawken rifle evolved, which had a much shorter barrel (26 to 38 inches), because its users had discovered that a long-barreled rifle, regardless of its advantages, was a damned unhandy thing to hunt with while on horseback.

It is a damned unhandy thing to hunt with in a lot of other situations, too. That's why I think the most practical length for a big-game rifle barrel is 22 inches. If you have a magnum, 24 is the most you want, and you can get away with 23 inches unless you're shooting something like a 7mm STW. Twenty-six is okay for varmint guns, and you can get by with 20 on a handy rifle chambered for small rounds, such as the .257 Roberts, .260, .308, 7mm/08 and the like.

24 ROLL OUT THE BARREL

Most custom barrels are produced by a process called button rifling, which was developed in the 1950s and is reasonably fast, but not nearly as fast as hammering. In button rifling, a tungsten-carbide button with a reverse imprint of the rifling grooves is pulled through a blank by a hydraulic press. If done slowly and with care, this will produce a truly superior barrel.

Some custom barrel makers, including Douglas, Shaw, and McGowen, make highly affordable barrels that are better than what the factories put out. I've shot a whole bunch of these. The worst of them was good, and the best would suck the breath out of your lungs—they were that accurate. This class of barrel is the best choice for a hunting rifle because any gain in accuracy you'd obtain from a more expensive barrel would go unrealized in the field. The cost, including chambering, threading, polishing, and bluing (which are performed by your gunsmith), will probably be a few hundred bucks.

25 CHOOSE YOUR METAL

Both stainless steel and chrome-moly make fine barrels. Chrome-moly can be blued, but stainless cannot. Stainless is somewhat more expensive but will last longer because it's more resistant to erosion from powder gas. No matter what it's made of, make sure you keep your barrel clean. You can have dirty thoughts, but your barrel should be spotless.

26 BUY IT FOR THE BARREL

A little while back I was talking with Chad Dixon, the gunsmith who builds Scimitar tactical rifles for Dakota Arms. Scimitars have to shoot 5 consecutive 10-shot groups that measure ½ inch or less before they leave the shop, so you could assume that Chad knows something about accuracy, and he said the following: "If someone wanted me to build him an accurate rifle, I would ask how much he had to spend, and then put 80 percent of that into the barrel. The rest I could improvise one way or another. Spend your money on the barrel."

27
PICK THE RIGHT BARREL WEIGHT

Weight is usually given in terms of taper, or diameter. Tapers vary from maker to maker, but not by much.

No. 1 For very light sporters only, such as the .243, .257 Roberts, and 6.5x55.

No. 2 In my eyes, the best weight for any non-Magnum cartridge.

No. 3 Just the ticket for the saner 7mm and .300 Magnums.

No. 4 For the powerhouses and the really hard kickers from .338 on up.

No. 5 For elephant executors and buffalo busters from .416 on up.

Straight For varmint rifles only.

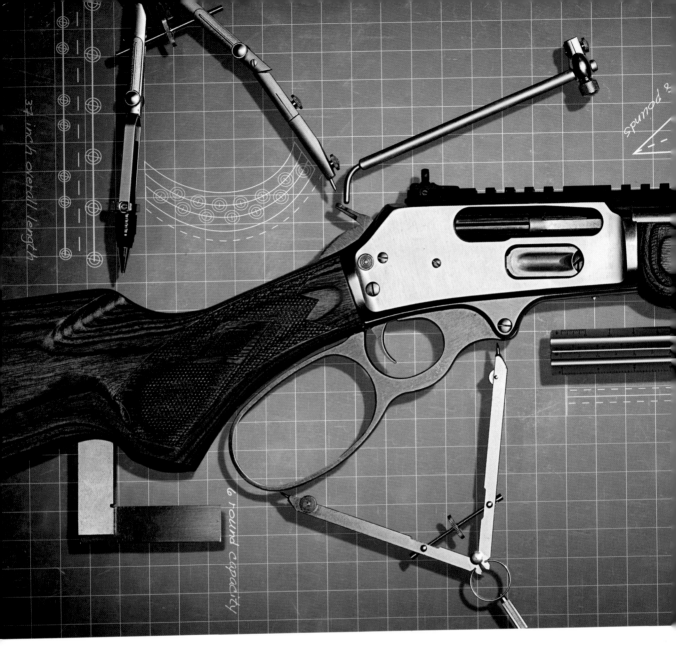

28 RESPECT YOUR TRIGGER

A trigger is to a rifle as steering is to a car. Steering that is too heavy or sloppy or gives you no feel of the road will have your car weaving all over the blacktop. Let me quote from *U.S. Army Field Manual 23-10*, Sniper Training: "Trigger control is the most important of the marksmanship fundamentals. It is defined as causing the rifle to fire when the sight picture is at its best *without causing the rifle to move* [italics mine]." If you have to wrestle your trigger, you're sunk, because your rifle will move.

If your trigger is a disgrace, you have two options: Have a gunsmith modify it or have him install a replacement. Usually, on a trigger that's not hopeless, an adjustment will cost you about $50.

It's the case that some triggers are made so that they cannot be tampered with in any way. That means you will need to get a replacement trigger, and there are several very good ones on the market, such as those from Timney, Jewell, and Rifle Basix.

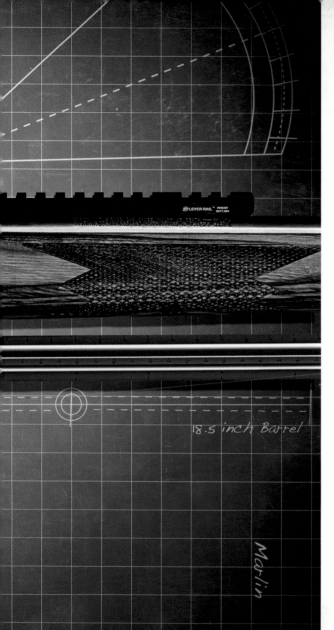

18.5 inch Barrel

Marlin

29 PULL IT LIKE A PRO

FINGER TECHNIQUE Triggers are best pulled with the first joint of the index finger, not the soft tip of the finger. The "give" in the tip makes it harder to know when the rifle is going to fire. For this reason, narrow triggers that fit into the index joint are better than wide ones that don't.

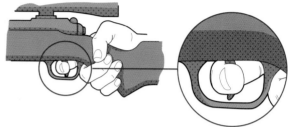

WEIGHTY MATTERS What about weight? Noting that the trigger on a Jarrett Signature rifle was set at $1\frac{1}{2}$ pounds, a reader once asked if that was a good pull weight for hunting rifles in general. To which I replied, "Great gobs of goose grease, no!" That Jarrett is a specialty gun. For general use, anything below 3 pounds is asking for it.

If you're excited, or your hands are cold, or you're wearing gloves, or any combination thereof, a trigger pull of less than 3 pounds is going to get you into trouble eventually—the rifle will go off before you're ready. Good dangerous-game rifles have their triggers set at 4 to 5 pounds, and I've pulled some heavier than that.

LIGHTENING UP If you must have a light pull, there are some excellent aftermarket triggers that will hold at a weight of as little as 2 ounces, but you had better practice with them, because controlling a trigger that light takes some thought and effort.

30 CARE FOR YOUR TRIGGER

A trigger has two natural enemies—water and oil. It can rust if it's left wet for days on end, and it will clog if you hose lubricant on it. There's an easy solution to both problems. If your rifle has been soaked repeatedly, take out the bolt and pump a few squirts of lighter fluid into the trigger so it runs down through the mechanism. That heads off corrosion pretty effectively. And before each hunting season, take the barreled action out of the stock and give the whole trigger mechanism a good hosing with lighter fluid. That will clean it out thoroughly.

If your trigger gums up due to cold weather, there are a couple of cures. Take the barreled action out of the stock and then pour either Coleman lantern fuel or boiling water through the trigger. That should clear up whatever gunk is stuck in there jamming it.

And remember, no trigger stays adjusted forever. Eventually, they'll all need to be tuned up. If yours starts to drag, creep, or otherwise misbehave, it's off to the gunsmith you go. If a friend says he can tune up your trigger for you, and he's not a gunsmith, get a new friend.

31 AVOID TROUBLE

The first rule of buying used guns is to only buy from dealers who will back what they sell you or from individuals whom you know and trust. Unless you are a firearms expert, don't buy from the guy with the table at the gun show. Tomorrow, he'll be down the road with your money, and you'll be at the gunsmith, fixing up the crummy rifle he sold you. In addition, you should avoid the following:

• Any rifle that shows sign of obvious abused and neglect: rust, a battered stock, or big patches of bluing worn off. No matter what the price is, just leave it be.

• Any rifle that shows signs of home gunsmithing. There are two kinds of people who work on rifles—those who know how and morons. Amateur tinkering can not only render a rifle useless, but dangerous.

• Any rifle with a rusted bore or chamber. There is no way that gun is going to shoot well, and the least you are looking at is a rebarreling job.

• Bargains that seem too good to be true. If someone offers you a rifle for a fraction of what it's worth, he may be genuinely desperate for quick cash, or he may be selling a stolen gun. As a rule, if you find a rifle in good condition that is selling for less than a third of its new price, it should be looked at with suspicion.

• Rifles chambered for obscure wildcat cartridges or famous wildcat cartridges. Unless you are an advanced handloader, you'll have problems getting ammunition, and you'll find it almost impossible to dump the thing when it aggravates you terminally.

32 TELL THE DEALS FROM THE LEMONS

RULE ONE If the rifle is in poor condition, forget about it. The only reason to buy a clunker is for parts.

RULE TWO If you buy a rifle sight unseen, insist on a trial period, during which you can send it back and get a refund if the rifle is not satisfactory.

RULE THREE Many used rifles are sold on consignment, and the prices are not unchangeable once they've gathered dust. That's when you leap up, checkbook in hand.

RULE FOUR A high price is no guarantee that a rifle will not have problems.

RULE FIVE Beware of dirty rifles. A bore that is fouled with copper is often pitted beneath it, and when you clean the stuff out, you'll probably find that you need a new barrel.

RULE SIX Some restoration work can get you a hell of a bargain. See if the seller will allow you to take it to a gunsmith to get an estimate on what it would cost to restore the gun. You may be surprised at how little it costs.

33 SPOT THE TOP TEN DEAL BREAKERS

ONE A dirty bore, or a bore with copper streaks. Who knows what lies beneath?

TWO Chips or dings at the muzzle. They ruin accuracy, and the barrel must be recrowned.

THREE Rust, anywhere, in any amount. Inexcusable.

FOUR Cracks in the stock.

FIVE Pits in the bolt face. These are a result of blown primers, which means that someone was firing injudicious handloads in the rifle.

SIX A rifle that fires when the bolt is slammed forward and down. There's not enough sear engagement, which is dangerous.

SEVEN A trigger that is heavy, creepy, or light, or shows signs of having been tampered with.

EIGHT A rifle that will fire when you cock it, put it on safe, pull the trigger, and then throw the safety to the off position.

NINE A chamber that is worn out of round. This comes from the poor use of a cleaning rod and means the rifle will not shoot accurately.

TEN Rifling that's scorched toward the rear of the barrel. This is a sign that the gun is near the end of its useful life.

34 GRADE THAT GUN

If you are looking to buy a used gun, the first thing you need to know is that they fit into one of six categories, depending on their condition.

POOR The gun is pitted and rusted, may not be in working order, and may not be safe to shoot. Forget it.

FAIR It works and is safe to shoot, but it has taken a beating. Consider it only if it's dirt cheap and you don't mind paying to have it touched up, or if you want to do the refinishing yourself, or if you just want something you can knock around.

GOOD It's in fine working order, but repairs or replacement parts may be needed. It should have 80 percent of its original finish.

VERY GOOD The gun should have more than 90 percent of its original finish, be in perfect working order, have no replacement parts, and need only very small repairs, if any.

EXCELLENT Just short of brand-new, it shows only the most minor signs of wear and use.

NIB (NEW IN BOX) It's just as it came from the factory, with all the tags, stickers, labels, and everything else. This category is more for collectors than shooters.

35 KNOW WHY THAT RIFLE'S FOR SALE

It's natural to think that people trade in rifles because there's something wrong with the gun. Usually that's not actually the case; instead they've likely gone on the used-gun market for one of the following reasons.

IT KICKS Owner falls for ad copy, buys gun, shoots it once, trades it in for something that kicks less.

DEATH Gun owner takes dirt nap. Kids are not interested in shooting, so the guns go on sale.

BOREDOM Owner loses interest in shooting for some reason.

IDIOCY Owner trades rifle to get something a gun writer wrote about (worst of all reasons to trade rifle).

POVERTY Owner gets into financial trouble; guns go to raise money.

MOVING Owner moves to new locale where guns are not welcome. Has to get rid of guns before relocating.

DIVORCE Husband and wife go to court. Judge hears both sides. Judge says, "Give her everything." Gun collection goes to pay settlement.

PETZAL ON: GETTING THE BEST BARGAIN

"Frequently, I'm approached by people who ask what the best bargain in rifles is, and my response is always the same: 'Get away from me or I'll hit you with this stick!' (I carry a stick for just such occasions.)

Once we have the correct social order established, I explain that the best bargain is not a particular brand of rifle, but a used rifle, and particularly at this point in history. As we continue our descent from the First World to the Third, people are having to part with some very good guns. The true bargains are not the cheap guns that are selling cheaper because they're used, but the really good ones that no longer cost big money."

36 JUSTIFY YOUR PURCHASE

There is no logical reason to buy a custom rifle. I love the things and use them almost exclusively, but there is nothing they can do that I couldn't get done by a good factory rifle. So why bother? What are you actually buying?

EXPERTISE When you pay all that money, what you are really buying is the ideas and skills of the man who made the rifle. If you get one of Melvin Forbes' Ultra Lights, you purchase the 20 years he spent as a country gunsmith fixing other peoples' mistakes, along with the two years he spent supporting himself as a shop teacher while designing a rifle that weighed 5-and-change pounds with scope.

PERFECTION When custom rifles leave the shop, they are supposed to work perfectly. Not well, not good enough, perfectly. If they do not, they will be made to.

EXCLUSIVITY Not every honyak in camp will be carrying a rifle made by Mark Bansner, or Nosler, or Kenny Jarrett. This is important to more people than you would think.

PERFORMANCE You're buying the cutting edge; the last 1 percent that money can purchase. No factory trigger will pull as well as a Jewell. No factory barrel will quite equal a Lilja, a Schneider, or a Pac-Nor, to name three. No factory stock will combine the uncanny light weight and strength of a High Tech Specialties stock.

If some or all of these factors are important to you, start saving your money.

37 BUILD IT RIGHT

Rule number one is to listen to your gunsmith. That said, you should go in with a basic idea of what you want and what you really don't. The first thing you don't want to do is cheap out. You should expect to spend a few thousand dollars on the right gun. If you find some guy who will build you one that's "just as good" for a few hundred bucks, run for your life. Here are some of the first things you'll want to consider.

WOOD OR CHEMICAL? If I were looking for a working rifle, there's no question that I would want a synthetic stock, and that's what many custom gunsmiths are using these days. Some offer laminated wood, which is a good compromise, especially for a larger-caliber rifle where you want some weight.

WATCH YOUR WEIGHT Extremely light rifles are every bit as accurate as standard-weight guns, but they are tougher to hold steady when you're winded or excited. For standard calibers, you don't want the rifle to weigh less than 7 pounds with scope. In heavier calibers, lack of weight can make a rifle unmanageable. I would not own a .338 that weighed less than 9 pounds or a .300 Magnum that weighed less than 8½.

IT'S THE BARREL, STUPID The most important component of your rifle is the barrel, because it determines how well your rifle will shoot. Most gun builders use premium barrels as a matter of course, but if yours doesn't, spend the extra couple of hundred dollars and insist on one.

SHUT UP AND LISTEN When it comes to scopes and mounts, just about every custom-rifle maker has strong ideas about what work bests, and you should shut up and respect his or her expertise. Most gun makers also insist on mounting the scope themselves, having endured bitter experiences when they let the customers do it.

38 DON'T BE AN IDIOT

You're spending a lot of money on this custom gun. Don't blow it. These rules will help you achieve that goal and get the gun you want, whether you know it right now or not.

ESCHEW THE ODD Years ago, Abercrombie & Fitch had a highly engraved used bull-barreled varmint rifle for sale. I think it was in their New York City store for 10 years, and I don't know if it ever did sell. Simply, no one wanted an engraved varmint rifle. Should the sad day come when you must part with your custom gun, and the gun is too strange, you will be unable to recoup any of your investment, at least not within a decade.

BEWARE OF REVOLUTIONARY IDEAS A few years ago, it was trendy to make barrels by wrapping fiberglass thread around a thin steel liner. All sorts of advantages were claimed until someone

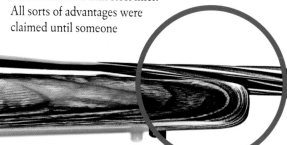

pointed out that if you put a nick in the fiberglass, the barrel would probably disintegrate. Most other radical attempts at improvement vanish just as quickly.

GET LESS POWER If you think you need a .300 Magnum of one kind or another, get a .30/06. Convinced you need a

7mm Magnum? Get a .280 or .270. For a deer rifle, think 7mm/08, .260 Remington, or 6.5x55 Swede. The less the recoil, the better you shoot, and the better you shoot, the more game you get.

PICK A SANE CARTRIDGE It is a given among custom-rifle builders that the clients with the most smarts pick the dullest, oldest cartridges: 7x57 Mauser, .30/06, .270, .375 H&H, and so on. That's because these rounds have been around longer than dirt and have proven themselves through many generations. They won't fail you, either. There are good reasons why few people build rifles for the .30/416 Eargesplitten Loudenboomer.

DON'T GET NUTS ABOUT ACCURACY Any big-game rifle that will shoot a minute of angle will kill anything you aim it at. A half-minute rifle won't make the beasts any deader. In all probability the gun you end up with will

shoot better than you can hold. What you're looking for is consistency above everything else. You want all your shots going to the same place all the time.

GET TO KNOW YOUR GUN The best rifle in the world will not transform a poor shot into a decent one or a mediocre shot into a good one. When you get your new rifle, burn some ammo.

39 KNOW YOUR GUNSMITH

Some gun builders will smile, take your money, and turn out exactly what you ordered, whether it's a crackpot gun or not. Others will tell you that you don't know what you're talking about. You want the latter. Any gunmaker with an ounce of pride does not want some screwball firearm out there with his name on it.

When shopping for the right gunsmith, ask for the names of half a dozen of his customers and then find out if they like their guns. You will have to listen carefully. Some people are chronic malcontents; others have unrealistic expectations. A guy who couldn't hit water if he fell out of a boat is not a good reference for a gunmaker who guarantees

half-minute groups. The fact is that all top makers shoot their rifles before they go down the road, and they know they are accurate, and they are likely to be short with the customer who says his gun won't deliver.

Once you choose your gunmaker, be sure to tell him how you're going to use the rifle.

I recently had a 6.5x55 Swede built but neglected to tell the builder that I wanted to use long, heavy bullets. He assumed I'd follow the current trend for light, fast bullets and gave me a barrel with a 1-in-10½-inch twist; fine for light slugs but all wrong for heavy ones. I had to return the gun and get a new barrel. The whole thing was my fault.

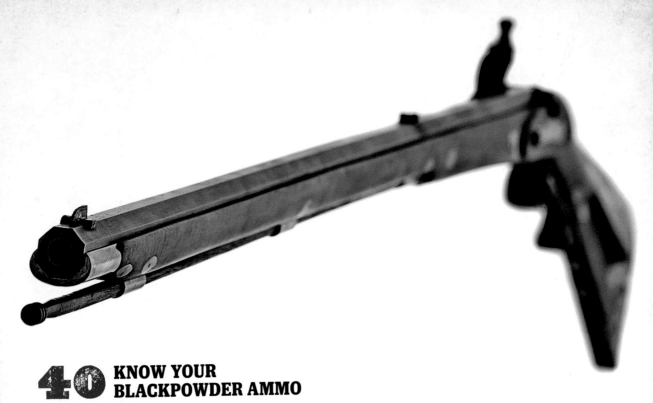

40 KNOW YOUR BLACKPOWDER AMMO

Here's a rundown of the most popular types of bullets used with muzzleloaders. Go with .54, .50, or .45 caliber for big game; .40, .36, and .32 are for small game.

PATCHED ROUND BALL On paper, the round ball's ballistics are pathetic, but it kills far better than it should at ranges inside 100 yards. The cloth patch seals the bore and engages the rifling. In general, round balls shoot best from traditional-style rifles with a slow rate of rifling twist, about one turn in 60 inches.

CONICAL BULLET About twice the weight of the same caliber round ball, a conical bullet hits much harder, shoots flatter, and loads easier. The Thompson/Center's Maxi-Ball was the first example made for modern hunters. Conicals shoot best from a fast-twist barrel.

SABOTED BULLETS The plastic sabot lets you shoot a slightly smaller bullet in a big-bore gun, resulting in higher velocities. Best of all, good-quality copper-jacketed hunting bullets can be united with a sabot, thus putting penetration and expansion on a par—or very nearly so—with that of centerfire rifle bullets.

POWERBELT Halfway between a conical and a saboted bullet, the PowerBelt is a full-bore projectile with a plastic base that expands to seal the bore, then pops off in flight. Unlike many saboted bullets, PowerBelts slide easily down a rifle's bore for fast loading.

Patched
Round Ball

Conical Bullet

Saboted Bullet

Powerbelt

41 CLEAN YOUR MUZZLELOADER

Single men fill a bathtub with hot, soapy water to clean muzzleloaders. The rest of us use a bucket. Add a squirt of any dish detergent, then fill it up with hot water. Take the barrel off the gun and put it in the bucket. With a cleaning jag and patch on the ramrod, pump it up and down, drawing water into the barrel. Run dry patches down the bore until they come out clean, then use one lightly oiled patch to lube the bore.

In-line guns with removable breech plugs can be cleaned from the breech just like a centerfire. With any type of rifle featuring a removable nipple, take it out, clean it, and dry it thoroughly. Finally, put a dry patch on the ramrod and run it down the barrel. Leave the ramrod in place and pop a cap. A burn on the patch proves the flash channel is clear.

42 KEEP YOUR POWDER DRY

There's a reason this catchphrase is used even by people who have only the foggiest idea what it means. Keeping your powder dry is essential, as a damp charge will not ignite or will behave unpredictably. Here are four handy hints.

TAPE IT UP Put a piece of tape over the muzzle on days when it's raining or snowing.

MAKE IT YOUR BEESWAX After capping your rifle, press beeswax around the bottom edges of the cap to keep moisture out.

BAG IT Keep your capper in a Ziploc bag.

KEEP IT COLD If you come in for lunch on a cold day, go ahead and leave the gun outside so moisture doesn't condense in the barrel and dampen the charge.

43

LOAD YOUR BLACKPOWDER RIFLE

STEP ONE Pour the powder down the barrel from a powder-measuring tool, which will ensure the correct charge. If you're using pelletized powder, just drop in the proper number.

STEP TWO Load the bullet. For a round ball, lay a patch over the bore and shove the ball down on it. You'll need a ball starter to get it going. A little lube helps; at the range, spit is all you need. In the field, use Crisco or a commercial lubricant. Conicals and PowerBelts go down fairly easily. Sabots can be hard to get down. A little lube helps here, too.

STEP THREE Push the bullet in and tamp it down with a ramrod. Afterward, leave the ramrod in and scratch a mark on it to show the proper seating depth. You can also use the mark to determine whether the rifle has been loaded yet.

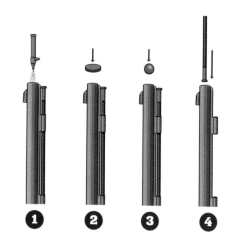

STEP FOUR Put on a primer cap if your black powder rifle is the percussion type, or fill the pan with powder if it's a flintlock. Remember to take out the ramrod before you even think about pulling the trigger; the only thing you should be firing is the bullet.

44 MEET THE MODERN SPORTING RIFLE

The AR (for AR-15, its original model designation) was first issued by the U.S. Army late in 1964 as the M-16 and has gone on to serve longer than any other weapon as our standard infantry rifle. It was a truly radical gun in terms of its weight, construction, and the small-bore high-velocity cartridge it uses.

Despite its military success, it made only very slow inroads with civilian shooters, but around the turn of the 21st century, people who didn't wear uniforms discovered that the AR (or Modern Sporting Rifle, or MSR) was something unique.

TRULY MODULAR The AR disassembles and assembles with ease and can be reconfigured with all manner of accessories to do all sorts of things. No skill is required, and few tools. It's our first shape-shifting rifle. Because the AR is modular, you can swap out triggers and sights (telescopic, red-dot, laser, and iron and mount them in any position you want thanks to the gun's Picatinny Rail bases), swap magazines, change buttstocks and fore-ends, and install a vertical fore-end grip, which makes eminent ergonomic sense. You can shift from one cartridge to another with minimal trouble.

A SOFT KICKER The cartridges the AR uses are light-recoiling to begin with, and unlike older rifle designs, the ARs kick straight back, shifting the jolt from your head, where you can't take it, to your shoulder, where you can. Its gas-operation system and spring-loaded bolt buffer drain off even more kick.

LOTS OF CHEAP AMMO This enables you to shoot for fun. Do know, however, that because MSRs are chambered for small cartridges (.223—or its military version, the 5.56mm—and .308 are by far the most common), you can't hunt everything on the continent with them, although you can hunt a great many species.

HIGHLY DURABLE It's a military arm, for heaven's sake.

Smith & Wesson Model M&P15 Carbine

45 DO YOUR RESEARCH

In a comparatively few years, the Modern Sporting Rifle has gone from a strictly military arm to a hugely significant part of the civilian market. Because it is so unlike anything else, the AR commands its own body of knowledge, and whatever you know about conventional rifles will do you no good here.

Do not rush out and spend your money before you know what you're doing. MSRs are not cheap, nor is the infinite array of accessories available for them. Think very carefully about what you want to do with your rifle, then research. You may want to have one built to order; there is no shortage of gunmakers who will do that for you.

And enjoy. They are, after all, fun. Remember fun?

PETZAL ON: ARS

" Because the AR is considered by some to be an assault weapon, whatever the hell that is, there are special laws and regulations governing it. In New York State, for example, you can't have an AR magazine that holds more than 10 rounds, and you can't have a muzzle brake. Does this make sense? Of course not, but then neither do most firearms laws. "

46 SHOOT ON THE RANGE

A few words of caution: An MSR basically encourages you to shoot as fast as you possibly can and ignore the fact that a rifle is a device for delivering aimed fire. But this gun's virtue lies in its ability to make multiple *aimed* shots easy, not to see how fast you can pop off 10 or 20 rounds.

Also, recall that unlike civilian firearms, where you can control cartridge ejection to a degree, the AR sends its empties flying. That hot brass really sails through the air, and if it hits the shooting bench or goes down the neck of the guy next to you, he may not take it in good humor.

Finally, remember that your rifle is a self-loader, and every time you pull the trigger it's going to shove another round in the chamber unless the magazine is empty or you lock the bolt back. Pay attention!

47 CHOOSE AMMO WISELY

AR chambers come in three varieties. Military chambers will handle just about any kind of 5.56mm ammo you want to stuff in them because their tolerances are very generous. However, they don't produce the best accuracy. Match chambers give the best accuracy but will probably not accept some kinds of ammo. The best compromise is a Wylde chamber, which was designed by a gunsmith of that name and will do a good job with either.

Military ball ammo is cheap, but tends to ricochet and can't be humanely used for hunting. Tracer is fun to shoot but will get you thrown off some rifle ranges because it starts fires. Lots of excellent civilian ammo exists for match shooting, varmint hunting, big-game hunting, and target practice, and I would stick to that.

48 KNOW THE ANATOMY OF AN AR

1. Buttstock Most AR rifles are sold with a collapsible, telescoping stock or a fixed stock; aftermarket options abound.

2. Lower Receiver Includes the trigger assembly, magazine well, magazine, magazine release and latch, fire selector, bolt stop, and pistol grip.

3. Forward Assist Added to later models of the AR, and absent from some modern models; helps move the bolt forward when normal charging fails to fully chamber a round.

4. Pistol Grip

5. Charging Handle Used to open the bolt or chamber a round from a closed-bolt position.

6. Upper Receiver Houses the bolt carrier assembly and attaches to the barrel.

7. Rear Sight Flip-down or fixed with multiple variations that serve as half the weapon's default iron sights.

8. Trigger

9. Magazine Release Button that releases the mechanism that locks the magazine into the magazine well.

10. Ejection Port Point where spent shells are ejected.

11. Magazine External box magazine that stores the ammunition and feeds it into the firearm during cycling.

12. Accessory Rail Mounting System Developed by the Picatinny Arsenal, the Picatinny Rail is a very simple, strong base for mounting sights. Many ARs have multiple rails for employing specialized sighting devices.

13. Fore-end Can include integral or attached rails for attaching lasers, tactical flashlights and other accessories.

14. Barrel

15. Front Sight Post Typically a simple iron post sight, but may also include a luminescent element for low-light shooting.

16. Flash Hider Disperses burning powder gas, and thus muzzle flash, making it harder to spot shooter's position.

Not Pictured:

Bolt Catch Activated when the bolt moves rearward on an empty magazine, allowing for faster reloads.

Fire Selector The rifle's safety; on a semiautomatic version, it's a simple two-position switch: Safe and Fire. Military and police models may include a setting for three-round burst or full automatic fire.

Gas Block Captures and directs gasses rearward.

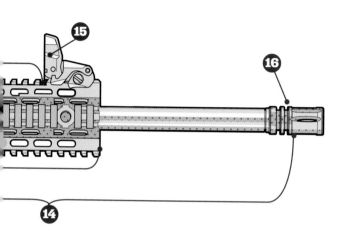

4⑨ GET OUT OF A JAM

Every once in awhile, especially when shooting large volumes of ammo or during rapid-fire shooting, you'll get a jam with your AR, and you need to clear it correctly and safely. Here's how.

When you first experience a malfunction, use the simple steps of the **SPORTS** method.

SLAP the bottom of the magazine. This ensures it is seated fully and correctly in the receiver.

PULL the charging handle completely to the rear and hold it there. The bolt should move back and expose the chamber.

OBSERVE the ejection port. See if pulling the charging handle ejected a live round or a spent cartridge that was holding up the works.

RELEASE the charging handle. If the jam has been cleared, this will fully lock the bolt forward and load a new round.

TAP the forward assist. This will help ensure the bolt is fully locked. Once the bolt is locked, pull the charging handle back slightly and do a brass check, ensuring a new round has been seated. Release it and allow it to snap closed fully. Remember to always keep the muzzle of the rifle pointed downrange.

SQUEEZE the trigger. Take aim and attempt to fire a shot.

If the above sequence doesn't clear it, or if the charging handle can't be manipulated, you have a more serious jam, and it's time to bring it to a professional gunsmith.

5⓪ BE SAFE WHEN CLEARING JAMS

Jams are a possibility with any type of rifle, but seem to occur more often in ARs. The directions that come with your AR will tell you how to clear a stuck case or live round, but there is one overriding principle to the business: Before you start working on the gun, make sure the rifle is pointed in a direction where the bullet will be stopped immediately if the gun goes off.

Keep the rifle level and point the muzzle at a backstop or a dirt bank or whatever else is safe and in plain view. A rifle bullet can travel 3 miles or more with the muzzle elevated 45 degrees and take a life at the end of its journey.

Be careful about pounding on a stuck live round from the muzzle with a cleaning rod. There are two cases on record of this being done in a way that in turn caused the powder charges to detonate, which propelled the cases from the chamber with such force that they killed people standing behind the rifles. Tap on the bullets very gently, and if you are in doubt, lock the action open and take the thing to a gunsmith.

51 BE TRIGGER HAPPY

Most everyone can sidle up to the gun range, aim a pistol in the general direction of the target, and squeeze off a round. Getting that round to go where you want it to go, though, is a different story. It's all well and good to achieve proper balance and stance, but if you don't know how to control your finger on the trigger, you might as well throw the gun at your target as much as shoot.

If you're shooting a semiautomatic pistol in single-action mode, correct hand placement is to put the pad of your index finger, the area just beyond the last knuckle, on the center of the trigger itself. For double actions, placement should be on the first knuckle joint rather than the pad. Take care to not put your finger too low on the trigger, as pulling your finger along the trigger guard will pull your shot low on the target.

When it comes to pulling the trigger, apply smooth, even pressure on the trigger until the shot fires. Avoid pushing or pulling the finger laterally across the trigger, which is a common mistake leading to inaccuracy. Instead, make sure the pressure on the trigger is applied straight back.

52 SIGHT IN RIGHT

If you can't aim, you'll never hit your target except by blind luck. Literally. When it comes to getting your round where you need it, nothing's more important than understanding a good sight picture. There are two parts to the proper sight picture: alignment and focus.

Quite simply, you align the front sight in the middle of the notch on your rear sight. The front sight should be level with the top of the rear sight, and there should be an equal amount of light on either side of the front sight. This line of sight, then, should be focused on the point downrange that you want to shoot.

If everything looks right, but you're still missing the target, chances are you're focusing on the wrong sight. Make sure that you focus your vision on the front sight, not the rear sight or the target. Too often, shooters try to bring the target into focus, leaving the sight picture blurry. That approach is no good. Remember: clear sight, blurry target.

53 STAND UP FOR YOURSELF

Getting your rounds on target starts with stance. If you're faced with a self-defense situation, the likelihood that you'll have time to consciously consider your foot placement is pretty slim. You simply do your best to aim, fire, and protect yourself. In a target-shooting scenario, however, where tight groupings are more important, proper stance is crucial to your success.

Begin by placing the foot on your weaker, non-shooting side forward. If you're right-handed, slide your left foot forward. If you're left-handed, well, you get the idea. Keep your feet shoulders' width apart. You'll want to slightly bend the knee of your non-shooting leg. This stance will give you a solid, balanced base. Keep your head up and shoulders facing square to the target.

If you're firing with both hands, the stance remains the same, but you'll want to place the fingers of your non-shooting hand around the off-side grip, over and around the fingers of

the hand holding the gun. Be careful of your thumb placement.

The key hint here is not to put your weakside thumb up and over the thumb of your stronger shooting hand. If you happen to be firing a semiautomatic pistol, you won't care much for what happens when the slide snaps back on recoil.

For proper hand placement, put your shooting hand on the backstrap of the pistol's grip. Extend your trigger finger along the outside of the trigger guard, placing your finger on the trigger only when you are ready to shoot. Keep the web of your shooting hand aligned as straight as possible with both your wrist and the pistol. Wrap your fingers around the grip, applying pressure both front and back.

Don't place your gun and shooting hand in the palm of your weaker hand, as it will lead to rolling when you fire, which in turn causes erratic bullet placement.

54 DO SOMETHING DIFFERENT

Having hunted deer with a handgun exactly once, I highly recommend it as a way to crank up the excitement level of gun hunting. When I realized a big doe was going to walk into range, and I was going to shoot it, my heart raced the way it did when I used to bowhunt.

I had practiced with my .357 revolver all the previous summer and fall. A handgunning novice, I practiced until I could hit a paper plate every time at 30 to 40 yards. That was my maximum range, making me less dangerous to a deer than a bowhunter with a top-of-the-line compound.

It was that range limitation that made the hunt thrilling. The doe stepped into a clearing at 70 yards, an easy shot for the scoped inline rifle I often hunt with. I had to wait patiently (and by "patiently" I mean "shaking while trying to remain outwardly calm") for the deer to come close. After standing behind a tree seemingly forever, the doe gave me a broadside shot at 35 steps. I rested the revolver on the shooting rail in the treestand and put the dot low just behind the shoulder. The heartshot deer ran for 50 yards and then fell over.

The revolver is an S&W 627 from their performance shop. I mounted the excellent Burris FastFire reflex sight on top and shot Federal Premium ammo loaded with 140 grain Barnes Expander copper bullets. I found the bullet in the hide on the far side of the deer. It weighed 138.2 grains on my reloading scale, which is pretty close to the advertised 100 percent weight retention. Bottom line, at least for me? If shooting a deer with a rifle has become routine for you, pick up a handgun.—P.B.

55 BUST A FOOT-POUND MYTH

When I chose my first hunting handgun I tried a .357 magnum. I picked it because it would have less recoil than a bigger bore, and because the .357 will chamber .38 special ammunition, meaning I could readily buy inexpensive, low-recoil practice ammo for it as I learned. I figured good bullet placement with a smaller caliber would be beat poor shooting with a bigger gun.

Opinions are split on whether a .357 is enough gun for whitetails. Many would consider a .357 with a 5-inch barrel marginal for medium-size game, especially given the old standard 1,000 foot-pound minimum recommended for making a clean kill on a deer.

Yet the .44 Magnum, which everyone agrees is enough gun for whitetails, doesn't make the 1,000-foot-pound cutoff either. Does that make handguns inhumane for deer?

Hardly. At ranges to 50 yards, a .357 penetrates to the hide on the far side. Premium bullets, found in more and more hunting loads for handguns, make them even more effective. The question I ask is not "Are handguns effective on deer?" but "Who came up with the 1,000-foot-pound figure?" My guess is some writer made it up, and we have all repeated it over the years, just as we all repeat the "fact" that pronghorns have 8X vision even though none of us has ever given a pronghorn an eye test.—P.B.

56 CHOOSE A DEER CARTRIDGE

Hunting deer with handguns has grown into a major part of the shooting sports. The challenge is far greater because the revolver is still a short-range arm, even with a scope. (Note: I have not included rifle cartridges that are used in handguns, such as the 7mm/08. Handgun means handgun.)

FIRST CHOICE: .44 MAGNUM

It's the cartridge that changed the way we thought about handguns, and for the average shooter, it's the best big-game round out there. The .44 combines serious power with recoil that almost anyone can master with a little practice. It comes in a wide range of loadings with both jacketed and non-jacketed bullets, but it's very hard to beat a hard-lead 240-grain bullet at 1,200 fps or so.
Favorite Load: Winchester Supreme 250-grain Partition Gold.

.44 Magnum

SECOND CHOICE: .480 RUGER

This wonderful cartridge provides a boost in power over the .44 Magnum without the knuckle-mangling recoil of the .454 Casull. It comes in two loadings—a 325-grain bullet at 1,350 fps and a 400-grain at about 1,200 fps, and if that ain't enough, maybe you should be using a rifle.
Favorite Loads: Hornady, either 325- or 400-grain.

HONORABLE MENTION: .45 LONG COLT

Yep, the same one that the Earps used to exterminate the Clantons and the McLowerys. If you are truly recoil sensitive, this ancient round will serve you well out to 50 yards. Handloaders can soup up the .45 Long Colt, but the factory version will do just fine within its limits.
Favorite Load: Winchester 225-grain Silvertip Hollow Point.—P.B.

57 TAME THE .44 MAGNUM

After I eased into handgunnning and handgun hunting with a .357 Magnum, I figured since nothing was broken I would fix it anyway and move up to a .44 Magnum.

First trip to the range, I started out shooting .44 specials—which can be fired safely from a .44 Magnum—to get a feel for the gun. The .44 special in a heavy revolver has no recoil whatsoever and is a lot of fun to shoot. However, I hunt with .44 Magnum ammo, so I loaded the gun with a full-power Magnum cartridge, pulled the trigger, and immediately realized why it is you so often see nearly new .44 Magnums for sale. People think they will be fun to shoot and then they find out the .44 kicks. The kick isn't horrendous, but it gave me a good enough whack on the heel of my hand that my groups grew bigger, not smaller, the longer my practice sessions lasted.

My first thought was just to go back to the .357. It has a lot less recoil and is effective at the close ranges I will

shoot, but I rejected that as being too wimpy a solution even for me.

Instead I changed out the hard rubber Hogue grip that came with the gun for a much softer Pachmayr Decelerator grip, which takes just a few minutes with a screwdriver. I found some padded shooting gloves. Next trip to the range, I noticed a huge difference in recoil, and my groups went down in size immediately.

If you are among those who finds that .44 you bought to be a handful, take heart. With enough padding, you can calm it down and make it do your bidding.—P.B.

58 IDENTIFY 15 ICONIC HANDGUNS

1. Colt Navy Revolver (1850)
Named for the cylinder's engraving of the Second Texas Navy's 1843 victory, this cap and ball revolver was mainly used by military land forces, and civilians such as Wild Bill Hickok.

2. Colt 1873 Single Action (1873)
Dubbed the "Peacemaker," the 1873 SAA was one of the most popular handguns on the 19th-century frontier. It has become the most copied handgun in history, and more than 137 years after its introduction, this classic is still being manufactured by Colt.

3. Mauser C96 (1899)
This semiautomatic pistol's distinctive features include the integral box magazine in front of the trigger, the long barrel, the wooden shoulder stock that can double as a holster or carrying case, and a broom-handle–shaped grip. The C96 was also the model for the blaster wielded by Han Solo.

4. Colt 1911A1 (1911)
The first successful military semiauto handgun, it served as the standard U.S. sidearm through four major wars and countless police actions. As popular today as ever, it is still carried by some law enforcement personnel and countless civilians. The most customized handgun ever, it's a mainstay for competition shooters.

5. Walther PPK (1935)
A semiautomatic pistol originally developed for German police forces in the 1930s, this gun quickly became popular with civilians as well, for its reliability and concealability. The PPK has gained literary and cinema fame as the gun used by James Bond.

6. S&W .38 Model 36 (1950)
One of the first guns S&W developed in the post-WWII era, this revolver was designed for police officers who wanted a small-framed gun that could handle the .30 Special load. Dubbed the "Chief's Special."

7. Colt Python .357 Magnum (1955)

Just as the Model 29 was the finest revolver Smith & Wesson could build, the Python was the best that Colt could do. It was a beautifully made .357 Magnum that came in 6- and 4-inch-barreled versions. Target sights, a vent-rib barrel, and a high price were all standard features. Nothing like it is made today.

8. S&W .44 Model 29 (1955)

Yes, this was Dirty Harry's gun, but that's not what's important. The Model 29 .44 Magnum is one of those rare firearms that force us to redefine what a gun can do. The .44 Magnum enabled handgunners to not only hunt big game but to shoot it at rifle-caliber distances.

9. S&W .38 Model 60 Chief's Special (1965)

The Model 60 was nothing more than a stainless steel version of the popular Model 36 snub nose .38 Special. Yet it was groundbreaking because it was the first successful handgun made from stainless steel, and it showed the handgun industry how to use this material.

10. Beretta 92 9mm (1975)

A semiautomatic pistol still used, in the M9 military version, by the U.S. Army, the Beretta 92 features a "double-stacked" high-capacity magazine.

11. Glock G17 (1979)

The polymer-framed Glock 17 was controversial upon introduction. But history validates it. As the first successful polymer-framed handgun, it spawned a sea change within the industry, and today every major handgun maker has a polymer-frame model. And they are wildly popular.

12. Desert Eagle (1982)

The .50 caliber gas-operated semiautomatic was designed in the United States, but until 1995 was manufactured by Israeli Military Industries. It is engineered using innovations from rifle design, including the gas-operated mechanism and a rotating bolt that strongly resembles that of the M16.

13. Freedom Arms Model 83 .454 Casull (1983)

The .44 Magnum reigned supreme in the handgun hunting fields for years, but the quest for more power resulted in the .454 Casull cartridge. More than existing handgun designs could handle, it found a home in the rugged, yet precise, Freedom Arms single-action revolver and ushered in a new era for handgun hunters.

14. SIG Sauer P229 (1984)

A full-sized service-type pistol designed by the Swiss SIG company and manufactured by German Sauer, the P229 and its variants are used by law enforcement and military organizations worldwide, including the U.S. Navy SEALs.

15. S&W Model 500 (2003)

Introduced in 2003, this 4$\frac{1}{2}$-pound monster of a double-action revolver is as much of a quantum leap over existing handguns as the Model 29 was 50 years ago. The immensely strong, very expensive Model 500 revolver is surprisingly easy to shoot, considering how powerful it is. You want it, the Model 500 can drop it for you, from deer to Cape buffalo.

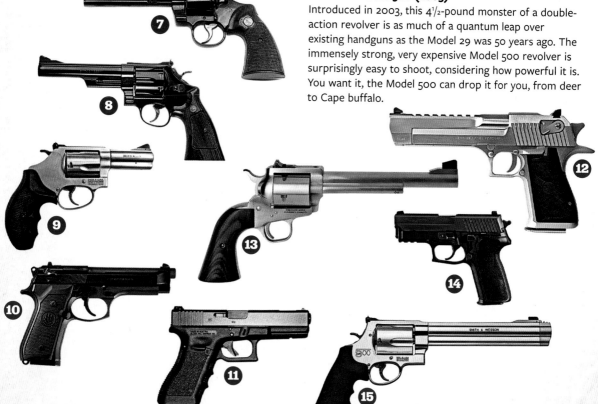

DECONSTRUCT A CARTRIDGE

1. BULLET The construction of the projectile has a major influence on the effectiveness of the cartridge.

2. NECK Holds the bullet in place and aligns it with the rifling.

3. SHOULDER Modern cases have sharper shoulders–30 degrees or more–than older ones. It's thought that this gives a cleaner, more efficient burn to the powder.

4. CASE A brass or steel shell for the bullet, powder, and primer.

5. POWDER It can be either spherical (ball) or extruded (log) and ranges in burn rate from fast to slow, depending on the bullet weight, case capacity, and shape of the case.

6. TAPER Modern cases have very little body taper; older ones have a lot. Low taper makes room for more powder, but more taper means more reliable feed.

7. RIM Rimless cases have rims that barely extend beyond the extraction groove. Rimmed cases lack the groove and have wider rims.

8. BASE The base of the case carries the primer pocket and the headstamp, which designates caliber and make.

9. PRIMER Composed of a cup, anvil, and a small charge of explosive compound. Primers come in several sizes, and there are some with longer-burning flames, for Magnum charges of slow powder.

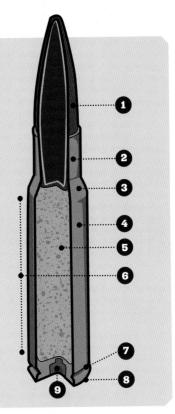

KNOW THE BEST CARTRIDGE EVER

The big-game cartridge that was most popular back in the repressed '50s, and is the most popular today, and probably will still be the most popular 20 years from now, is an ancient number developed three years after the Wright brothers flew at Kitty Hawk. What we know today as the .30/06 was originally known as "U.S. Cartridge, Model of 1903," and was loaded with a slow-moving 220-grain bullet; the whole package was designed for the Springfield Model 1903 bolt-action rifle.

This was all very well and good for two years—until, in 1905, the Imperial German Army came up with an 8mm (.323) round, which fired a lighter, faster bullet that badly outranged the '03. Not to be outdone, the U.S. Army modified the '03 to take a 150-grain bullet and renamed it "U.S. Cartridge, Model of 1906." Because that was a mouthful, people have called it the .30/06.

What the Army achieved in the '06 was a cartridge that struck an ideal balance between power and recoil. It has killed every kind of big game in North America, but its kick can be managed by just about everyone.

The '06 can also handle a wider range of bullet weights than any other cartridge. At the light end, you can go as low as 110 grains, whereas at the upper, 220-grain slugs are available. This will take you from mice to moose.

Because there are so many bullet weights available, '06 users often snort and fart in confusion over which to use. Here's a brief guide.

125- AND 130-GRAIN These lightweights are suitable for varmints, but the '06 kicks too much for high-volume shooting, and anyway it would be like swatting flies with a sledgehammer.

150-GRAIN For my money, this is the best of all the deer-shooting weights—it travels fast, expands violently, and puts them down in their tracks more often than not.

165-GRAIN A number of knowledgeable shooters think this may be the best all-around weight, combining relatively high velocity with enough heft to take on most critters.

180-GRAIN It's the consensus favorite for best all-around weight. There is very little out there that a good, tough 180-grain bullet can't handle.

200-GRAIN For big beasts only. A 200-grain .30-caliber bullet is not the fastest thing around, but it bucks wind well, retains plenty of impact downrange, and provides incredible penetration. It's my choice for elk, moose, bear, or the bigger African plains game.

61 MEET THE BALLISTIC BUFFALO

Back in the 1970s, when great bullets did not abound and bad ones definitely did, I corresponded with a very knowledgeable gun writer named Bob Hagel, who told me that I should do my own testing to see which slugs would penetrate and hold together before I took them hunting. The following target is based on what Hagel used and is made to tear apart weak bullets. In the Ballistic Buffalo, only the strong survive.

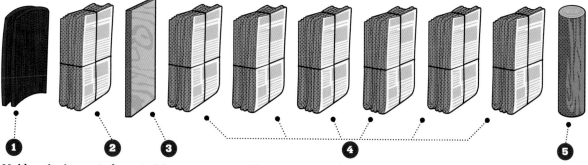

Making the beast: In front, I stick two thicknesses of worn-out truck inner tube [1], which you can get for free at any tire shop. Behind it goes a bundle of water-soaked newspapers [2], and behind that, an 11x14-inch piece of ¹/₂-inch plywood [3]. Behind the plywood, I place bound bundles of water-soaked newspaper [4] that total 2 feet thick, and behind that, if I'm testing an extremely tough bullet (usually it's not needed), more plywood. In the rear, I use a post [5] or tree stump to lean it all against.

In the buff: With an orange aiming dot marked on the upper left-hand quadrant of the tire, I fire a shot from 50 yards. Then, I go up to the buffalo and carefully start pulling the paper bundles apart to see how far the bullet has penetrated, taking note of the size and shape of the wound cavity and the depth of penetration. When I find the slug, I remove it with a pair of pliers because it is as hot as hell.

Weight up: The slug goes into a handloader's scale. I divide the resulting measurement by the original weight of the bullet to find the percentage of weight it retained. Try this yourself, and you will know how far your bullet penetrated, how big a hole it made, and how well it survived the trip.

62

PICK THE RIGHT RIFLE CALIBER

There are almost as many opinions about best cartridges out there as there are hunters. And most of them are wrong. Why? Because most opinions about cartridges are formed by a combination of shuck, jive, ad copy, and the ill-informed advice of friends. For the unvarnished, always unglamorous, and sometimes downright ugly truth, read on. These cartridges won't make a bad shooter into a good one, but they might help a good shooter get better.

● Petzal's Picks

Small Game Light recoiling and easy on the wallet, these rimfire rounds are the perfect choice for hunting squirrels and rabbits. These are also used on short-range varmints.

1. .22 Long Rifle
2. .22 Winchester Magnum Rimfire
3. .17 Hornady Magnum Rimfire

Varmints Long-range, flat-shooting, hyper-accurate calibers with light recoil.

4. .223 Remington
5. .220 Swift
6. .22/250 Remington

Varmints and Big Game Heavier bullets than straight varmint rounds make these a choice for deer hunters as well.

7. 6mm Remington
8. .257 Roberts
9. .243 Winchester

Big Game: The Light Kickers These calibers are powerful enough to drop deer in their tracks but light enough to shoot enough to make you accurate enough to do it.

10. 7x57 Mauser
11. 7mm/08 Remington
12. .308 Winchester
13. 6.5x55 Swede

Big Game: The All-Around Rounds For everything in between antelope and moose, these calibers excel.

14. .30/06 Springfield
15. .270 Winchester
16. .280 Remington
17. .338 Winchester Magnum

Big Game at Long Range These calibers are ballistically capable of killing elk and bear some four football fields away. They demand similar capabilities from whoever pulls the trigger.

18. .300 Weatherby Magnum
19. .270 Winchester Short Magnum
20. 7mm Weatherby Magnum

Heavy or Dangerous North American Game These are large, tough calibers for large, tough game. Warning: They kick both ways.

21. .338 Winchester Magnum
22. .338 Remington Ultra Mag
23. .340 Weatherby
24. .325 Winchester Short Magnum

63 UNDERSTAND WHY THESE ROUNDS RULE

I promised you the ugly truth, and one of the ugliest facts is this: Choice of cartridge ranks fairly low in determining whether you will succeed as a hunter. If you're a good shot, it doesn't matter much what you use. On the other hand, choosing the wrong round can screw you up royally. With that contradiction firmly in mind, here are my top choices in each category, and why I chose them.

SMALL GAME

.22 Long Rifle This gun has no recoil, a comparatively mild report, extraordinary accuracy, and a lack of destructive force, which is just what the job calls for. You can choose between regular velocity, high velocity, and hypervelocity, and between solid-point and hollow-point ammo. I rule out hypervelocity (too destructive and not accurate enough), which leaves regular or high velocity, both of which are fine. I prefer hollow points over solids because they're more certain killers.

Favorite Load
Winchester High Speed Hollow Points

VARMINTS

.223 Remington Known to the military as the 5.56mm, this hugely popular cartridge shoots a 50-grain bullet at 3,300 fps muzzle velocity. When being considered as a military round, it has its detractors, but for varmints (which these days basically means prarie dogs), it is a standout. Among its virtues is low recoil, which is very important because your sight picture must not be disturbed. It also heats up barrels far less than larger .22 centerfires, it's as accurate as anything out there, and, as an extra bonus, there's tons of cheap .223 ammo around.

Favorite Load
Winchester 50-grain Ballistic Silvertip.

VARMINTS AND BIG GAME

6mm Remington Through no fault of its own, the 6mm is less popular than the .243, but it's still a better cartridge. I used both of them for years and found I could always get better velocities with the 6mm. The best factory bullet for varmints is the 80-grain at a listed 3,500 fps; for deer, the 100-grain at 3,100. (In the typical 22-inch-barreled 6mm, you'll find these figures to be wildly optimistic.) Fifteen years ago, I'd have told you that the 6mm is an uncertain killer on big game because the bullets are just too small; however, bullets are now so much better that the objection is withdrawn.

Favorite Load
Remington 100-grain Core-Lokt.

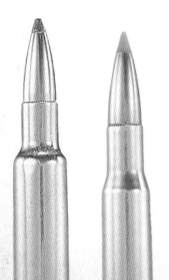
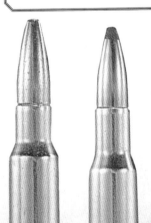

BIG GAME: THE LIGHT KICKERS

7x57 Mauser and 7mm/08 Remington Why two? Because even though one is very old (the 7x57) and one is comparatively modern, ballistically they are alike as peas in a pod (140- or 150-grain bullets at 2,700 fps, give or take a couple of feet). Lots of 7mm/08 rifles are around, and tons of 7x57s. Here is what these cartridges will not do: knock you sideways with recoil or deafen you with muzzle blast. If you wish to use them in short, light rifles, you may do so and the recoil will not cause your lamentations to reach unto heaven. Here is what they will do: kill most species of big game within any reasonable range. Right now. Dead.

Favorite Loads 7x57 Federal Power-Shok 140-grain and Speer Hot-Cor SP. 7mm/0 Winchester Supreme 140-grain Ballistic Silvertip.

BIG GAME: THE ALL-AROUND ROUNDS

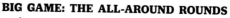

.30/06 Springfield You thought I was going to pick something else and get drummed out of the Gun Writers' Guild and spend the rest of my life being hunted like a criminal? Fat chance. Nope; sorry. The '06 is the unquestioned champ in the do-everything category. Now in its 101st year, the '06 is loaded with bullets ranging in weight from 125 grains to 220 grains, but of these, the most useful are 150 grains at 2,900 fps, 165 grains at 2,800, and 180 grains at 2,700. And you can find all sorts of inexpensive military ammo floating around. Among handloaders, it is no secret that with caution and slow-burning powder, factory ballistics can be significantly bettered. Handloaders also know that one of the most useful bullets for the '06 is the 200-grain slug, which is not available from the factories.

Favorite Loads Of the endless variety out there, I'll try to narrow it down to two Federal Premium Vital-Shok with the 150-grain Nosler Ballistic Tip (shown) and the same brand with the 180-grain Barnes TSX.

BIG GAME AT LONG RANGE

.300 Weatherby Magnum Let me be the first to acknowledge the various huge .30s made by Remington, Lazzeroni, and Dakota, all of which will do everything this one will do, but the Weatherby got here first, and its track record on game is equaled by few other cartridges. If you'd like to kill something, especially a big something, far, far away, use this. Weatherby loads the .300 with bullets ranging in weight from 150 grains (at 3,500 fps) to 220 (at 2,850). But there are only two weights you should consider: the 180-grain at 3,150, or the 200 at 3,000 or just a bit under. The heavier slugs carry just as well as light ones, fight the wind better, and do not result in a lot of ruined meat. Recoil and muzzle blast are for experienced shooters only. Take that to heart.

Favorite Loads Weatherby 180- or 200-grain Nosler Partition.

HEAVY OR DANGEROUS NORTH AMERICAN GAME

.338 Winchester Magnum Despite its serious recoil, this thumper is highly popular because it's amazingly versatile. With 200- or 210-grain bullets (which travel around 2,900 fps), it is a terrific long-range round that will make the deer drop. With 225- to 250-grain slugs, it will handle really large critters with aplomb. A strong 250-grain .338 slug gives tremendous straight-line penetration that you do not get from anything else. You wanna break an elk's shoulder? Here's your cartridge. Recoil is stiff, and if your .338 weighs less than 9 pounds with scope, you will regret it.

Favorite Load Remington Premier 225-grain Swift A-Frame.

64 KNOW YOUR GAME BULLET OPTIONS

Game bullets come in three types: varmint, deer, and controlled-expanding.

VARMINT BULLETS are very accurate and very fragile. They're intended to do a maximum amount of damage and not ricochet. This is achieved through the use of a hollow point, very thin copper jacket, and soft lead core.

DEER BULLETS are built so they combine a reasonable amount of penetration with rapid expansion, and all of them use some or all of these elements: a lead core, copper-alloy jacket that is thin at the nose and thick at the base, "skiving" (grooves that are cut in the jacket's interior to ensure rapid expansion) and—in the better ones—a jacket that is chemically bonded to the core to ensure that the bullet holds together.

CONTROLLED-EXPANDING BULLETS give modest expansion while retaining nearly all of their weight, even when fired into thick hide and heavy bones and muscles. Where a deer bullet might retain 50 percent of its weight after striking an animal, a controlled-expansion slug will keep 90 percent plus, and this greater mass ensures it will penetrate nearly anything. Controlled-expansion bullets come in two types—conventional, which employ lead cores and heavy, bonded copper jackets, and the newer variety, which are all copper or copper alloy. These bullets, although quite expensive (copper costs a lot more than lead), are extremely effective and, very often, exceedingly accurate.

Varmint Bullet

Deer Bullet

65 IDENTIFY BULLET SHAPES

SPITZER A pointed bullet, more streamlined than a round-nose, but structurally less strong. All bullets designed for use at long range are spitzers, as are all military bullets.

ROUND-NOSE A bullet with a blunt nose. Round-noses are employed on dangerous-game bullets and on bullets that are used in rifles with tubular magazines, where a spitzer point could detonate the primer of the cartridge ahead of it.

SEMI-SPITZER A shape that falls somewhere in between and combines the advantages and disadvantages of both types.

FLAT-BASE A bullet with no taper at its base. Not aerodynamic, but strong.

BOATTAIL A bullet whose base tapers toward the bottom, like a boat's stern when viewed from above. Boattails and spitzer points are usually combined.

REBATED BOATTAIL A boattail that curves inward, leading to a base that is of markedly smaller diameter than that of the bullet. It's more streamlined than a simple boattail.

VLD Very Low Drag is the most extreme type of bullet streamlining, incorporating a very sharp point with a long taper and a rebated boattail.

Flat-based Spitzer

Flat-based Round-nose

Boattail Spitzer

VLD

Conventional Controlled-Expanding Bullet

All Copper Controlled-Expanding Bullet

66 FORGET ABOUT HYPERVELOCITY

With every decade, cartridges get bigger and muzzle velocities get higher. Maybe it's time to ask why. Now it's true that you can kill a tiger with a .250/3000, or with a .22 Long Rifle (and I will come to visit you in prison), but it is a stunt. High velocity by itself does not kill anything faster than standard velocity. I started out believing devoutly in lots of speed, but 40 years later, having shot creatures of all sizes with just about everything that goes bang, I've never been able to find any correlation between bullet speed and sudden animal demise. For 15 years, I hunted whitetails in South Carolina, where you can shoot lots and lots of deer, so I had the ability to draw some valid comparisons. The smallest cartridge I used was the .257 Roberts; in other years I used the .270 Winchester, .257 Weatherby, and 7mm Weatherby. None of them killed anything any faster or deader than any other cartridge. Same with the .338, .340 Weatherby, and .338 Remington Ultra Magnum, all of which I have used a lot. The latter two give anywhere from 250 to 300 fps more than the former, which is a bunch, but the beasts do not go down any quicker. In addition, consider the following.

RECOIL A high-velocity-loaded rifle can generate 28 to 40 foot-pounds of recoil, which is tolerable only to experienced shooters and the criminally insane. In addition, muzzle blast also rises proportionately.

IMPACT When you get bullets traveling at 3,000 fps and more (sometimes way more), even the strongest and slowest-expanding of them makes a mess of whatever it hits unless the shot is long enough to let some of the velocity drain off. If you are a trophy hunter and don't mind an acre or so of hamburger around the entrance hole, this is not an objection. But if you like wild meat and are disturbed by the waste of same, it is a problem.

BARREL LIFE It's considerably shorter for the super-speed than it is for standard-velocity loads. A well-cared-for .30/06 (60 grains of powder per cartridge) will give you about 5,000 rounds of first-class accuracy. Any of the super .30s (80 grains of powder) will get perhaps 1,500 before they start to deteriorate. This gets expensive fast.

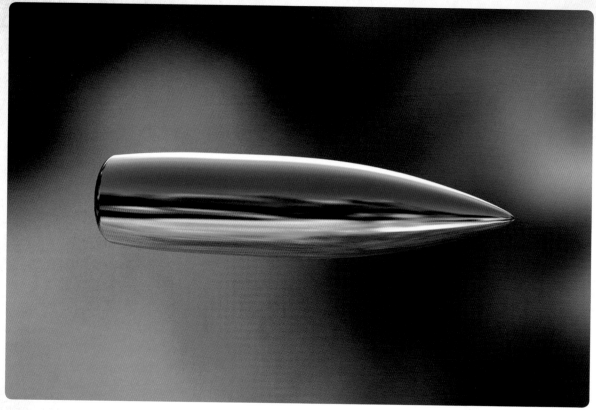

67 DO HIGH VELOCITY RIGHT

Why does high velocity keep getting higher, and horrific super loads keep appearing? Because nothing makes hitting at long distances easier than a good dose of feet per second. If you think you will ever need to take a shot at 300 yards and more, high velocity is your very best friend.

However, it's also the case that speed alone will not solve all your problems in hitting at long range. You also need resistance to wind drift and momentum, or the ability to sustain velocity way out there. The way you get it is by going not to light bullets that give the highest initial velocity, but to the heavier slugs in a given caliber, and to bullets that are streamlined.

For example, if you have a 7mm Magnum, you want 160-grain bullets in preference to 140- or 150-grain. If your rifle is one of the real 7mm monsters, you may find that 175-grainers are the way to go. In .30 caliber, look for nothing lighter than 180-grain, and so on. As for bullets, you want sharp points (preferably polycarbonate) and boattails, both of which increase a slug's ballistic coefficient.

The truth about high velocity is that it is a mixed blessing. But when your target is a dot in the distance, it is the deadliest thing since cholera.

68 REMEMBER BILLY DIXON

In the 1870s, at a place called Adobe Walls in Texas, a group of buffalo hunters was trapped in an abandoned mission by a band of Comanche warriors who looked forward to slitting them from crotch to brisket with a dull deer antler. Things looked bad for the hunters until one Billy Dixon shot the Comanche leader dead at what was probably close to a mile, and the rest of the war

party remembered they had pressing business elsewhere. Dixon made this shot with a .50 Sharps buffalo rifle, which hurled a lumbering 500-grain bullet at roughly 1,200 fps. Instead of a scope, he had a peep sight called a vernier sight. Rangefinder? Nope. Ballistics program? Nope. Shooting experience? Plenty. Incentive? Loads. It worked for him, and it can work for you.

69 SHOOT MORE, SHOOT BETTER

In 1965, I worked up my first handload, took myself to the range, and sat cowering behind the rifle for five minutes before I got the nerve to pull the trigger. I was convinced that I was about to splatter important parts of my person up and down the firing line. Many thousands of handloads later, I'm still intact. I've also saved a ton of money, become a better rifle shot than I would have otherwise, and gotten superior accuracy from legions of rifles.

I know a number of very good rifle shots, and without exception, they load their own ammo. The reason for this is that if you want to shoot well, you have to shoot a lot. The only way you can afford to shoot a lot is to make a lot of money or load your own ammo. I've found that it's a lot easier to load your own ammo.

The most expensive component in a round of centerfire ammunition is the brass case—just under 50 percent of the total cost, in fact—and if you can save that case and

substitute your labor for the factory's in loading it, you can suddenly afford to shoot in volume. Once you buy your basic tools—press, scale, dies, primer seater, etc.—you're pretty much done, because nothing wears out.

Your only expense over the long term is the components, which is to say powder, bullets, primers, and cases. (Yes, the cases do wear out eventually, but unless your pressures are high, you can get 10 to 15 loadings out of a brass case without much trouble.) Look for bargains. Someone is always having a sale or going out of business, and that is where you jump in.

In addition, there's the fact that only the handloader knows the joy of switching to a different powder, or using a half grain more or less, or changing primer brands, or seating the bullet a little farther in or a little farther out, and seeing mediocre groups turn into bragging groups. It's magic, is what it is.

70 LOAD YOUR OWN AMMO

Getting started requires less money than you'd think, and the equipment never wears out. (I'm still using a lot of the gear that I bought in the mid '60s.) You need: a press, a powder measure, a die set, a powder trickler, a caliper to measure case lengths, a case trimmer, a deburring tool, a primer pocket cleaner, case lube, a powder scale, a powder funnel, and a loading manual. That's the basic gear list. If it all seems like too much to keep track of, you can buy a starter kit that will have almost everything you need.

Loading your own ammo requires no mechanical aptitude and no manual dexterity.

It's a series of very simple steps. The exact details vary depending on the ammo in question, which is why you need to get a couple of loading manuals and read them before you even start. You will then have a grasp of the basics. What the manuals can't supply is judgment—how to gauge pressures, how to look at a group that's not so tight and be able to tighten it. This is something you get from experience and from consulting with other handloaders who know what they're talking about.

All of that said, here are the very basic steps.

1. Clean inside the case's neck with a bristle brush.

2. Lubricate the case lightly on the lube pad.

3. Run the case through the sizing die using your bullet press; this will also remove any used primer.

4. Check your case's length with the caliper. Trim the case with the trimmer if needed.

5. Use your deburring tool to smooth the inside and outside of the case's mouth.

6. Clean the primer pocket with your primer pocket brush.

7. Prime the case using your priming tool.

8. Weigh out the powder on your scale and pour into the case using a powder funnel.

9. Seat the bullet into the case using the bullet seating die.

71 KEEP IT SAFE

Handloading is considerably safer than driving. When assembling ammunition, you do not have to share a road with homicidal maniacs texting away at 70 mph. What the hobby does require is that you understand what you're doing, do not assume that you know more than the loading manuals, and pay attention. I feel a lot easier about smokeless powder in my house than I do about gasoline cans in the garage. Primers are very stable; all they ask is that you handle them with the respect they deserve. It's both unwise and unnecessary to keep a lot of powder on hand. Although smokeless powder is no more dangerous than cleaning fluid or propane or gasoline, you don't want a ton of it in your house because if you do have a fire and it catches, you will have a really dandy blaze to contend with. On top of that, there may be legal restrictions on how much you can store in a residential dwelling, so check. Then keep only what you need on hand, and no more. And if you have kids around, keep all your reloading gear (including primers and powder) locked up.

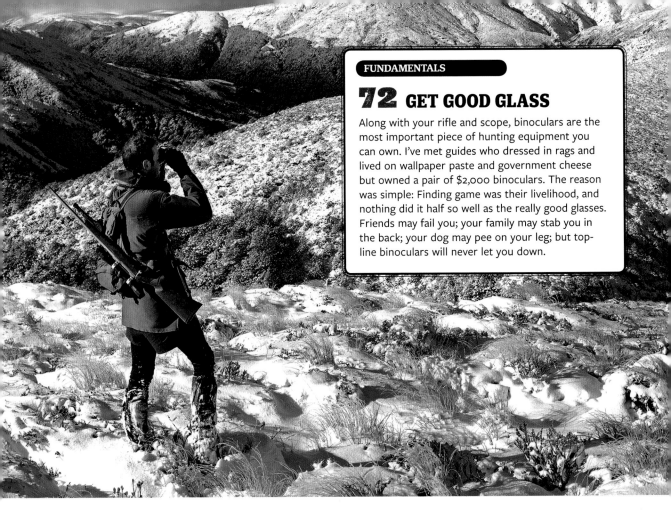

72 GET GOOD GLASS

Along with your rifle and scope, binoculars are the most important piece of hunting equipment you can own. I've met guides who dressed in rags and lived on wallpaper paste and government cheese but owned a pair of $2,000 binoculars. The reason was simple: Finding game was their livelihood, and nothing did it half so well as the really good glasses. Friends may fail you; your family may stab you in the back; your dog may pee on your leg; but top-line binoculars will never let you down.

73 SPEAK FLUENT BINOCULAR

LENSES AND PRISMS A lens brings an object into focus. But when you look at an object through a lens, it appears upside down, and you need to put the image right side up before it reaches your eye. That's the job of the prism, a wedge-shaped assemblage of glass pieces that bends the light coming through a lens. There are two types: roof and porro. Roof-prism binoculars demand greater precision in manufacture than porros and are usually more expensive. But most hunters choose them anyway because they are more compact than porro-prism models. Lenses are often used in combination to cancel out each other's optical faults. A lens that is alone is called a singlet, two lenses used together is a doublet, three is a triplet.

POWER Another term for magnification, *power* is almost always expressed along with the size of the objective lenses in millimeters. Therefore, a 7x35 glass magnifies seven times, and its objective lenses are 35 millimeters in diameter. The most popular strengths for hunting are 8X and 10X.

The lower the power, the wider your field of view and the easier it is to hold the binocular steady. Still, I have always preferred 10X glasses. The field of view shrinks, and it's harder to hold them steady, but you get to see in detail. I own two pairs of binoculars in 12X that I have used for elk hunting and varmint hunting, and I love them madly.

BRIGHTNESS The objective-lens diameter determines the amount of light that enters the glass. The bigger they are in relation to magnification, the brighter the glass (in theory at least). A 7x42 binocular will be brighter than a 7x35 because of the larger objective. The other number you need to know when thinking about brightness is the diameter of the exit pupil. All else being equal, the bigger the brighter. The way you calculate the size of the exit pupil is by dividing the diameter of the objective lens by the magnification of the instrument. So a 10x42 binocular has an exit pupil of 4.2. The same glass in 8x42 has an exit pupil of 5.3 and will be brighter.

74 KNOW YOUR COATINGS

When light passes through glass, it tends to reflect in all directions. This causes the image to dim, distorts the colors you see, degrades contrast, and may give you leprosy for all I know. The solution is to apply a coat of magnesium fluoride that is .00004 to .00006 inch thick. Much shuck and jive about coatings is foisted on the public. There are four levels of the process, which Thomas McIntyre admirably describes in his excellent little book *The Field & Stream Hunting Optics Handbook* as follows.

COATED A single layer of coating has been lavishly slapped on at least one lens surface, somewhere.

FULLY COATED A single layer has been applied to all the "air to glass" surfaces, which includes the two sides of any air-spaced elements inside the optics.

MULTICOATED Several layers of antireflective coating have been applied to at least one lens surface.

FULLY MULTICOATED All air-to-glass surfaces have received multiple layers of antireflective coating.

But we are not yet done with coatings. When light passes through roof prisms, the wavelengths of different colors of the spectrum do so at different rates, and the result is a degraded image. The cure is a process called "phase coating." All self-respecting roof-prism binoculars are phase-coated.

75 SHUN CHEAP BINOCULARS

Cheap binoculars are worse than no binoculars. You need to spend a little money, but bargains are out there. Go cheaper than a few hundred bucks, and you are likely to end up with an inanimate hideosity. I've never known someone to spend money on good binoculars and regret it. The usual reaction is "Why did I wait so long?"

COMFORT If you are using a binocular properly, you will look through it by the hour. If your glass is a good one, you will be able to do this with no trouble. But poor binoculars, as my late friend Gary Sitton once said, "will suck the eyeballs out of your skull."

LONGEVITY Top-line binoculars, though they may become technically obsolete because they lack some sensational new feature, will still be top-line binoculars long after you have fired your last shot.

VALUE People who just have to have the latest and most advanced of everything will trade off a pair of first-rate binoculars quicker than you can say "exit pupil." For this reason, there are spectacular deals online and at gun shows for used top-line glass.

76 FOLLOW THE LIGHT

Not sure what happens when you peer through a pair of binoculars? Here's a quick overview.

Light, and the image it carries, does what it wants, not what you want, so the job of a binocular is to keep it under control. The objective lens **[a]** gathers the image, simultaneously inverting it, and sending it down the binocular barrel to the focus lens **[b]**, which is set in a housing that moves forward and backward and is in turn controlled by the focus wheel **[c]**.

The image next encounters the roof prism **[d]**, whose job it is to turn the image right side up. (In order to avoid light loss by all this bouncing around, the prism's surfaces are given what is known as phase coating to prevent light dispersion.) This is done by reflecting it from as many as 16 surfaces, until it arrives, exhausted but erect, at the ocular lens **[e]**, which magnifies it.

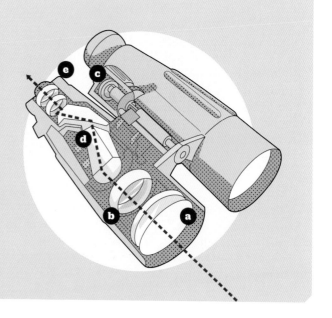

77 SCOPE IT OUT

TUBES Today's rifle scopes are drawn from aircraft-grade aluminum and are available in two finishes: shiny and matte. A shiny scope tube is nothing more than a warning light that says to animals, "Why die when you can run?" A hunter needs a shiny scope tube like he needs a freshly polished tuba.

Tubes come in two diameters—1 inch and 30mm. It's claimed that 30mm tubes allow more light in. I doubt it. But they are structurally stronger and allow more latitude of adjustment, which helps you get your rifle on the paper even if something is out of alignment somewhere.

BELLS At either end of the scope tube are the objective-lens housing, or bell, and the ocular-lens housing, or bell (this is the one that cracks you in the eyebrow). As the power of the scope increases and/or the manufacturer wants to admit more light, the size of the objective bell increases. Most for hunting are between 40mm and 50mm. I'm perfectly happy with 40mm or 42mm most of the time. The bigger the lens, the more the scope weighs, the more it costs, the clumsier it makes the rifle to handle, and the more difficult it is to mount on the receiver.

ADJUSTMENTS All scopes have adjustments for windage (lateral) and elevation (up and down). The elevation dial is at 12 o'clock, the windage dial at 3 o'clock. What these dials are supposed to do, via a system of small, fragile, and treacherous parts, is adjust where you place the crosshairs to match the bullet's point of impact. Most scopes claim to change the point of impact 1/4 inch per click at 100 yards. In reality, they do what they please, and you just have to live with it. The best windage and elevation adjustments move with a solid, firm click or a thunk, and this is one of the things to look for when you buy a scope. Some scopes also have adjustment for parallax, to adjust the sight-picture's focus at precise distances, which is handy if you'll shoot at long range or at small targets.

The simplest of all adjustments is focus. To focus a scope, point it at the sky or a wall and turn the ocular-lens bell until the reticle appears sharp. Then lock the bell in place. If there's no locking ring, you need to get a better scope.

EYE RELIEF This is the distance between the ocular-lens bell and your eye when you're looking through it; if you don't have enough of it, you will eventually hear the melodious sound of aluminum splitting your eyebrow. Eye relief decreases in proportion to scope power. Depending on how much your rifle kicks, you need an absolute minimum of 3 inches. On a heavy-kicking rifle, 4 is the least you can get away with.

LENSES The quality of the glass and the coating applied to it determine in large part how good a scope is. Even if you know nothing about scopes, you can look through a $200 scope, and then a $1,200 scope, and know instantly which is which. The difference in image quality is startling, and is what you pay all that money for.

RETICLES In the 1960s, Leupold developed the Duplex crosshair, and that has been the standard for hunters ever since. It pulls your eye to the center, which makes for fast aiming, and also makes it possible to aim with precision. Of all the reticles out there, I believe it's the best.

In recent years, manufacturers have added LED lights to reticles, and here's what I can tell you about them: First, they function extremely well. Second, I'm not quite sure why we need them.

Range-compensating reticles consist of crosshairs on the vertical stadia wire of the scope that show where to hold for a given distance, sometimes out to 600 yards. They work extremely well provided you read the directions and pay strict attention to them.

Duplex-type Reticles

Range-compensating Reticles

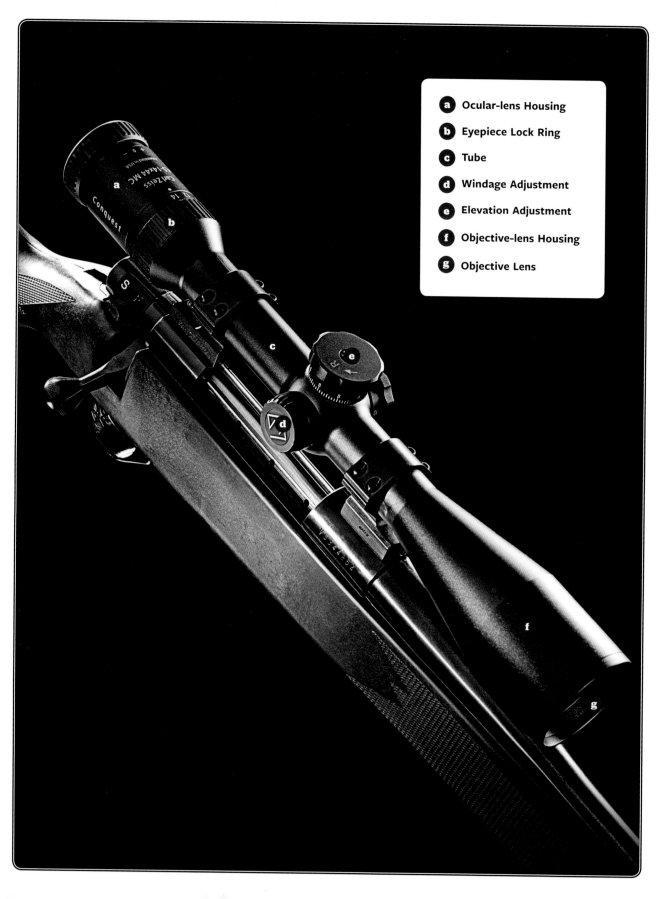

a Ocular-lens Housing

b Eyepiece Lock Ring

c Tube

d Windage Adjustment

e Elevation Adjustment

f Objective-lens Housing

g Objective Lens

78 POWER DOWN (OR UP)

The more power you have, the more difficult it is to keep a steady hold, and the greater the effect that mirage has on your sight picture. In addition, powerful scopes are bulky, heavy, and expensive. On the whole, less is more. Today, the variable-power scope is supreme because it offers a degree of flexibility that is genuinely useful. Here's a rough guide to the power ranges that work best:

BIG GAME

3X–9X or 2X–10X

DANGEROUS GAME

1X–4X

VARMINTS

6X–24X

79 DIAL IT BACK

Because of the current tactical craze, an increasing number of scopes have exposed dials with no caps over them. I believe these have no place on a big-game rifle. Snipers need them because they routinely crank in windage and elevation adjustments to compensate for the extreme ranges at which they shoot. But because these knobs are exposed, they can turn accidentally, or be damaged by a blow that a capped dial would survive.

QUICK SHOT

80 SEE THE TARGET

A deer-size animal looks very small at 400 yards; that is why variable-power scopes that magnify up to 10X were invented. Here is what the typical whitetail looks like with the scope cranked to 9X. More magnification means more reticle movement with each twitch.

| 100 yds | 200 yds | 300 yds | 400 yds |

81 MARK THE SPOT WITH A DOT

Red-dot sights are optical sights, but unlike scopes they don't magnify, and there's no crosshair—just a red dot. Red dots offer some distinct advantages over scopes: They're smaller, lighter, tougher, and faster to get on target. They have unlimited eye relief, which makes them a natural for a heavy rifle. For a firearm that will be used inside of 200 yards, they deserve very serious consideration.

Their disadvantage is, they don't magnify. So if you have geezer eyesight, or are going to shoot at long range or at small targets, you'll need some Xs in your scope.

82 AVOID FOGGED LENSES

When you hunt in truly cold weather, develop the habit of holding your breath as you raise the rifle to aim. If you don't, you may breathe on your scope's ocular lens, and you'll find yourself trying to aim through a fogbank. You can cloud up even the fog-proof coatings on the newest scopes; they're designed to deal with water droplets, not breath vapor. This applies to binoculars as well.

83 MOUNT IT RIGHT

When mounting a scope, many shooters set it in the rings so that the vertical crosshair tilts right or left. That's because when you rest your cheek on the comb and look through the sight, your head is canted. The problem with an out-of-kilter vertical crosshair is that it is out of line with the axis of the bore, and your bullets will not fly in line with it.

To ensure a straight crosshair, you want to simply put the fore-end of the rifle on a solid rest, then position your head behind the butt of the rifle and sight through the scope. You'll be able to see very clearly whether the crosshair is tilted. If it is, correct accordingly.

KEEP IT CLEAN

Some time ago, I was asked how to clean a rifle. There are as many different ways to do this as there are to summon Beelzebub, and there is no single "correct" method. Whatever works, works. Think of cleaning as a two-stage process. First you get out the powder fouling and then you get out the copper.

For powder fouling, I use Shooter's Choice solvent and phosphor-bronze brushes. When you're finished with a brush, give it a toot from a can of Birchwood Casey Gun Scrubber; this will get the dirt off the brush and will keep the Shooter's Choice from eating the bronze bristles.

COMBAT RUST

Bluing, by itself, is not protection. Bluing is created by controlled rusting, and its only contribution in the fight against corrosion is its ability to retain oil.

Oil prevents rust, but not for long. If you're interested in serious protection for your firearm, a very thin coat of floor wax works better than oil, particularly on the bottom of the barrel and receiver where they are in contact with the stock.

Body chemistry also causes guns to rust. This occurs via fingerprints; it's why you see arms-collection curators handling their treasures with white gloves. Some people's fingerprints are positively poisonous; other folks can grope guns forever without leaving a speck of the red stuff.

Stainless steel is not immune to rust. That's because the "stainless" steel used in firearms is not truly stainless. It will rust the same as chrome-moly; it just takes a little bit longer.

Dirty guns rust faster, and rust worse, than clean guns. This is because dirt attracts and holds moisture.

Light surface rust can sometimes be removed by rubbing gently with oooo steel wool and Shooter's Choice powder solvent. If actual pits have formed, a gunsmith will have to polish them out and reblue the afflicted part. And if the pits are deep enough, too bad; you'll have to live with them.

Storing guns where air cannot circulate is like hanging out a sign that says, RUST WELCOME! Some prime examples are storing guns in a vinyl case that can't breathe, or plugging the barrel with grease at one or both ends. The new "freeze-dry" storage cases, from which you pump out all the air, are the exception to this rule.

If you're hunting in a heavy rain and decide to put off wiping down your rifle at the end of the day until you've had a cup of warm milk or two, you may find yourself with a hell of a case of rust. Your rifle comes first, always.

86 DEAL WITH POWDER FOULING

CLEAN YOUR BORE For copper fouling, I use J-B Non Embedding Bore Cleaning Compound. Other copper-killers will not work on some barrels, or take forever, or will pit your bore if you leave them in too long. This stuff works fast and will get all the copper out for sure.

KEEP YOUR RODS CLEAN This is why God gave us paper towels. A dirty rod is an instrument of destruction.

NO SLOT-TYPE PATCH HOLDERS You do not want to drag dirty patches back and forth through the bore. Each patch gets one trip only.

BE SURE When you think you're done, leave the bore wet with Shooter's Choice for a couple of hours and then run a dry patch through. If it comes out with no green on it, you're done. Then run a Rem-Oil patch through the bore and a dry one after it.

CLEAN THE CHAMBER with a dry patch. You don't want anything at all left in there.

87 ASSUME NOTHING

Just when you think you know everything you get a lesson in humility. I have a very, very accurate .22 with a Lilja barrel that was installed by gunsmith John Blauvelt. After a while, the rifle wouldn't extract the fired brass. So I went whining to John and asked him to see what was wrong with the extractors. It turned out there was nothing wrong with them. Instead, when he put the bore scope up its bore, lo and behold there was a disgusting ring of lead and burned powder near the front of the chamber. It had not been removed even by regular cleaning with a bronze-bristle .22 brush. It turns out that tight-chambered .22s often suffer from this type of loathsome deposit, and the way to get it out is to take a 6mm phospor-bronze brush and scrub the hell out of it. A .22 brush won't do because it doesn't fit tightly enough.

88 SPEND SMART

Extensive work on firearms, particularly older ones, should be thought out very carefully. If a rifle is inaccurate, working on it may not make it a shooter. With so many incredibly accurate guns available right out of the box, my attitude these days is that if it doesn't shoot, sell it. Most old guns are not worth redoing. Leave them alone and accept their scars and dings as badges of honor. That said, you may own guns that have a sentimental value and wish to improve their appearance. Such work does not increase the gun's worth to a collector but nonetheless enhances the owning experience to you. If that's the case, go right ahead.

89 KEEP YOUR GUN HAPPY

The tragedy of rifle neglect (like dandruff or flatulence) occurs in even the finest people. But that doesn't make it right. Your rifle wants to be your friend and will perform faithfully for you. All it needs to succeed at this is some careful but cheap attention, outlined in these 10 steps.

SCRUB THE BARREL Scrub away with powder solvent, patches, and a phosphor-bronze brush, and then polish all the little grooves and lands with J-B Non-Embedding Bore Cleaning Compound. When you can no longer see copper streaks from the muzzle end, you're done.

FIX THE DINGS Major dents in a wood-stocked rifle can often be raised by laying a damp cleaning patch over the depression and heating the cloth with the tip of a hot iron. The steam will work its way into the wood fibers, causing them to swell, and the dent will either diminish or vanish.

HOSE DOWN THE ACTION Get a can of Birchwood Casey Gun Scrubber. Next, take your barreled action out of its stock and remove the scope. (If you have a lever or pump or auto, remove the buttstock.) Now, working outdoors and wearing safety glasses, spray down the action, and in the case of a bolt gun, the trigger as well. The most amazing stuff will come out. Do not re-oil. I will say that again: Do not re-oil.

REMOVE THE GOO While the barreled action is out of the stock, wipe off all the accumulated goo that's on the underside of the barrel and the receiver. Do this to the corresponding surfaces in the stock as well. Re-oil the metal surfaces you've just cleaned. Lightly.

INSPECT THE BASE While the scope is off the rifle, make sure the base screws are tight. If you're really conscientious, remove the bases and check for oil that's seeped underneath. Wipe it off. Degrease all surfaces, including the base screws and screw holes, and replace the bases. Be sure the screws are as tight as they were before.

CLEAN YOUR SCOPE LENSES Treat your delicate optics kindly; use camera lens cleaning solution and lens tissue. You can find them at any photo-supply store.

REMOVE RUST Light rust can be removed by scrubbing with 0000 steel wool and a little oil. A rusted trigger is a more serious problem; a gunsmith will have to take it apart and clean it or replace it.

REBLUE WORN AREAS Some shooters consider bright spots to be the equivalent of campaign ribbons. I do, to an

extent. But they are more likely to rust than blued surfaces, so you may want to get rid of them with a bottle of gun blue.

REPLACE BURRED SCREWS The best way to get new ones is from a gunsmith. They buy spare screws by the bushel and can sell you the exact number and size you need. This includes not only ring and base screws but also bedding screws.

UPGRADE TO TORX Even if your slot- or hex-head base and ring screws are not damaged, consider replacing them with torx screws. These rank among the great inventions of man because you can drive the suckers in tight and they are almost impossible to bugger up, even by the most ham-handed people. Base screws should be tightened until blood seeps from under your fingernails. Ring screws should be tightened firmly, not obsessively, because you may have to take your scope off in the field, where a screw that won't budge is the last thing you need.

90 EXORCISE DEMONS FROM YOUR RIFLE

Rifles do not suffer from demonic possession; it only seems that way sometimes. They will not swivel their heads 360 degrees and hurl in your general direction, but they will cause you to miss, which is probably worse. Life is hard enough without inaccurate rifles. Here's how to cure them—and avoid them.

CHECK THE SCOPE In many cases, "inaccurate" rifles are not inaccurate at all but are wearing ruptured scopes. To see if the scope adjustments work, try "squaring the circle." Fire a shot; then, aiming at the same point each time, move the reticle 12 clicks (3 inches) up; then 12 clicks right; then 12 down; then 12 left. You should end up with four shots forming a square. If you don't, send the scope back to the manufacturer for repair.

CLEAN THE BARREL Rifle barrels must have absolutely uniform dimensions (to the ten-thousandth of an inch) for the length of their bores in order to be accurate. So when you don't clean a barrel and the copper fouling starts building up, accuracy goes out the window.

SHOOT DIFFERENT AMMO If the gun still won't group the way you'd like, try all the different ammo you can get your hands on because some rifles "prefer" one brand and weight of bullet over another.

BACK IT GOES If you experiment as far as your budget and your patience will let you and the rifle still won't group, your next step is to send it back to the manufacturer.

91 CURE A SICK TRIGGER

From the 1980s until about 2000, rifle makers routinely put out guns that were excellent—except for the trigger. Today's triggers are infinitely better, but there are still plenty of dogs out there. If you shoot less than a box of ammo a year and take your rifle out of the case only during deer season, don't worry about your trigger—you're not a serious shooter. But if you don't shoot well, want to improve, and your trigger is part of the problem, you can adjust or replace it. A gunsmith will take it completely apart, polish the engaging surfaces, and/ or replace the spring that controls the pull weight. He or she may also tell you that nothing can be done with your trigger, and that might be true. You can replace it with a much better model for a good price. If you are a serious shooter and/or have a fine rifle that you would like to turn into a super gun, you will not begrudge a penny that you spend.

92 JOIN THE (ACCURACY) REVOLUTION

What makes a super-accurate rifle? It must be three things: stiff, concentric, and stress free. To see how this works, let's start with stiffness.

Back in the 1950s, benchrest shooters discovered that bolt actions flex upon recoil, literally squirming in the receiver, and that all this fidgeting did not make for small groups. So these folks began "sleeving"—welding massive reinforcements to actions in order to give them some backbone. Today, the most accurate rifles all have receivers that are cylindrical in cross-section and have a minimum amount of steel cut out of them for magazines, bolt-lug raceways, and so on. Some have flat bottoms to make precise bedding easier, but otherwise, those suckers are round.

The same principle extends to the barrel. A bullet passing through causes it to vibrate in a complex pattern, resembling the writhing of a serpent. The less and more consistent the writhing, the better the rifle will shoot. Short and/or heavy barrels writhe less and more consistently than thin and/or long barrels.

Concentricity is simple. If everything is not in line with everything else, your rifle will not shoot well. When a barrel blank is first drilled prior to rifling, the hole must go dead straight through its center. When the finished barrel is screwed into the receiver, it must be perfectly aligned with same. The chamber into which the bullet goes must be precisely centered with the bore, and when a cartridge is seated in the chamber, its bullet must be centered, too.

And finally we come to stress, which is bad for people and very bad for rifles. When a rifle is fired, the entire mechanism—lock, stock, and barrel—vibrates like a tuning fork. Stress causes that vibration to become inconsistent, and inconsistency in any form is death to accuracy. Stress occurs when one part of the rifle bears too tightly, or with uneven pressure, against another part of the rifle. It's eliminated by having everything fit together correctly.

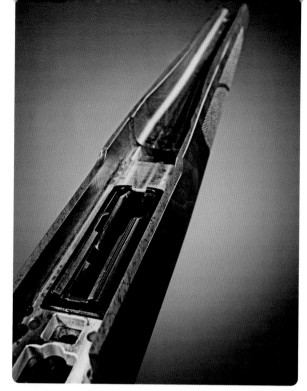

93 KNOW WHY IT WORKS

LOCK TIME is the interval between when the sear releases the firing pin and the primer ignites. Long lock times invite aiming errors, because you can flinch in those fractions of a second. Most modern bolt guns have fast lock times.

TRIGGERS If you have to haul on something that does not want to give, you are not going to shoot well.

THE BARREL must be straight, and its rifling grooves and lands must be of the same depth for the whole length of the bore. A maker of first-rate barrels is obliged to let the depths of his grooves vary no more than .0005 of an inch.

BEDDING Back in the good old days (up until the late 1950s), most rifle barrels were full-length bedded with a bit of upward pressure on the barrel to damp its vibrations. With a good, stable piece of wood and a stockmaker who knew what he was doing, it was a satisfactory system. If, however, the wood shrank or swelled, or the inletting was poorly done, the result was wretched.

The modern solution is to free float the barrel—to bed it solidly to the end of the chamber and let the rest of it wave in the air. The theory is that since there's nothing to interfere with the tube, it will vibrate the same for every shot. For the most part, this theory works very well, especially with heavy barrels. But there is one drawback. The gap between the barrel and the barrel channel, if there's a lot of it, is ugly. I've seen free-floated barrels with enough room under them to start a small nutria ranch.

Some gunmakers believe in full fore-end contact. Melvin Forbes, who builds New Ultra Light Arms rifles, glass-beds his barrels to have complete contact (but no pressure) from action to fore-end, but because his stocks are made of Kevlar and graphite and don't shift, he doesn't have to worry about warping or shrinking or swelling.

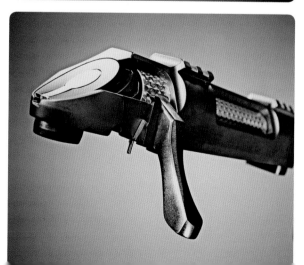

STOCKS In the late 1970s, the first practical synthetic stocks made their appearance. Disdained by traditionalists, they were pretty crude looking, but they were stronger, lighter, stiffer, and unaffected by changes in humidity. For the first time, they gave rifle builders a truly stable platform to build on. Along with synthetic stocks came pillar bedding. In its simplest form, it consists of two thick aluminum tubes that are epoxied into the stock. The front and rear bedding screws pass through them, and the action tang and the front of the receiver rest on them, giving you complete metal-to-metal contact. You can't compress them no matter how hard you turn the screws.

94 KNOW WHAT YOUR BULLET IS DOING

Dime-size groups fired on the range are one thing, but hitting game under hunting conditions is quite another. What you see here are some of the practical problems involved in the latter. The cartridge involved is one of the most effective long-range rounds available, the Federal version of the .270 Winchester Short Magnum, loaded with 140-grain Nosler AccuBonds—real-world velocity in a 24-inch barrel, about 3,100 feet per second, or fps.

MEDIUM DISTANCE What applies to 100 yards applies here. The problem is one of appearances. Two hundred yards looks much farther than 100 yards and causes people to compensate for range and wind when they don't need to.

IN CLOSE At 100 yards, you don't need to think about ballistics. The trajectory is flat, and even a strong crosswind is not going to move the bullet enough to matter. All you have to do is pick an aiming point and not aim the rifle at the whole deer in general.

MOA = minute of angle

THE SHOOTER Offhand shots are sometimes a necessity, but you should always try for a rest or a more stable position. Only a fool shoots offhand past 100 yards.

Sighting and Aiming The best system of all, for those without range-compensating reticles, is to sight in 3 inches high at 100 yards. With the .270 WSM, that will give you an effective point-blank range of 300 yards, or a bit more. If you want to shoot at 400 yards, you had better get a reticle with mil dots that will allow you to avoid the horrors of holding off target.

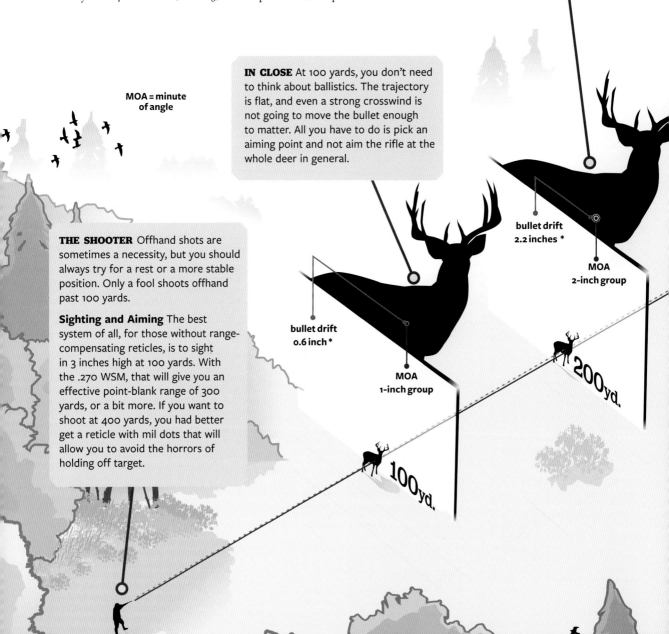

bullet drift
2.2 inches *

MOA
2-inch group

bullet drift
0.6 inch *

MOA
1-inch group

200yd.

100yd.

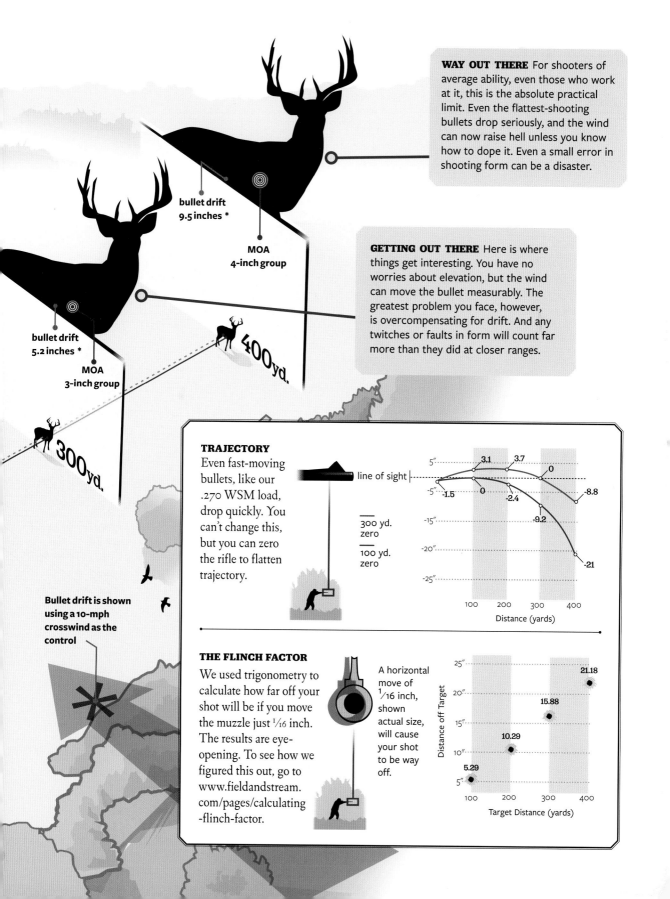

WAY OUT THERE For shooters of average ability, even those who work at it, this is the absolute practical limit. Even the flattest-shooting bullets drop seriously, and the wind can now raise hell unless you know how to dope it. Even a small error in shooting form can be a disaster.

bullet drift
9.5 inches *

MOA
4-inch group

GETTING OUT THERE Here is where things get interesting. You have no worries about elevation, but the wind can move the bullet measurably. The greatest problem you face, however, is overcompensating for drift. And any twitches or faults in form will count far more than they did at closer ranges.

bullet drift
5.2 inches *

MOA
3-inch group

400 yd.

300 yd.

Bullet drift is shown using a 10-mph crosswind as the control

TRAJECTORY
Even fast-moving bullets, like our .270 WSM load, drop quickly. You can't change this, but you can zero the rifle to flatten trajectory.

line of sight

300 yd. zero
100 yd. zero

5"   3.1   3.7   0
-5" -1.5   0   -8.8
           -2.4
-15"   -9.2
-20"
-25"   -21

100   200   300   400
Distance (yards)

THE FLINCH FACTOR
We used trigonometry to calculate how far off your shot will be if you move the muzzle just ¹⁄16 inch. The results are eye-opening. To see how we figured this out, go to www.fieldandstream. com/pages/calculating -flinch-factor.

A horizontal move of ¹⁄16 inch, shown actual size, will cause your shot to be way off.

25"   21.18
20"   15.88
15"
          10.29
10"
5"   5.29

100   200   300   400
Target Distance (yards)

Distance off Target

95 FIGURE OUT YOUR BULLET'S TRAJECTORY

From the instant a bullet leaves the barrel, it begins to drop. How much? The only way to find out for sure is to go out with your rifle and whatever ammo you favor and shoot at 100, 200, and 300 yards. Sight in your rifle to hit 3 inches high at 100. Then, set up a National Rifle Association 50-Yard Slow Fire Pistol Target (the one with the 8-inch-diameter bull) at 200 yards, hold right on the center, and fire five shots. You'll probably see no drop at all. If you do, make a note of it.

Move back to 300 yards and try the same thing. If your rifle produces at least 3,000 fps, you'll probably get a drop of 3 inches below the center of the bull. If you're working with 2,600 to 2,850 fps, then you'll see a drop of 6 to 8 inches from center.

When the time comes to shoot at something that's alive, you'll have very little to do in the way of calculation. If your

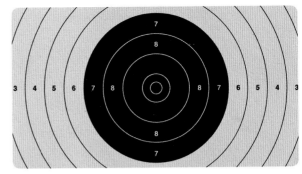

bullet drops 3 or 4 inches from center, hold where you normally would, more or less on the center of the body. If the drop is 6 to 8 inches, you may or may not have to allow for it. On a big animal like an elk or a caribou, I would hold a handbreadth (4 inches) high. On something small (an antelope or a ratty little whitetail, for example), I'd allow two handbreadths. Whatever you do, as long as you know that the range is no more than 300 yards, never hold out of the hair. Untold numbers of animals have fled from bullets whizzing over their backs.

When you're shooting uphill or downhill, hold low. The closer to vertical a bullet flies—either high or low—the less it drops over distance. How much to hold? I can't tell you. I can only advise that you'll probably miss more shots by overcompensating rather than undercompensating.

96 CALCULATE WIND DRIFT

I've seen numerous formulas for calculating wind drift in the field, none of which are any good when your brain is boiling prior to a shot. The only workable one comes from my friend and colleague Wayne van Zwoll. According to Wayne, if you're shooting 180-grain .30/06 bullets at 2,700 fps, and the wind is coming at 10 mph from a right angle, allow 1 inch at 100 yards, 2 inches at 200, 6 inches at 300, and 12 inches at 400. If the wind is coming from 45 degrees instead of 90, you halve these allowances. If it's blowing 20 mph, you double them.

Watch the wind out where the animal is. The wind where you are is not going to have much effect on the bullet. The most important thing is to practice shooting in the wind. A couple of years ago, I was shooting a .308 at 600 yards in South Dakota and being coached by a former member of the Marine Corps rifle team. He was giving me very accurate wind adjustments out of his head, and I asked him how the hell he did it. "Easy," he said. "You watch ten or twenty thousand 7.62 bullets go downrange and you get to know just what the wind will do. If it were another cartridge I wouldn't have a clue."

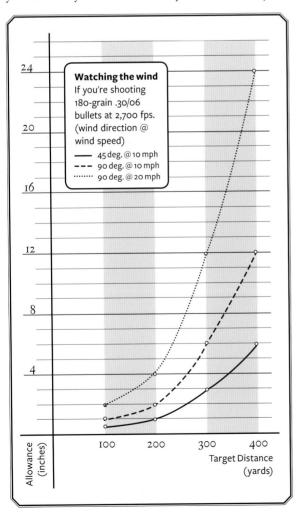

Watching the wind
If you're shooting 180-grain .30/06 bullets at 2,700 fps. (wind direction @ wind speed)
— 45 deg. @ 10 mph
- - - 90 deg. @ 10 mph
····· 90 deg. @ 20 mph

Allowance (inches)

100   200   300   400
Target Distance (yards)

97 PERFORM UNDER PRESSURE

A few people can become fine riflemen. Most people can become competent. A few are advised to take up badminton instead. What separates them in the end is nerves and knowledge. Good shots and great shots know exactly what they're doing every step of the way and they can, when it counts, tell their nervous systems to f**k off. Poor shots are ignorant of the marksman's mechanics. And they twitch, jerk, and panic. To be among the former, it helps to have or to develop several key qualities, including:

DILIGENCE You must practice regularly. Shooting at game is shooting under stress, and the way you perform under stress is through constant drill and rehearsal. When it's for real, you fall back on what you have learned instead of succumbing to panic. At the U.S. Army Sniper School, the conventional wisdom is that you expend 5,000 rounds in practice for every round you fire at the bad guys.

COLD BLOOD This means you are not undone by pressure, but in hunting it also refers to a willingness to kill. I think a good many cases of buck fever are caused by a reluctance to take life. Good shots do it impersonally; they don't relish it, but they don't shy from it, either. If you are able to kill with complete indifference, perhaps you should take up another sport.

FAITH That is, faith in your rifle—and the way to become a true believer is to use a gun you shoot really well. Yet we often go astray. We read about which cartridges will do what, at which ranges, on which animals. We obsess about making shots far beyond our practical limit. Then we go out and buy veritable cannons whose recoil and muzzle blast keep us from shooting as well as we can.

EXPERIENCE A friend of mine who has been hunting for six decades and has the skills to show for it said that after you've taken 300 head of game or so, you start to calm down and figure out what you can and can't do. This is one part I can't help you with, but I hope you have fun figuring it out.

WILL I've known at least two shooters who simply willed themselves into a state of excellence. A couple of weeks ago, I was shooting against one of them at a contest in which a perfect score is 50, and there are very few of those. I had a 48. So my competition sat down and stared at the ground awhile, thinking I know not what, but willing himself to beat me. And he did.

98 TAKE MY RIFLE-RANGE CHALLENGE

Everyone needs a plan, and this is a simple one. Performed regularly, it should prepare you for the three most common shooting situations in the field. Use the NRA 50-Yard Slow Fire targets, because their 8-inch bulls are roughly the size of the vital zone on most big-game animals. And keep score so you can track your process. Your hypothetical field situations are below; your scoring system for each is at right. Good luck.

1. SHORT-RANGE SHOT

THE DRILL

Phase 1 Stand 25 yards from the target and have a friend with a stopwatch there to time you. Starting with the butt at waist level, round in the chamber, safety on, you have 5 seconds to raise the rifle, aim, flip off the safety, and shoot. Take five shots here.

Phase 2 Do the exact same thing, but at 50 yards. For both distances, score 5 points for a hit anywhere. A hit outside the black, or a shot that takes longer than 5 seconds, counts for zero.

Shooting Tip The instant the crosshairs look about right, pull that trigger. As the folks at Gunsite Academy put it: "A good fast shot is better than a perfect slow shot, because you're not going to get the time to take the slow shot."

Maximum Points: 50 Points

2. MIDRANGE SHOT

THE DRILL

Fire two shots each, at 100, 125, 150, 175, and 200. You must take at least two from prone and two from kneeling or sitting, with or without a sling, improvised rest, or bipod. For each shot, you have 1 minute from a standing start, rifle loaded, chamber empty, to get into position and shoot. Each hit in the black within the time is worth 5 points.

20-Point Bonus After your second shot at 150, stay in position and take a third shot within 4 seconds.

Shooting Tip Create a routine. Settle into your shooting position, begin taking aim, take a breath, let most of it out, and shoot. Then do it the same way on the next shot. Consistency pays.

Maximum Points: 70 Points

3. LONG-RANGE SHOT

THE DRILL

With your chamber empty, hold the rifle diagonally across your torso and go to both knees. Lean forward and place the toe of the stock on the ground about 2 feet in front of your right knee. Now, using the toe as a pivot, lower your carcass flat on the ground. The butt should come right up into your shoulder. Get a good prone position and take five shots at 300 yards, either supported or unsupported, in 5 minutes. Same scoring as above.

Shooting Tip I gave you 5 minutes here, but you may do a lot better if you use a hell of a lot less. Wind varies, s**t happens, and the longer you take, the more of it is going to happen. If you get a calm stretch, start pumping lead and don't stop.

Maximum Points: 25 Points

1. SHORT-RANGE SHOT
Quick Buck You look up from the fresh tracks you've just cut and a very nice whitetail buck emerges from a blowdown just ahead. Shoot or watch him disappear.

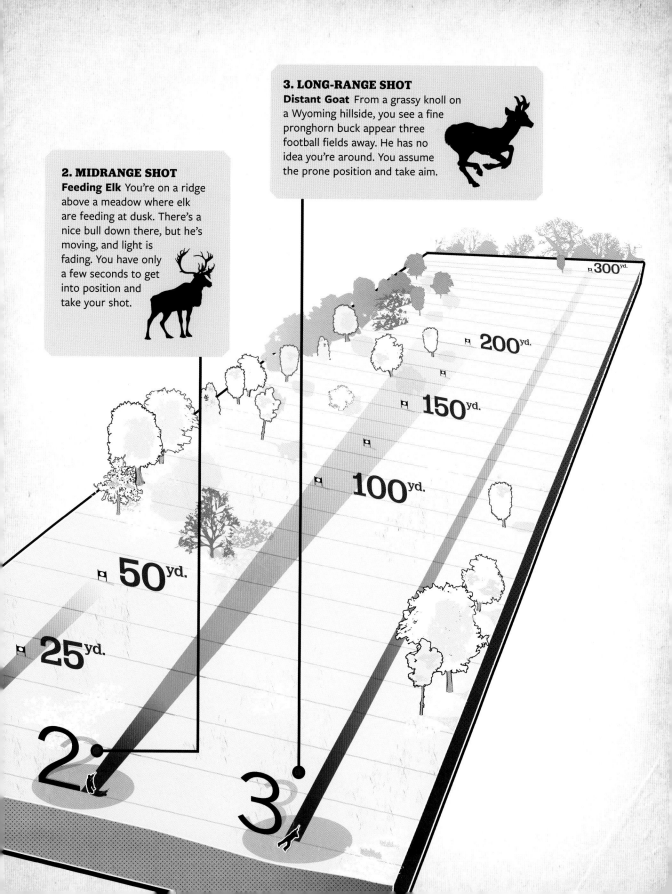

3. LONG-RANGE SHOT
Distant Goat From a grassy knoll on a Wyoming hillside, you see a fine pronghorn buck appear three football fields away. He has no idea you're around. You assume the prone position and take aim.

2. MIDRANGE SHOT
Feeding Elk You're on a ridge above a meadow where elk are feeding at dusk. There's a nice bull down there, but he's moving, and light is fading. You have only a few seconds to get into position and take your shot.

300 yd.

200 yd.

150 yd.

100 yd.

50 yd.

25 yd.

2

3

99 SHOOT BETTER WITH THE RIMFIRE REGIMEN

I never took well to rote memorization. I can remember a day in fourth grade when, bored to near insanity, I yanked out one of my baby teeth and waved the bloody fang under the nose of the girl sitting next to me. She shrieked, and I was sent to the principal's office.

All of that aside, and 50-plus years later, I've come to believe deeply in drudgery, especially the kind that results in one-shot kills. The course of shooting that follows is something I worked out about 20 years ago, and it's been successful for me and for people to whom I have

recommended it over the years. It's hard, you may find it boring, and it can be very discouraging at first. But I guarantee it will make you a better shot.

In the steps that follow, you should use a high-quality .22 rifle to save costs in ammunition as well as to save the wear and tear on your shoulder. By going smaller, you'll develop the muscle memory necessary to handle just about any shot you'll take in the field. The trick is in not just shooting for shooting's sake, but in building a detailed regimen that fosters nothing but good habits.

100 GET READY TO GET BETTER

How to improve your shooting? First on the list is a good .22 rifle, as close as possible to what you use for hunting—not some piece of junk you got at a tag sale, but a serious, accurate firearm. It should be wearing a good scope.

Next comes the ammo. In order to follow the rest of the plan below, you're going to need every bit of accuracy you can muster, so you're obliged to buy at least half a dozen different boxes of ammo (skip the hypervelocity stuff, which I've never seen shoot really well). Get high and standard velocity, both solid and hollow point.

Shoot five-shot groups from a bench at 25 yards with each box. Eventually you'll see that one type of ammo is much more accurate in your rifle than anything else. Get at least a brick of the stuff, which is 500 rounds.

Last on the list are targets. You're after either the NRA 50-Foot Rifle Target (A-36) or the NRA Rifle Silhouettes Target (TQ-14), which are printed by the National Target Company. The former has a dozen bull's-eyes each about the size of a silver dollar. The latter reproduces the four iron targets used on actual silhouette ranges—chickens, wild pigs, turkeys, and rams, five of each to a row.

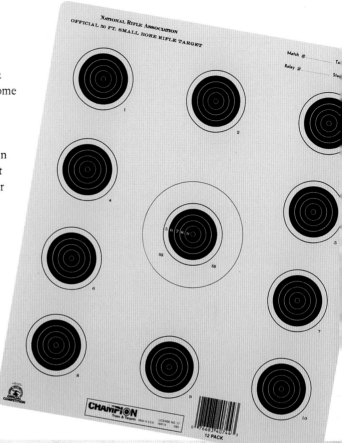

101 SHOOT, SCORE, AND SHOOT AGAIN

Post your target sheet at 25 yards. The choice of shooting positions is up to you, provided that you dedicate at least half your practice to the offhand position, which is by far the hardest and one that comes up in the field a surprisingly large percentage of the time. You can shoot kneeling, sitting, or any way you please as long as you don't use a rest.

If you're shooting at the bull's-eyes, give yourself five shots at one bull, taking the absolute minimum amount of time to shoulder the rifle, find the bull in the scope, put the crosshairs on it, and fire.

With the silhouette target, take one shot at each little critter in a single row. Your goal in this regimen is speed as much as it is accuracy. Squeeze the trigger no more than five seconds after you shoulder the rifle.

Score yourself after every five rounds. A hit anywhere in the bull's-eye counts. I find that if I'm really concentrating, 12 bulls (or 12 rows on the silhouette target) is about all I can handle in a session before my mental focus wavers and the crosshairs start jumping uncontrollably.

You may find that this drill is less discouraging if you move closer than 25 yards at first, and you may not want to shoot up a whole target.

Over the course of a month or more (or 500 rounds, whichever comes first), you should get to the point where you put either four or five hits on every bull on a target. Once you can do that, go sight in your centerfire rifle, because you're ready for anything the wonderful world of rifle hunting can deal you.

102 ASSUME THE POSITION

Tragically, we can't take our benchrests with us into the woods. Still, you can get very steady if you're willing to practice and have the presence of mind to use what's available as support. Here are the positions I've found most useful.

OFFHAND Everyone hates it, no one practices it, and that's why so many animals escape so many bullets. To shoot offhand, first make sure that your trigger-finger arm **[a]** is more or less parallel to the ground. This forms a pocket for the butt (the rifle's, not yours) and keeps you from placing it out on your arm. This is the old-fashioned method. It's now considered more effective to raise your arm, get the butt into your shoulder, and then let your arm sag down again. Maybe. But the old method looks better, and looking good is as important as shooting good. A sling in the offhand position is worthless. Unless you can get your left arm down on something solid, you get no benefit from it. As for the arm that supports the fore-end **[b]**, keep it directly under the rifle. Or try to. I can't manage it for more than a second or two. My arm invariably wanders off to the side. But if you obey the first principle of offhand shooting, it won't matter. That principle is to shoot fast. I repeat: Shoot fast. You are not going to be able to hold very steady for very long, and the longer you screw around, the worse it's going to get.

PRONE I love prone because I get to lie down and because it's the steadiest position of all. Sadly, you don't often get a shot this way because nature usually puts something between your muzzle and your target. To take advantage of prone, you have to have some kind of support for the rifle in addition to your quivering left arm. (I assume you are one of those degenerates who shoots right-handed.) This can be a sling, a backpack, a rock with your hat on top of it, or best of all, a bipod. If you're using a sling, your left forearm **[a]** should be directly under the rifle, as close to vertical as you can get it. The sling should be tight enough to turn your left hand blue with red streaks. Purple is also acceptable. Instead of lying flat on the ground with both legs splayed out, bring your right leg **[b]** up toward your chest. This raises your torso and minimizes the effect of your heartbeat and breathing. Finally, avoid a bloody noggin by making sure you have enough eye relief **[c]** because prone gets your forehead closer to the scope than any other position.

SITTING Next to prone, this is the steadiest position, but it takes time to get into and often doesn't get you high enough off the ground. That said, the key here is to rest the points of your elbows on the flesh of your legs, just behind the knees **[a]**. If the bone of either elbow rests on the bone of either knee, you will wobble. When you're sitting in a tree stand, it's all but impossible to get your knees high enough to use for support. So install a shooting rail, or at the very least, bring a shooting staff.

KNEELING I would like to be buried in the kneeling position. It's very fast to get into. It gets you over most ground cover and is steady if you execute it correctly. Your right butt cheek rests on your right heel **[a]**, and in this case, your left elbow should be thrust past your left knee **[b]** so that your tricep, rather than the point of your elbow, is resting on the knee. I've tried using a sling from the kneeling position, but I don't seem to get any benefit from it. You, on the other hand, may have better luck.

103 AVOID THE LOW BLOW

In rifle shooting, it's axiomatic that the closer you get to the ground, the more accurate you are. But the corollary to that is, the lower you go, the more you get pounded because your body gives less and less with the force of recoil. With a gun that really kicks, it behooves you to shoot offhand and look for some kind of support rather than use the sitting or (shudder) prone position.

104 HUG A TREE

Shooting offhand is very unsteady, and many hunters tend to stand there and wobble as the agonizing seconds tick by. Instead, head for the nearest tree. Take off your hat and hold it against the tree with the back of your left hand. Now grasp your gun and aim. You'll find that you have a nearly dead-solid hold and that you can get the shot off almost instantly. (Why the hat? Because you can take the skin off the back of your hand if you don't have something to cushion it.)

105 KNOW YOUR AMMO

The first thing you need to do is chose the right brand of ammo for your gun, but that's not enough. You also need to test out your top pick.

COMPARE BULLETS Never assume that one brand of ammo will shoot the same as another or that two different bullets of the same weight will shoot the same. I once gathered many different brands and bullet weights of .30/06 ammo and fired them in a very accurate rifle without changing the rifle's zero. When I was done, the target looked as if I had hosed it down with a machine gun. Bullets went everywhere. The fact is, some rifles are wildly inaccurate with certain loads and Tack Drivers with others. Some will shoot only one load, period. I have a .270 that will shoot only the old Trophy Bonded bullets that were made in Houston back in the 1980s. I would never sell that rifle because it is Death Its Own Self, but I'd never trust it with any other kind of bullets.

SHOOT GROUPS I recently watched a fellow sight in his rifle for a competition shoot. He fired a shot. Then he cranked the dials. He did this ten times in a row: blam, crank, ka-pow, twirl, bang, twist. Later, I got to score his target, and he was all over the place because he broke a cardinal rule of sighting in: One shot tells you nothing. You need at least a three-shot group. Only after determining where the center of that group is should you make compensating windage and elevation adjustments. Then repeat until you're dead on.

QUICK SHOT

106 DRESS TO KILL

To ensure a rifle's scope is correctly mounted, put on the clothes you'll wear while hunting. With the scope loose in the rings, set it on a low power. Close your eyes and throw the gun to your shoulder. Now open your eyes. You should see the full field of view, and the scope's ocular lens should be 4 inches from your eyebrow. If not, adjust until you get the right distance, and then tighten the rings.

PETZAL ON: GETTING ANTSY

"I witnessed my all-time favorite sighting screw-up on safari in Africa in 1978. A group member whined perpetually about the trackers, the game, and his rifle's alleged inability to hold its zero. The professional hunter did not appreciate the nonstop bitching at all, and finally he had had enough. 'Tom,' he said sweetly, 'I think you should resight your rifle again. Why don't you rest it on that little hill there and shoot at that mopane-tree knot?' The hill he pointed to was a safari-ant apartment complex, and when its residents were serenaded by the bellowing crack of a .375 H&H, they decided on payback. In the best safari-ant tradition, they swarmed into Tom's clothing and, at the same precise instant, started biting."

107 REST EASY (BUT NOT TOO EASY)

When you sight in, you have to do it on a rest that is firm but not hard. If the fore-end is sitting on a hard surface, it will bounce at the shot, sending your bullet high. If you'd really like to get a false zero, rest the barrel on something—it doesn't matter whether it's hard, soft, or pleasingly firm—your bullets are going for a ride upward. It also pays to rest the fore-end at exactly the same place for each shot. In other words, don't have it resting nearly at the sling swivel for one round and near the floorplate for the next. That breeds inconsistency. And some rifles are very fussy about their

preferred degree of firmness. I've owned numerous guns that I could not shoot accurately over a hard sandbag because they'd bounce. Only a softer sandbag made them happy.

108 SHOOT GROUPS RIGHT

Nowadays, just about everyone uses three-shot groups as their standard of performance, the theory being that three is the minimum number of rounds required to see what is what, and that few big-game animals are going to stand around for more than three rounds anyway.

If you really want to see how your rifle will shoot, however, try five-shot groups. This was the standard number a couple of generations ago and is still used by target and varmint shooters whose need for consistent accuracy is more pressing. A five-shot minute-of-angle group is much more difficult to shoot than a minute-of-angle three-shotter.

And if you go back before World War II, people used 10-shot groups to measure rifle accuracy. They was men back then.

Want to measure your groups accurately? You'll need a caliper (digital-readout calipers are much easier to use than dial-readout models) and the ability to subtract. First, measure the outside spread of the two widest shots in the group. Then, subtract from that figure the diameter of the bullet you're shooting. Let's say you take your .270 and shoot a group that measures 1.313 inches. Subtract from it .277, which is the actual diameter of the bullet, and you get 1.036 inches, which is your group size.

109 KEEP COOL

As rifle barrels get hot, two things happen to them—both bad. First, any stresses that are present in the steel will cause the tubes to warp. And second, you will create a mirage from the heat that rises off the barrel, causing you to see your groups as being higher than they are. If you shoot a magnum rifle, or a rifle of any caliber with a lightweight barrel, you are going to have problems with overheating. Fire no more than three shots at a time and let the barrel cool to where it is no hotter than tepid (it's way too hot if you can't hold on to it and count to 10) before you continue. I've found it useful to bring two or three guns to the range. This lets me shoot one while the others are cooling. (You don't have three rifles, you say? Buy until you do.) If there's an electric outlet near the firing line, plug in a fan and let its breezes cool your barrel's fevered brow. To really make certain of where your rifle is shooting, try this as a final step: After you've sighted it in over a rest, shoot from the prone or any other position where you get your hand on the fore-end as you will in the field. If you use a sling to shoot when you hunt, use it now. The same applies to bipods or any other kind of support that you might rely on. Now shoot a group and see where it hits. You may need to make some changes. Picky? You bet. But picky people make the best rifle shots.

110 LEARN TRIGGER CONTROL

Your trigger should break at no less than 3 pounds, no more than 4, and at the same weight every time. It should not creep and should have an absolute minimum of over travel.

That said, when you acquire your sight picture, take a deep breath and let most of it out. You now have 7 seconds in which to shoot. If you don't, your vision begins to deteriorate, and you have to start all over again, which can cost you a shot. Therefore, discipline yourself to aim and get the round off forthwith. Screw around, and miss.

It's common advice that you should squeeze the trigger so that you're surprised when the rifle goes off. This assumes you can hold the rifle perfectly still. I can't do that in the field. I wobble and weave—not much, but enough. Instead, I pick the precise instant when the crosshairs are where they should be and then pull that trigger smartly.

If you have a bolt-action centerfire, you can work on your trigger pull by dry firing. After making sure the rifle is unloaded, pick a target 50 yards or so away and practice getting it to your shoulder, acquiring the perfect sight picture, and pulling that trigger, over and over. Be discreet about this. If your neighbors see you aiming a rifle out your window, you will shortly get a visit from the local SWAT team who will inquire, politely but firmly, what you're up to. After they fire a warning shot through your heart.

111 DRY FIRE YOUR WAY TO SUCCESS

One of the most useful tools in the ongoing struggle to shoot well is dry firing—aiming and snapping the trigger with no ammo in the chamber. Dry firing had no greater champion than the late Creighton Audette, a gunsmith, a friend of mine, and a high-power competitor who was good enough to shoot on the Palma Team and coach it. "Recoil," he said, "is a form of distraction."

He believed that any serious shooter should do far more dry firing than practice with live ammo. (Creighton also said, "Everyone should have at least one gun the government doesn't know about," if you need any further proof of his wisdom.)

The Marine Corps used to start its marksmanship training with a solid week of nothing but "snapping in"—dry fire from the basic shooting positions—to show the maggots how to do things correctly before they got live ammo. Dry fire allows you to concentrate, without distraction, on that moment when the trigger lets go and the instant immediately afterward, when so many other things can go wrong.

Dry fire, however, is not for every firearm. It's okay to dry fire most bolt-action rifles, but the practice can damage most .22s, just about all shotguns, and some handguns. If you are in doubt about its effect on your firearms, you should consult your gunsmith.

It's invaluable, costs nothing, won't give you a flinch, and makes no noise. Dry fire a lot and you will shoot better. As Ed Zern said, "Keep your powder, your martinis, your trout flies, and your fire dry."

112 HEAR WHAT YOUR RIFLE IS TELLING YOU

Were this the best of all possible worlds, we would fire three rifle shots at a target, peer downrange, and see three holes clustered within the area of a dime at precisely the right place. But this is not the best of all possible worlds, in that it has a place for chiggers, bad cholesterol, rabies, and abdominal fat. And in this vale of sorrow, we often look at our targets and see nothing but horror, chaos, and disorder.

In any event, we know that something is wrong, but what? Rather than burst into tears, you should regard this as a heart-to-heart talk with your rifle, which, if you can speak its language, will tell you what ails it.

DIAGNOSTIC TOOL Shooting from the benchrest will tell you just what your gun is thinking.

COMPLETE BREAKDOWN
Problem Your shots are all over the place, and you can't get a group to save your life. There could be several causes. First is a ruptured scope. The way to test this is to put a different scope on your gun and see if it groups better. Second is loose bedding screws on the rifle. Check to see if they're tight. Third is loose ring or base screws. Sometimes, one particular bullet weight will give results this bad. If this is the case, it's usually because the barrel's rifling twist is wrong for that bullet weight.

CONSISTENT FLIER
Problem Your ammo is almost, but not quite, right for your gun. Usually this shows up as two holes close together and the third one off to the side by an inch or two. At 100 yards, this is not a problem, but at farther distances, it will begin to cause some trouble. It's caused by bullets traveling just above or below the optimum speed for that barrel, causing it to vibrate inconsistently. Hand-loaders can cure it by raising or lowering the powder charge. Non-handloaders will have to try different ammunition.

INCONSISTENT FLIER
Problem Most of the time you get good groups, but sometimes you have one shot go astray, and then sometimes all three go where they're not supposed to. Most likely you're flinching, and if you don't think that it's possible to flinch from a benchrest, think again. You can buy or experiment with a sled-type shooting rest, which can virtually eliminate felt recoil, or try putting a soft gun case or sandbag between your shoulder and the butt. Or, if all else fails, get a less punishing rifle.

RISING GROUP
Problem Your groups are usually okay, but they seem to keep moving up on the target, sometimes up and to the left or right, sometimes straight up. This is caused by an overheated barrel. When a tube gets too hot, it warps slightly, sending bullets errantly, and in addition, the heat waves rising from it give you a distorted view of the target, sort of like shooting through a swimming pool. The cure is easy: Let your barrel cool down. Start each group with a cold barrel and never let it get beyond lukewarm.

STRINGING
Problem In this situation, your groups string vertically or horizontally. First check the barrel bedding. Most barrels today are free-floating; there should be no contact from 1½ inches forward of the receiver right out to the end. If there is, take the gun in for a rebedding job. The horizontal grouping can be caused by wind at the target that you don't feel at the bench. The vertical groups can be caused by the fore-end jumping on too hard a surface.

113 WATCH YOUR FORM

Much of proper rifle-shooting technique is designed to spare you pain, and if you simply pick up a gun and start blazing away, you are going to take needless punishment. For example, if you don't get the butt into the "pocket" that forms when you raise your right arm to shoulder the rifle, it is going to ride out on your bicep and pound you. If you lean back from the waist to support the gun's weight (women are especially guilty of this), you will be rocked back on your heels. If you crawl the stock, the scope will sooner or later say hello to your forehead. Get competent help. A range officer or an NRA instructor can assist you. A shooting class will also work wonders.

114 LEARN TO TAKE A PUNCH

When Tommy Hearns, the great welterweight boxer, was just starting to learn the manly art, he was sparring with a much better fighter who promptly broke his nose. Hearns grabbed his nose with his glove, wrenched it back in place, and kept right on fighting. Some people are much tougher than others, and just as the Motor City Cobra could ignore a busted beak, some of us can take a lot more recoil than others. There are two types: real recoil, measured in foot-pounds; and perceived recoil, what you feel. There is a formula for calculating real recoil, but it's easier to go online and find any of the several sites that can do it with the click of a mouse. Perceived recoil is affected by the makeup and design of the rifle, and it can't really be calculated.

One of the most sadistic rifles ever built was the Winchester Model 95 lever action. The majority were made in .30/06 and .30/40 Krag, and a fair number used the .405 Winchester. The 95 had all the requirements for a truly painful rifle. Its stock had loads of drop, so when it recoiled, the barrel whipped up and back, directing much of the recoil into the shooter's head. The stock's comb was sharp, guaranteeing a bruised cheekbone, and the butt was small, curved, and capped by a steel plate, ensuring the maximum amount of hurt in your shoulder. In .30/40, which is a mild-kicking cartridge, and in .30/06, which is moderate, the Model 95 was brutal. In .405 it must have been unthinkable. Muzzle blast is not physically connected to recoil but can also seem to make a rifle kick harder. You can develop a raging flinch from shooting a muzzle-braked rifle or a short-barreled rifle without hearing protection. You'll swear it kicks like a mule even though it doesn't. Even your build is a factor: recoil flings around small, slender people in a spine-chilling manner. But they are actually suffering less than heavyset people because they give with the shove, whereas the fire-hydrant types soak up every bit of it. Of the people I know who have been permanently screwed up by kick, all of them are close to 6 feet tall and weigh over 180 pounds. There is not a lightweight in the lot.

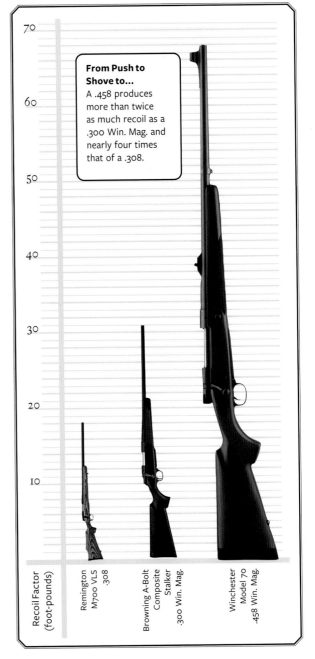

From Push to Shove to...
A .458 produces more than twice as much recoil as a .300 Win. Mag. and nearly four times that of a .308.

Recoil Factor (foot-pounds)

Remington M700 VLS .308

Browning A-Bolt Composite Stalker .300 Win. Mag.

Winchester Model 70 .458 Win. Mag.

115 LOWER THE KICK

In case you're really suffering, here are some things that will bring you instant relief.

RECOIL PAD Get rid of your aluminum or hard-plastic buttplate or your cheap, unyielding-as-granite factory recoil pad and replace it with a soft, squishy, premium recoil pad.

MUZZLE BRAKE They're not cheap, they'll rip your ears to shreds if you're not plugged and muffed, and you'll need to have a gunsmith do the work, but they really do save you a lot of foot-pounds. Some shooters opt to have Mag-na-ports cut in their barrel. This will reduce muzzle jump but not recoil, and bullet jacket fouling tends to collect at the rear corners of the ports, eventually cutting accuracy.

STOCK If you have an older rifle with loads of drop at the comb, get a more modern stock with a lot less drop. Unless your rifle is extremely rare or odd, you can choose among wood, laminated wood, and synthetic stocks. See your gunsmith.

INERTIA RECOIL REDUCER Have a gunsmith install one (or better yet, a pair of them) in your stock. They will change the balance of your rifle and increase its weight by about a pound, but they work.

TRIGGER A heavy trigger pull will add greatly to the unpleasantness of a hard-kicking rifle. A light, crisp trigger will make it easier to set the thing off, rendering the whole experience more tolerable. Don't even think about diddling with a trigger. Take it to a gunsmith who can alter or, if necessary, replace it.

116 KNOW YOUR LIMITS

For most shooters, the cutoff for real recoil is around the .30/06 or 7mm Remington Magnum level, which is about 25 foot-pounds. When you add 10 foot-pounds, the average shooter really feels it—and will not shoot the rifle very well.

There is a huge divide between the .375 H&H and the .40-caliber and larger rounds. I believe a considerable number of shooters can't or shouldn't shoot anything bigger than a .375. My own personal limit is the .458 Lott. Bigger rifles exist: the .460 Weatherby, for example, develops just over 100 foot-pounds. I have shot one on several occasions, but I'm not about to do so anymore.

Here are some approximate figures for 9 popular cartridges. All weights are for the rifle alone; a scope and mounts will add about a pound, and the recoil will decrease proportionally.

Cartridge	Rifle Weight (lb.)	Recoil (ft.-lb.)
.243	7	12
.270	7.5	21
.30/30	7.5	10.5
.308	7.5	18
.30/06	8	24
7mm Rem. Mag.	8	27
.300 Win. Mag.	8.5	31
.338	9	35
.375 H&H	9.5	39

PETZAL ON: FEAR

" Don't ever fall for one of the more pervasive myths in riflery, which goes: Even if you flinch when you're shooting at targets, you won't flinch when you're shooting at game because you won't feel the recoil. If you are afraid of a particular gun, you are going to stay afraid of it, and you'll miss. Period. "

117
GO LONG IF YOU HAVE TO

Shooting at long range is a last-ditch measure that should be in the repertoire of every skilled hunter, but it should not be used as a substitute for being able to hunt.

118 SHOOT LIKE A MARKSMAN

Once upon a time, someone asked Willie Mays how he hit so well, and the Say Hey Kid said that you watched the ball come to you, as big as a pumpkin, and you just put the bat in the middle of it. Now if you've ever seen a fastball come at you at 90 mph plus, you know that it looks like a kid's aspirin tablet—if you can see the thing at all. But Mays was gifted. He did with ease what normal people can't do at all.

Depressingly, in the world of rifle shooting, there are people just like him. A friend of mine, a marksman of the first order, once competed against Gary Anderson, who was one of the great American rifle shots of the 20th century. My friend summed up the experience thus: "I didn't think it was possible to be beaten that badly." Anderson, of course,

was supremely gifted. But what if Nature has not lavished her gifts on you? No sense in worrying about it; there's no use worrying about it. But you can get a lot better by applying some basic fundamentals of marksmanship, which far too many hunters don't bother with.

Though some shooters tout the need for upper body strength in order to shoot well, the ability to bench-press 300 pounds won't make you a better shot. Far better is the ability to make your hands do what the eyes and brain tell them to. This hand-eye coordination is the same quality that makes for good ping-pong players and golfers.

It's pretty simple: First, learn to shoot correctly. Then, practice. A lot.

119 DOPE THE WIND

There are all sorts of devices that will tell you how far away something is or what your holdover should be, but nothing that scopes out the breezes that make your life a waking hell. So, filled with despair, I offer these rules.

LOOK AHEAD Don't worry about what the wind is doing where you are; watch it midway to the target.

MORE IS LESS The faster a bullet is moving, the less the wind pushes it. The heavier and more streamlined it is, the less the wind pushes it. This doesn't apply to short, fat bullets, which despite their weight do not slip easily through the air.

INCH CLOSER It's easy to outsmart yourself by holding off too much. If you have wind-resistant bullets and lots of velocity and are not shooting from terribly far away (say, 250 yards or less), then a moderate wind is going to push your slug a couple of inches one way or another, but no more.

120 ACCESS YOUR LIZARD BRAIN

Rifle shooting is a great many different things, ranging from slow, calculated precision work at long range to fast shooting at point-blank range. To excel at one (or both), you need a reptilian nervous system. It is to all other factors as three is to one.

If you can't stomp on your nerves, you will never be able to shoot a rifle well. I've known two men who could not shoot and could not be taught to shoot. The problem with both was not their eyes or their hands or their shoulders; it was their psyches.

Gifted shooters, on the other hand, are able to tap into their lizard brains, which make them immune to whatever devils beset the rest of us. They can shoot under intense pressure. This can mean anything from an African professional hunter sticking a bullet in a buffalo's eye just as old nyati is about to get a horn into him to an Olympic shooter not blowing it when she needs one more squeeze of the trigger to secure the gold medal. Whatever the situation, they know that when they pick up a rifle they are going to hit what they aim at, period.

121 DO THE MATH

A gifted shooter can not only access his or her lizard brain—he or she can also exit that cold-blooded mode instantly to perform something much more cerebral: mathematics. I know of a candidate who washed out of sniper school because, as one of his instructors said, "He couldn't do the math." "Doing the math" means calculating bullet drop, bullet drift, the effects of wind, air temperature, altitude, and even the Coriolis effect. Gifted shooters can not only do this but do it under pressure.

Recently, I listened to a talk by David Tubb, who is an 11-time National High Power champion and one of our leading thinkers on shooting at long range. Mr. Tubb can solve math problems in his head, on the firing line, in competition, that I could not unlock with the aid of three computers and eight professors from Princeton University.

The ability to do the math quickly can spell the difference between success and failure in the field. If you're throwing down at something 592 yards away that's going to get into Boone and Crockett, do you fling lead and pray, or do you figure it out? I don't need to tell you the answer.

122 SHOOT FASTER

In Montana in the early 80s, I was hunting a ridgeline in deep, soft snow and jumped a nice whitetail buck out of his bed. He whirled and started to accelerate, and I had perhaps two seconds to get my rifle up, find him in the scope, figure out the lead, and pull the trigger. As it was, two seconds was enough, and he was the only deer I saw that whole trip.

In the best of all possible worlds, we would be able to watch a critter stroll into view, raise our rifles in a leisurely manner, and shoot with all the time we need. In this world, we are sometimes forced to shoot at an animal that is about to get or is getting the hell out of there—or we go home empty-handed.

(And before we go any further, you should understand that I'm not presenting you with a rationale to blaze away at anything you please. Speed becomes a factor only after you've identified your target beyond the shadow of a doubt. If you're not sure of it, keep your rifle down and watch through your binoculars until you are.) Here are the basics.

DEFEAT DITHER Speed is achieved by the absence of dither—a brew concocted from indecision and clumsiness that saves thousands of animals' lives every year. Much indecision comes from not knowing clearly what you want to shoot. Should I settle for a forkhorn? What if a better deer comes along after I shoot this one? While you are debating, the deer becomes aware of you and leaves. Decide what you want beforehand, and stick to your decision.

TAKE THE SHOTS YOU CAN MAKE If you think you can't make a shot, you are probably right. As you become experienced, you will develop a very good sense of which shots you can take and which you can't. Until you reach that point, play it cautious.

KNOW YOUR RIFLE Much hesitation is caused by unfamiliarity with your firearm. Omigod, where's the safety on this thing? If you have a new rifle, or a different type of action from what you're used to, or you only pick up your rifle once a year, you will dither—unless you practice.

123 DEVELOP A SENSE OF TIMING

It's important to learn to distinguish between those times when you have to shoot fast and those when you can take your time. Many shots are missed because hunters are slow or because they panic. What to do? Use your common sense. If an animal is right under your tree stand, it can get your scent at any instant, and you are going to have to shoot right now. If it's 300 yards away, you're not likely to have your cover blown unless you stand up and cheer. Also, look at the critter. Animals have body language that reveals whether they're spooked or placid.

If a deer stamps with a front hoof he has you spotted and is trying to get you to do something stupid.

If the tail comes up, that tells you that he is leaving right now.

A deer puts his head down and pretends to feed, then yanks it up to see if anything is going on. Let him do this a few times, and he'll settle down.

124 DRILL FOR SPEED

I'm sluggish and torpid by nature, so by rights I should never get fast-breaking game. However, for 25 years, I've practiced shooting quickly every chance I get. This drill will help you do the same.

The drill consists of two parts. At home, I practice shouldering a rifle that I've checked very carefully to make sure is unloaded, aiming at a lichen patch on an oak tree 50 yards away and snapping the trigger, all in as close to one motion as I can make it. Do this regularly, and you'll get pretty fast and pretty smooth. Don't do this if you live where the neighbors can see you. You'll be visited by a SWAT team, and they'll show you how fast they can shoot.

Then, at a 100-yard range, I put up a target with an 8-inch bull and load five rounds. I shoulder the rifle, aim, and allow myself 3 seconds to get off the shot. If I can't get the crosshairs where I want them in that time, I lower the rifle and count it as a miss. (If you shoot at a public range, check first to see if this kind of practice is permitted.)

Hits anywhere in the black count; anything outside the black is a miss. I go through 20 rounds, and if I can put at least 18 bullets through the black, I'm okay, provided that the other two are no farther out of the bull than the nine-ring. Speed kills—and it puts venison on the table.

125 LEARN TO SWITCH HIT

On more than one occasion, I've had to endure the shame of shooting right-handed when I was up in a tree stand and a deer came from my left-hand side. As I shoot southpaw, I couldn't turn enough to aim at him without getting busted, so I moved the butt of the rifle into my right shoulder and shot that way. If you have a strong master eye on your shooting side, you are going to have to close it to shoot from the weak side. As shown for a right-hander, switching sides lets you cover everything in front of you. Practice helps.

126 PERFECT THE UPSIDE-DOWN CARRY

There is a way to sling a rifle that allows you to bring it into action quickly and use the sling as a shooting support at the same time. In the past when I have recommended this technique, I set all the Safety Nazis in a frenzy. To them I say: One hand is always on the rifle and has it under constant control. It's not as though the gun is swinging freely, doing whatever it pleases. I learned how to do this in 1958 from a gun writer named Francis E. Sell, who had probably used it for 50 years at that point. I have been using it for 46 years. Sell did not shoot himself in all that time, and neither have I, so spare me.

It works like this: Assuming you have a smooth rifle sling and not one of the grabby kind that won't slip off your shoulder, and assuming you're right-handed, you sling the rifle over your left shoulder, muzzle down, trigger guard forward. Your left hand should be on the fore-end to control the movement of the gun.

When it comes time to shoot, you simply haul the rifle up and put the butt in your right shoulder. The sling remains looped around the upper part of your left arm as a brace. This can be done in one motion with a minimum of movement and is very fast. And as the signs correctly say, speed kills.

127 UNSLING IT

Rifle slings have saved the lives of more critters than PETA. Used incorrectly, a sling (or more properly, a carrying strap) can place your rifle out of reach for more than enough time for an animal to bolt and die of old age.

Sling misuse can have even more serious consequences. Many years ago, I was on the trail of a highly irritated lion in the Kalahari Desert of Botswana, .375 slung over my shoulder. Ian Manning, the professional hunter whose job it was to keep me from becoming lion poop, said, "David, do you really think the bloody lion is going to wait for you to unsling your bloody rifle before he bites you in your bloody arse?" I had offered to fight Manning the day before when he said my rifle looked like it belonged to a French nobleman, but there was no doubt he was making sense about the sling.

The only situations in which your rifle should be slung is when you have no intention of shooting anything or when you have to use both hands for something. (You should not sling a rifle while getting into a tree stand; instead, get in the stand first, then pull the unloaded gun up with a rope.) The rest of the time, put the sling in your pocket and be ready to shoot.

128
PROTECT YOUR RIFLE FROM THE ELEMENTS

The worst-case scenario for rifles is if you get snow or ice in the bore. This will put your gun out of action. Firing a rifle or shotgun with a plugged bore will get you a new nickname—Stumpy, for example. The way to prevent this is to wrap a small piece of plastic electricians' tape or bowhunters' camo tape over the muzzle. I've had people assure me that this will blow up the rifle, but it's perfectly safe as long as you observe two precautions:

One, don't use heavy tape. Two, don't let condensation form in the barrel. If the condensation freezes, you have trouble. If you're going to expose the rifle to drastic temperature changes, take off the tape and air out the barrel.

Rifles rust, including stainless-steel rifles; they just rust slower than blued steel. The solution: Wipe the metal down with an oily rag at the end of the day. Pay particular attention to the bolt, which is bright metal and prone to rust. If you're hunting in a dry climate, such as in the Rockies, rust doesn't seem to occur, no matter what the weather is. But elsewhere, beware.

Triggers are especially vulnerable. I've seen at least a couple of triggers that were ruined by rust from being wet day after day. The temptation is to put oil on the trigger, but you will regret doing this, as the oil will eventually congeal, and your trigger will cease to move.

The proper course is to remove the bolt and squirt the trigger from above with lighter fluid, being sure to hit the sear. Do this every time the rifle gets soaked. This appears to flush out whatever water lies lurking. Also, while the bolt is out of the rifle, wipe it down with a lightly oiled rag and to the same with the bolt raceway.

As for the rest of the metal, don't worry about it. Getting at it requires that you remove the barreled action from the stock, and unless you know for a fact that the gun will shoot to the same point of impact when screwed together, let it be.

Another thing you must not do is put your wet rifle in a case. This practically guarantees rust. Dry it off completely and then put it in a case.

129 COPE WITH BAD WEATHER

One of my more vivid memories of the Army is standing in a driving sleet storm watching the warm ugh in my mess tray turning rapidly to cold, congealed ugh and thinking that when I left the Green Machine I was never going to stand around in the sleet again. And so I left the service, took up big-game hunting, and have stood around in sleet—and much worse—forever after.

Cold, wet weather can not only affect the stuff on your mess tray; it can affect you, your gear, your scope, and your rifle. Let's start with you. That's easy. If you dress wrong in inclement weather, you will become hypothermic and die. Your rifle—that's a bit more complicated. The Army looked very unkindly on a rusted rifle, and we learned that, above all, you took care of your weapon (not your gun, thank you very much) first, no matter what kind of shape you yourself were in. Finding rust on a rifle was enough to get you a night in the mess hall scrubbing pots and pans, which, for sheer loathsomeness, could only compare to a contemporary political campaign. Much better to take care of your rifle, we were told, because only then would it take care of you.

130 SEE UNDERWATER

These days, no good rifle scope or binocular is going to be damaged by the weather, but they can be rendered temporarily useless, which is almost as bad. Water—in whatever form—has an unfortunate way of collecting on lenses, and when that happens, you are not going to see anything but a blur. (Some scopes do have a superhard exterior lens coating upon which water cannot condense and which, therefore, cannot fog or be disabled by rain. This is good stuff.)

The way around this problem is to always have caps on your scope if the sky is anything but blue and to not pop them off until you're actually ready to shoot. By the same token, take them off the scope when you come in from the weather. Good scope caps will create an almost airtight seal over the lenses, and whatever water is trapped there will condense when you bring the rifle from the cold outdoors into a warm tent. (If at all possible, I leave my rifle outside, under the eaves where it won't get wet. The fewer temperature changes, the better.)

Be careful as you bring the rifle up to aim that you don't exhale a cloud of moisture-laden breath onto the cold lens. This will fog your scope in an instant. Inhale as the rifle comes up and hold the breath until you squeeze off the shot.

Binoculars are more of a problem. I haven't found a way to keep binoculars out of the wet, since they should be in use almost constantly. For now, we just have to suffer.

What I said about exhaling on your rifle scope goes double in the case of your binoculars. Suck in your breath as you bring them up and exhale once they're at your eyes. If it's really cold, the heat from your face will be enough to cloud them. The only way around this is, if possible, to keep them under your coat where they won't get warm but they won't get ice cold, either.

131 KEEP YOUR POWDER DRY (OR NOT)

Ammo, unlike you, is almost impervious to water. On many occasions I have had the same three cartridges in my magazine through a week of torrential rain and have never had a round fail to fire. Modern smokeless powder is nonhygroscopic, meaning it won't absorb water.

About 15 years ago, a friend of mine who was a shipwreck nut brought me a couple of rounds of .30/06 military ammo that had been aboard the *USS San Diego* when that ship was torpedoed off the New Jersey coast in the early days of World War II. These cartridges had lain beneath the Atlantic Ocean for 40-plus years, and their cases were so badly corroded that I could punch a hole in one with my fingernail and pour out the powder. Which I did. I then put some in an ashtray, touched a match to it, and it flared right up.

If you handload, and water worries you, you can buy a cartridge-sealing adhesive from Loc-Tite. But, really, it isn't necessary. Mike Jordan of Winchester says that his company seals military ammo (which must pass an immersion test) and the primers of handgun ammo (which is used by cops and other people who shoot people) but that hunting-rifle ammo is unsealed, and it doesn't leak.

132   CHOOSE YOUR DEER-HUNTING RIFLE

In 1956, the year I bought my first firearm, hunters who were interested in a deer rifle had seventeen guns to choose from. There were eleven cartridges that could be considered deer sized. Today, there are something like sixty rifles and more than thirty cartridges that are suitable for deer. All of this choice leaves the average deer hunter perplexed, which is why one of the questions I hear most often is "What do you use?" But there's no simple answer. The are some 30 million individual deer in the United States alone, and they range from the 90-pound whitetails of the Deep South to the 300-plus-pound muleys of the northern Rockies and inhabit just about every big-woods thicket, farmland woodlot, prairie river bottom, desert scrubland, and mountain crag in North America. No one rifle is ideally suited to all deer everywhere. The first question you'll have to ask yourself is just how you intend to make use of that gun—where, how, and what you'll be hunting the most.

133 GO TRADITIONAL WITH A BRUSH GUN

Brush guns are the traditional "deer rifles." They're short-barreled, compact light, handy, and chambered for cartridges of modest power. These rifles are designed to be used for shots at 100 yards, more or less. When considering a brush gun, the speed with which you can get off a second shot should not be a factor, but the speed with which you can get off a first shot is vital.

As a world-class high-power competitor once said, "Rapid fire is the crutch of the incompetent." You don't need a Tack Driver. A rifle that will shoot 3-inch groups at 100 yards will do. Tighter is better, but 3 inches suffices. Levers, pumps, and autos dominate this category, but quick-handling bolt action can do the job quite well.

134 USE AN ALL-AROUND GUN

These are the guns that should be able to handle everything from shots in the brush at 25 yards to shots down a powerline right-of-way at 300. They have to be handy, but they also have to be considerably more accurate than the average brush gun. A good all-around deer rifle should group inside a minute and a half of angle at 100 yards. This is a high degree of accuracy, and it pretty well limits the field to bolt actions. Bolts are, without question, the most accurate of rifles, and they are very likely the most reliable as well. The perfect all-purpose rifle will not be ideally suited for either the brush or the beanfield but can handle both. If you must own only one deer rifle, this is it.

135 RULE THE BEANFIELD

This category very likely owes its existence to pioneering South Carolina gunsmith Kenny Jarrett and other Southern gun makers who catered to people who sat in tree stands and shot at long range across beanfields. These rifles are not meant to be handy, well-balanced, esthetically pleasing, or anything else except accurate. Very accurate. A typical beanfield rifle has a 26-inch-long heavy, stainless-steel barrel, a tuned trigger that is lighter than average, and a synthetic stock and is chambered for speed-merchant cartridges.

A good beanfield gun will group into ½ inch or often well under. To get it, major manufacturers lavish care on their beanfielders that they don't have to on the rest of their lines, particularly on the barrels, which are the best they can make or buy. Most beanfield rifles weigh between 9 and 10 pounds, and some go heavier. I once met a beanfield rifle whose owner had nicknamed her "Miss Piggy" because she weighed in at a porky 11 ½ pounds. Miss Piggy would put three shots through one hole at 100 yards.

Beanfield rifles are utterly useless for anything but shooting from stands, but they are exceedingly good for that, and their owners love them.

136 SHOOT THE BEST DEER RIFLE

There are more than 12 great deer rifles, although I can't think of any that are better than these, which are all truly special in one way or another.

BRUSH GUNS

Marlin Model 1895G Guide Gun, .45/70 Very short, unstoppable, and a proven deer killer.

Remington Model 7600, .35 Whelen Quick-shooting, very reliable, and in .35 Whelen, capable of a lot more than deer hunting.

Ruger Gunsite Scout, .308 Not designed for peaceful purposes, but it excels in the deer woods nonetheless.

Blaser R8 Professional, 7x57 A unique rifle that is, among many other things, very compact and gets off aimed shots with blinding speed.

BEANFIELD RIFLES

Savage Model 11/111 Long Range Hunter, 6.5/284 So accurate it will leave you talking to yourself.

Kimber Sonora, .25/06 Just as wonderful as all the other Kimber rifles, and like them, a bargain, considering what you get.

Weatherby Mark V Accumark, .257 Weatherby A truly hellish combination that makes it hard to be a deer.

McMillan Long Range Hunting Rifle, .300 Win Mag Simply, a superb firearm. Nothing better anywhere.

ALL-PURPOSE GUNS

Weatherby Vanguard Series 2, .270 One of the great rifle bargains around, and a damned near flawless firearm.

Winchester Model 70, .270 This is a far better "rifleman's rifle" than your daddy ever dreamed of.

Ruger American Rifle, .243 Ruger's break with the past, and a terrific gun.

Thompson/Center Dimension The first affordable interchangeable-barrel rifle ever, so you have a choice of 12 deer cartridges.

Best Sights For very short, very quick deer shots, use iron sights. The best rear sight is a large peep, with a front sight consisting of a sizeable gold or white bead. With cover open enough for longer shots, use a compact low-power scope that's bright with a large field of view; 1X–4X is ideal.

Best Cartridges .30/30 Winchester is the classic deer cartridge; .35 Remington is a dandy big-woods round, light-kicking but with plenty of thump. .308 Winchester is a great choice, too. .45/70 Government is more than you need, but highly effective at close range in thick cover.

Best Sights These rifles are too heavy to carry far; you do no harm by adding a big scope. Thirty-millimeter tubes and 50mm objective lenses are favored for gathering light, and a magnification of up to 20X is in vogue—all of which help you make the long shots these guns are made for.

Best Cartridges .257 Weatherby Magnum: Roy Weatherby's favorite cartridge, for good reason. .270 WSM: Faster than the .270 Winchester, with just a bit more kick. 7mm Remington Magnum: Simply hard to beat. .300 Winchester Magnum: more than you need, but incredibly accurate.

Best Sights An all-purpose deer rifle needs to be light enough to carry all day. Don't undermine this by adding a monstrosity of a scope. A 2X–7X model is dandy for a lightweight bolt; 3X–9X is all you need; 12X should be the limit. Keep the objective lens under 40mm.

Best Cartridges .25/06 Remington: A great deer cartridge that could be more popular. 7mm/08 Remington: Low in recoil, but accurate and powerful. .270 Winchester: Perennial finalist for "best all-purpose deer cartridge." .30/06 Springfield: A bit much for deer, but very popular.

137

GET THE 8 MUST-HAVE PIECES OF DEER-HUNTING GEAR

You can hunt deer with only a rifle, a cartridge, and a pair of boots. But you will do better if you also have, at a minimum, these additional items.

COMPASS Yes, I know all about GPS and how it can get you to within a yard of where you want to go. And it will do that unfailingly unless its batteries die, or you're under heavy tree cover, or unless the satellites are off shopping somewhere. Compasses work, period.

PARACHUTE CORD At least 50 feet of parachute, or 550 cord. You can use it for everything from tying a dead deer to a tree so it won't slide down a hill as you gut it to lowering your rifle from a treestand. I know one hunter who rappelled down a cliff with parachute cord, thereby saving himself from death by exposure.

TAKEDOWN CLEANING ROD of the proper diameter for whatever rifle you're using. This is to clear stuck cases, or worse, stuck cartridges, from the chamber. Tap gently for best results. It beats the hell out of a stick, assuming you can even find a stick that fits..

THREE MEANS OF STARTING A FIRE Who knows what's going to happen out there? I carry waterproof matches, a spark-striker, and a butane lighter with a clear reservoir so I can be sure it's full. To have tinder on hand, saturate half a dozen cotton balls with petroleum jelly and carry them in a watertight container.

THREE SMALL FLASHLIGHTS At least one should be of the headlamp variety. Why three? Because at least one is almost guaranteed to crap out on you in the course of a hunt, and at the worst possible time.

SWISSCHAMP SWISS ARMY KNIFE People will laugh at all those blades...until they ask to borrow it. There is hardly any problem this knife will not solve.

FIRST-AID KIT A small one will do. You can go for years without using it, and then some day you'll need it very badly. Check it at the start of each season to make sure that nothing needs replacing.

RUBBER GLOVES If you like blood all over your hands, you can skip this. However, if you have an open cut and get deer blood in it, you will probably change your mind after said cut gets badly infected.

PETZAL ON: BULLETS FOR DEER

" Among deer hunters, there are two schools of thought as to what comprises a good bullet. The first says that violent expansion is necessary: That all the bullet's energy should be expended in the deer. The second holds that few deer are dropped where they stand and to reliably track a deer you need an exit hole, and therefore must have a bullet that penetrates through and through. I vote on the side of penetration. You need some expansion, certainly. But the tough bullets are better; they give you a blood trail you can follow."

138
FORGET BRUSH-BUCKING BULLETS FOR DEER

Putting the crosshairs on a tangle of branches with a deer on the other side and pulling the trigger results in tofu for dinner. No bullet bucks the brush. Would you like a real brush bucker? Get a 20mm cannon. I'm sure you can work something out with the ATF, fish and game wardens, and the state police before next season. Or you can always hold your fire until you have a clear shot.

139 BELIEVE IN MAGIC

I've been lucky enough to hunt lots of different critters, and I can tell you for a fact that there is nothing to send you instantly into adrenaline bloat like the appearance of a big whitetail. Elk and Cape buffalo will churn your ductless glands, but they are amateurs compared to *Odocoileus virginianus*.

Part of the whitetail's mystique is its ability to materialize out of thin air. If you've hunted them, you know that you can be looking at a perfectly empty field one instant and in the next instant there is a deer standing where you were looking. You never see them approach; they just seem to assemble themselves from free-floating molecules in the space of a nanosecond.

It's possible that they learn this from their mothers as fawns: "Pay attention now, children. This is important."

It's possible that they had help from aliens, eons ago, before the aliens went to Egypt to build pyramids.

Who knows? In any event, it's a good part of why they drive so many people nuts, including myself.

140 WATCH THE DEER DROP

It just occurred to me that this title may be insensitive. That's okay; I'm insensitive. But I digress.

For about a dozen years, I hunted whitetails in South Carolina every year. Because I was hunting on a private plantation, and because South Carolina has extremely generous bag limits, I could shoot two deer a day for four days. This adds up to a fair number of deer. During that time I carried a number of different rifles, the smallest of which was a .257 Roberts, the largest a 7mm Weatherby Magnum. I could see no difference whatsoever in "killing power" between the various cartridges.

I've killed whitetails and mule deer as small as 70 pounds and as large as 300 with cartridges as small as the 6mm Remington and as large as the .340 Weatherby. No difference. Deer, of any size, are not hard to kill. There are animals that require some horsepower, but not these.

If called upon to kill a deer these days, I will choose either a 6.5x55 or a 7mm/08, or if there may be a long shot, a .270. Just shoot well and the deer will drop.

141 HAVE THE HUNT OF YOUR LIFE

Elk hunting is special. Once you've had a taste of chasing bulls in the vast Rocky Mountain wilderness, you'll wonder why you bother to hunt anything else. Okay. That's just my opinion. After 30 years of hunting elk, I think nothing can compare. But it takes planning, hard work, and some money to pull off an elk hunt, and, for most sportsmen, it's a rare opportunity. Here's how to make any type of trip a success.

THE GUIDED HUNT If you can swing the price, a fully guided hunt is the way to go. When you spring for a guided hunt, you're not buying an elk. You're paying for the things that make a week in an elk camp an unforgettable experience—pack strings and wall tents and wilderness. Above all, you're getting the leadership of men whose devotion to hunting elk and living in the mountains often costs them things like wives and 401(k) accounts.

THE DROP CAMP For self-sufficient hunters who want an easy, affordable way into the mountains, this is the perfect trip, as it puts you in the middle of elk country, where you hunt on your own and do your own chores. Drop camps work if you're looking mainly for transportation to a place from which to hunt elk. Be aware, however, that it denies you some important benefits of a full-service camp.

The key element lacking here is, of course, a guide. If you don't know the country, you'll spend valuable time looking for elk. And don't expect them to stampede between the tents. Most outfitters who offer drop camps also sell full-service hunts. If you were an outfitter, where would you put your guided, and higher-paying, hunters? Say "Where the most elk are," and you get a gold star. Drop camps are second-tier. It's not criminal or even devious—it's good business.

DO IT YOURSELF If you really want to earn your bull, forget guides and outfitters and go it alone. Success will never taste so sweet. It's not as difficult as most hunters think. But preparation is crucial. Not only do you have to find the elk; you must first locate a good campsite or a hunting area accessible enough for day trips. You can plan hunts without an outfitter anywhere, but I do so only in states with big blocks of lightly roaded national forest and relatively light human presence. Wilderness gives you a better chance of finding undisturbed elk.

INSIDER ADVICE Be ready to accept some problems. Sometimes major ones. One of my *Field & Stream* colleagues once rode 27 miles in sleet to a drop camp, only to find that a bear had raided it: The tent was down, poles were scattered, and ropes were broken. It was one of those headaches no outfitter can prevent.

PETZAL ON: ELK HUNTS

"Take the first decent elk you see. Big bulls are rare, and any elk is hard to find. Last October, hunting on my own, I watched 18 average bulls in a herd of 120 elk on opening morning. I declined the shots and never saw them again.

Don't be afraid to ask your guide to change hunting strategies. Twice I've had to talk to a guide about giving me more rein or trying a new tactic. Both times I killed a bull. The same goes for hunting on horseback; if you'd rather walk more, say so."

142 EARN YOUR ELK

You can, if you are frail of body and timid of spirit, hunt elk on a ranch where you will be driven to a herd, make a brief stalk, and pull the trigger. You may then *consider* yourself an elk hunter, but you won't *be* one. Elk are animals of the Rocky Mountain wilderness, and they are properly hunted on horseback and on foot, many miles from the nearest road, out of tent camps. At the end of such a hunt, you will be dirtier, colder, and more exhausted than you have ever been in your life, and you may or may not have meat on the pole to show for it. But you will be an elk hunter.

A former Marine I know saved for years to hunt elk, and when he finally did get the chance for his hunt, he was well into his seventies. He spent two weeks on horseback, never walked normally again, but he got a magnificent bull. He had no regrets. He was an elk hunter.

A good-size whitetail buck will scale 200 pounds; a big bull elk will go as high as 600 or better. A spooked whitetail will travel up to a mile. An elk that is looking to protect his hide will run into the next zip code. Deer hunters can work a square mile in a day successfully; elk hunters must cover 10 to 20 miles to get their shot at an elk.

Your chance to down a bull probably will come when you are footsore and fed up and your mind is elsewhere. Then you will see a bull, and you must put everything out of your mind but the act of shooting. If you miss, it is no worse than drinking straight vinegar. If you do get an elk down, it is triumph tinged with sorrow. But you will not be a hero or a goat until you return to camp, where the final judgment of your peers awaits. And when the day comes to mount up and leave for the flatlands, you will turn in the saddle and take a long look back, because you never know if you will be lucky enough to do this again.

143 CHOOSE YOUR ELK RIFLE

Half a million years ago, hunters had to contend with the critter called Megaloceros, or Irish elk. It dwarfed anything pooping on the sagebrush today. This giant deer stood 7 feet at the shoulder, had antlers that spread 12 feet, and weighed twice what a modern elk does. And I am willing to bet that, around Paleolithic campfires, there were screaming arguments about the right tool for getting Megaloceros into the cooking pot: heavy spear or accurate atlatl. The same argument still is going on today, so I'll weigh in on both sides.

The first school of thought on elk rifles states that any gun will do if you shoot well. There is massive evidence that any big-game rifle is a good elk rifle. Years ago, I hunted the same Montana divide as a fellow who got an elk nearly every year with a .30/06 and factory ammo. He was smart and patient and had loads of time, so he could pass up shot after shot. Only when things looked perfect did he pull the trigger. In the 20 years that I kept track of him, he never missed, and he never had to track a wounded elk. If any kind of tally were to be kept, it would probably show that more elk have fallen to the .30/06, .270, and .30/30 than everything else combined. Even I once killed an elk with a .270. However, I was pale and shook for days afterward.

The second school of thought is: you get one shot, and it will be tough. Unlike that Montana hunter who could afford to pass up shots, most of us are lucky to get an elk tag and a week in the mountains and to see a shootable bull. Few of us are going to hold our fire if the shot is less than perfect. That is where the big guns come in. By big, I mean .300 Weatherby Magnum and up, mainly up. A .300 Weatherby or a .300 Remington Ultra Magnum can shoot a 200-grain bullet at 3,000 fps, more or less, and is a fearsome proposition. A .338, .340 Weatherby, or .338 RUM can shoot much heavier bullets—up to 250 grains—at speeds ranging from 2,600 fps for the .338 to 2,900 fps for the other two.

Heavy, medium-caliber slugs cause more damage than smaller bullets. If you're using the very strongest, like Swift A-Frames, they'll pass through any amount of hide, bone, and muscle. The problem with guns of this size is that they kick—hard. To counteract the kick, they must either weigh a lot (9 pounds, with scope, at the minimum) or they must have a muzzle brake, which means you will have to hunt with some kind of ear protection since the noise produced is simply unbearable. Which side of the argument do I favor? I go with the big guns. But if you have any doubts about your ability to carry and shoot one, use your deer rifle. An elk that's gut-shot with a .338 will die just as protracted and miserable a death as an elk that's badly shot with a .270.

144 BUILD YOUR ELK ARSENAL

Choose a rifle that is powerful enough to put elk down nearly every time. And it must have enough weight to counteract recoil so that you won't flinch when you get your shot. If you don't like the idea of lugging around a heavy, hard-kicking rifle, that's tough. This is elk hunting.

ALL PURPOSE These are bolt actions that fire heavy bullets at high velocity and will put an elk on the ground, near or far. They are no fun to carry, but they are what I use, given my druthers. Notice that I opt for .33 magnums over .30s. The .30s are easier to hit with on very long shots, but a 250-grain .338 bullet moving at 2,700 to 3,000 fps is the better choice.

Sako 85 Classic
.338 Winchester Magnum
The Model 85 Classic is a beautifully finished, finely made traditional wood-stocked rifle, and the .338 Win Mag is regarded by many as the greatest elk round of all. How can you lose?

Remington Model 700 LSS in .338
Remington Ultra Mag
As delicate as the average boulder and as stable as a synthetic-stocked rifle. The barrel is better at 23 ½ or 24 inches than at the factory-issue 26. Although you lose maybe 100 fps, which is meaningless, you get a much handier rifle.

Weatherby Mark V Accumark
in .340 Weatherby Magnum
Courtesy of a composite stock, a specially tuned trigger, an aluminum bedding girder, and a fluted, 26-inch stainless Krieger barrel, this rifle could shoot the eyelashes off an elk. You will curse its weight—until you see the job it does.

TIMBER Much elk hunting takes place in dark timber where you are walking either nearly straight up, nearly straight down, or sideways on a 45-degree slope, constantly ducking under downed limbs. If you get a shot, it will be at under 100 yards, and for these circumstances, several specialized rifles work to perfection. Here are three examples.

Remington Model 673 Guide Rifle
in .350 Remington Magnum
The 673 is a nonpareil elk rifle—compact, powerful, and manageable. Its barrel length is 22 inches, and it weighs about 7¾ pounds. The vent rib is silly and useless, but that is about the end of the gun's faults.

Ruger No. 1S Medium Sporter in .45/70
It has a 22-inch barrel, but because the receiver is so short, the overall length is quite short. The front sling swivel is sited far forward on the barrel, riding very low on your shoulder. You only get one shot at a time, but you aren't going to need more than one shot if it's a good one.

Marlin Model 1895G Guide Gun in .45/70
With a stubby 18 ½-inch barrel, this rifle is very short (only 37 inches overall) and light (7 pounds) as well, but with the right cartridge it will knock an elk down flat. This little rifle works great with iron sights but is so accurate that it begs to be used with a low-powered scope.

145

GO SLOW TO GET YOUR MOOSE

I was hunting the Tsiu River region in southeastern Alaska when I shot an attractive bull moose with an Ultra Light Arms rifle chambered for the .340 Weatherby Magnum. It took one bullet high in the lungs at 60 yards to put him down, which is rare for moose. Usually, you shoot them three or four times, and they stand around thinking the matter over and then head for the nearest body of water and die.

I was using handloads, specifically 275-grain Swift A-Frames that develop a muzzle velocity of 2,550 fps in that rifle. If you're familiar with the .340, you're aware that it can shoot 250-grainers at plus-2,800 fps, and 210s at 3,000 fps. So why did I settle on such a long, slow projectile?

Because it works. Called-in moose are usually shot at ranges of 20 to 40 yards, where high velocity is worse than useless. At best, it will produce blown-up bullets that cause horrendous meat loss. At worst, the bullet will blow up on the shoulder, and the animal will run away and die at his leisure, and you may not ever find it. What you want is a bullet that will hold together and pass intact through 4 feet of bone, hide, and muscle. Which is exactly what the Swift did.

For years, I've been handloading all my hellish magnum cartridges with long, heavy bullets at substantially less velocity than factory specs. One of the very best of these cartridges is a 7.21 mm (actually, .284) Lazzeroni Tomahawk, which is capable of sending a 140-grain bullet along at nearly 3,400 fps, and a 160 at just under 3,200. I load 160-grain Nosler Partitions to 3,000 fps even, and guess what? The critters fall down just as fast either way.

Velocity is fine and dandy in its place, but in a great deal of big-game hunting you don't need nearly as much as is available, and in a surprising number of cases it can actually work against you.

146 SHOOT FAST, SHOOT ACCURATE

When I bagged a bull moose on a hunting trip in 2006, after two weeks of slogging through the bogs of southern Alaska, he was approaching at a rapid trot. I was out in the open, and if I moved, he would see me. This position meant that, as he came abreast, I would have to mount the rifle, take aim, and get the shot off, all in the space of a second or two before he figured out that something was amiss, or amoose, as it were.

Sometimes you have to shoot fast. Additionally, you have to be able to hit where you're aiming. Guides and outfitters whine that far too many hunters these days are no more capable of getting off a fast, accurate shot than they are of flying. One outfitter told me, as he approached apoplexy, "You work your butt off to get them a perfectly easy offhand shot, and they look around for a benchrest."

In areas where the game population is hunted hard or where you will have to shoot at close range, you had best fire right smartly. On the other hand, there are places where the critters are more curious than concerned about humans. If you're one of the growing numbers of nimrods who shoot

at more than 300 yards, you probably have time for a leisurely first shot and two or three more as well. Get in touch with your inner Wyatt Earp, who said that you get your revolver clear of the holster just as fast as you possibly can, and then you take your sweet time aiming.

Translated into rifle shooting, this philosophy means getting the gun to your shoulder quickly, with no wasted motion, all the while keeping your eyes on what you want to shoot. Remember that you don't yank the stock straight up; you bring it forward, up, and back in a short semicircle.

When your gun is up and you're aiming, you have to make a fundamental decision: How much time do I have? Experienced hunters can judge by an animal's behavior whether they have no time at all, 5 seconds, or 5 minutes. Whatever time they think they have, they'll take all of it.

If you're not an experienced hunter, it's better to assume you have no more than 3 seconds. So, pick a spot on the critter, aim for it, and when the crosshairs are on it or close, pull the trigger. Don't keep aiming, hoping your sight picture will get better. It won't.

147 DON'T BE STUPID

In almost every situation, some basic rules apply. If you're going for the larger, more dangerous prey, all the more reason to review your fundamentals. Get to the range and burn some ammo. Doing so will at least keep you from making the following four mistakes:

MISTAKE ONE Finding out the hard way that you can't shoulder your rifle because what you are wearing out there in cold moose country is so thick that you can't get the scope close enough to get a proper sight picture.

MISTAKE TWO Sighting in your rifle with the scope on 10x and leaving it there instead of cranking it down to 4x.

MISTAKE THREE Forgetting where your safety is, or how it works, or that you even have a safety.

MISTAKE FOUR Keeping the rifle slung over your shoulder, or worse, across your back as you hike across the tundra in search of moose.

148 GET YOUR GOAT

I am not a fan of the 6mm or .243 for most big-game hunting, but goat-hunting is one place where they shine. However, you have to be wary of two things. First, if you do happen to get a long shot—300 yards or more—those little bullets get pushed very hard by the wind, and a goat is a small target. Second, .243 and 6mm ammo comes loaded with both varmint and game bullets, and you want game bullets. Usually, this will mean a slug of 90 or 100 grains at about 2,900 fps (real-world velocity).

Far better than either of these are the .257 Roberts and the .25/06. Both of them are older guns, but they're unbeatable. They allow you to use 115- and 120-grain bullets that buck the

wind better, penetrate better, and are generally more effective than 100-grain slugs. The Roberts is not hugely popular ammo for it can be hard to find, and most of that is badly underloaded. But what a handloader can do with the .257 is nothing short of wonderful. The more powerful .25/06 has never set the world on fire, but if I were building a rifle just for antelope, that's what I'd chamber it for.

The .270 makes a superb antelope rifle, provided you use the 130-grain bullets available for this round. The .30/06 will also do, but you must limit yourself to the 150-grain loadings.

Don't head for the sagebrush flats with your '06 and the 180-grain ammo you would use for elk. These bullets

are too tough for goats; they'll punch right through without expanding and your antelope will run off, seemingly unhit, to suffer and eventually die.

If you would like a rifle that will really lay those goats out at long range, get one of the short .270 magnums by Remington, Winchester, or Lazzeroni. These guns shoot so flat I can hardly credit it, and they don't kick much, considering the ballistics they develop.

.257 Roberts

149 USE THE LANDSCAPE TO YOUR ADVANTAGE

Goats (antelope actually are a species of goat, whereas mountain goats are actually antelope, if you care) are not the most adaptable of creatures. For eons, they have gotten by on a mixture of wonderful eyesight and tremendous speed, but they lack the cerebral qualities of whitetails and elk, and they suffer from insatiable curiosity.

If they lived in truly flat country, you'd stand no chance with them, but the land on which the buffalo roam and the deer and the antelope play (I've never seen antelope actually playing; maybe I just don't know what to look for) is not flat. It is filled with buttes and mesas, coulees, washes, and arroyos, all of which allow you to creep and sneak where the goats can't see. This means you can get fairly close, if you

don't mind making the effort. Also, antelope have to drink, and where there are water holes, there they will gather, and there you can lurk.

Pronghorn hunters stand a good chance of getting a steady prone shot, so learn to shoot over your day pack or to use a sling from your prone. Or buy a bipod and clamp it to your fore-end. You may have to crawl to get into position, and, if so, you'll find that the sagebrush is carpeted with small cacti, yuccas, rocks, and serpents.

To deal with the first three, order a set of knee and elbow guards. If you encounter a prairie rattler while creeping up on a goat, just go home. Only lunatics crawl around with venomous serpents.

150 SCOPE OUT GOATS

I think the best goat scope you can use is a variable in the 3X to 10X range. And make sure to bring a good binocular or a good spotting scope, or both, particularly if you're looking for a trophy.

Most of the antelope bucks you see will have horns (not antlers) that measure 12 inches to 14 inches. A 12-inch goat is a respectable trophy, while 14 inches is considered quite good in many places. Two inches of horn is not all that much, particularly when you're hundreds of yards away, so before you begin your stalk you want to make sure that the buck in question is worth shooting, and that you can pick him out of the herd.

Smart antelope hunters glass much and walk as little as possible. Walking is an intrinsically disgusting activity that makes you sweaty and tired and spooks the wildlife, and no one does it when he doesn't have to.

It has been said that the average goat's eyesight is roughly equivalent to a human who is using 8X or 10X binoculars. Maybe. What I do know is that if you see them, they see you. Keep that in mind.

151
GET A GOAT IN YOUR SIGHTS

Many of the people who hunt antelope come from the East, where they rarely see an animal in the open or at long range. When they spot a goat, they assume it's much farther away than it is, aim over the critter's back, and send the bullet high. Assuming that they aimed too low, they hold still higher and keep missing until the critter wanders off or they run out of ammunition.

Remember that these creatures are small, and the antelope that seems a whole section away is probably 200 yards off, which is an easy point-blank shot. The golden rule is: Never hold out of the hair for the first shot. If you think a goat is really, truly, a long way off, hold right on its spine—no higher.

But no matter how you go after them, or with what rifle, do it as a sportsman. Antelope have been here a lot longer than we have, and they deserve our respect.

PETZAL ON: ANTELOPE

"When it comes to writing about hunting antelope, my joy is less than total. The little critters have had more rotten things done to them by way of 'hunting,' and suffer more as a result of lousy shooting, than any other animal.

Antelope are not the brightest of creatures (although an old buck can be very good at staying alive), and they've never learned to jump fences, so it's considered great sport among certain pickup-driving yahoos to panic a band of goats (which is what most folks call them in the West), herd them against a fence, and start shooting. Sometimes these heroes don't even bother to take aim at a particular animal but fire into the flock, and some antelope run off gut shot, others with shattered legs swinging.

With the growing craze for long-range shooting, the poor goat has another problem in the form of shooters who fire from many hundreds of yards, where it's easy to accidentally hit an antelope in the paunch or leg or jaw. No thanks. To hunt antelope–and I mean the word 'hunt' to the fullest–takes skill, patience, and the proper equipment."

152 HUNT THE HUNTERS

Coyotes are mostly small; however I've shot Maine coyotes that were nearly the size of wolves. Coyotes are not hard to bring down—I have killed coyotes virtually at the muzzle of a shotgun and at 500 yards.

I use my beanfield gun, a custom rifle built on a Savage action, in .25/06, using handloads. The scope is a Trijicon AccuPoint 2.5X–10X 56mm, which will let you deal with coyote at long range or paw-shaking distance and in poor light. The handloads are 100-grain Swift Sciroccos, and they are not only dandy on deer, but they will bring eternal rest to any sort of coyote up to the size of a dire wolf.

Not following my advice to the letter? In that case, my ammunition picks would be .223, .22/250, .25/06, and .270 Win Mag.

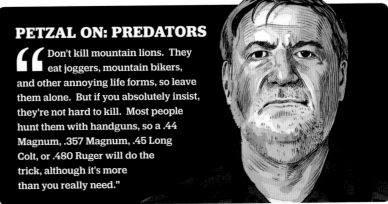

PETZAL ON: PREDATORS

"Don't kill mountain lions. They eat joggers, mountain bikers, and other annoying life forms, so leave them alone. But if you absolutely insist, they're not hard to kill. Most people hunt them with handguns, so a .44 Magnum, .357 Magnum, .45 Long Colt, or .480 Ruger will do the trick, although it's more than you really need."

Marlin Guide Gun

153 SCORE A SWINE

Forget about Babe. These piggies can be huge and very tough, and believe me, you don't want to deal with a wounded swine. I can't remember taking any kind of wild pig at more than 100 yards, if that.

My choice of rifle for pig hunting is a highly worked-over Marlin Model 95G Guide Gun with a Leupold VX-III 1.5X–5X scope, chambered for .45/70. It holds six rounds in case you encounter a plethora of porkers, and when used with Garrett hard-lead-bullet ammo or Buffalo Bore jacketed-bullet rounds, it will stand even the biggest swine on its nose.

These two brands of ammo are loaded far beyond standard .45/70 specs, and they will make believers out of whatever you shoot with them.

154 SCOPE OUT PREDATORS

You may be asking if pigs are technically predators. My answer? If they're not, they will do until the predators come along. When it comes to hunting pigs, something in the low-power range is nice. I'd say anything whose bottom end is 1X to 2.5X. At the top end I'm not all that particular, because I've never shot a pig where I need more than, say, 4X. Quite often, you'll shoot pigs at dawn or dusk from a deer stand, so you need a reticle that's visible in poor light, or a red dot.

It's a bit different for coyotes, because some coyotes are not much bigger than foxes, and often you'll be taking them at long range. At the bottom end, I'd recommend 2.5X, and at the top end no less than 10X. A range-compensating reticle can be a big help. As with the pig scope, poor light is a factor, and I would definitely go for a scope that has a red dot in it.

155 LEARN FROM A RODENT

Set aside the "aww" factor for a moment and recognize that cute little varmints and rodents provide great opportunities to improve as both a shooter and a hunter. If you're interested in becoming a true long-range rifleman, the prairie dog can teach you better than any other instructor. Two or three days of shooting can do wonders for your appreciation of distance, mirage, wind, and proper shooting technique. Here are seven lessons prairie-dog hunting has taught me about shooting that I never would have learned anywhere else short of sniper training.

ONE There's no substitute for shooting a lot. I think that the minimum ammo expenditure needed for a good shot to stay that way is about 200 rounds of centerfire ammo a year, and I doubt if most big-game hunters fire 20. When you've sent 500 bullets downrange at all distances, and with all different kinds of wind to account for, you'll have a much better idea of how ballistics work in the real world.

Scope with Mil-dots

TWO Learning how to estimate range without using a laser rangefinder will make you a better hunter. The prairie dog's small size, and the fact that it inhabits country with few prominent landmarks, makes it tough to figure out how far away the little rodents are. You'll find that after a few days with the dogs, you can estimate distances pretty well out to 300 yards.

THREE He who holds off is lost. Kentucky windage may work in Kentucky, but it will not work where you are. Long-distance shooting requires shooting from multiple aiming points. It's fine to learn this skill when you're hunting prairie dogs. It's not fine to learn this skill shooting at a 12-point buck in the waning light on the last day of the season. Use a scope with mil dots and stop aiming at empty chunks of air.

FOUR The bipod is your friend. For a rock-steady hold, no matter what you're hunting at long distance, go with a bipod. They're equally useful on a big-game rifle that's going to be used for long-range work.

FIVE You gotta have a spotta. Another shooter, of equal or greater ability than you, is invaluable when it comes to reading the wind, making sighting adjustments, and spotting bullet splashes. The alternative is to get yourself a recoilless rifle. The latest custom prairie-dog guns I've seen weigh in the neighborhood of 12 to 15 pounds and have muzzle brakes to boot. That's because the only way you can spot your own bullet splashes is if the rifle doesn't move at all.

Savage 12 LRPV Dual Port

SIX A lot of shooting at small targets makes shooting a deer seem like shooting a tame elephant. What I discovered very early on was that unless you had an accurate rifle and you were a pretty fair shot, you were not going to hit a small creature like a woodchuck. For most prairie dogs, which are about a third the size of a woodchuck, I use a .223 and a .22/250. The latter will put five shots in ¼ inch; the .223 will actually do better than that.

SEVEN Lay off the caffeine. The slowest heartbeat makes for the steadiest hold, and if you drink three coffees before you take your rifle out of the case, your life is going to be a lot harder and the rodent's a lot longer.

.223 and .22/250

156 BE BEAR AWARE

Even if you're not actually hunting bear, you may well need to know how to most effectively shoot one. In fact, you're most likely to have a bear encounter of the violent kind when you're after something else. If you're hunting caribou or moose you'll be thinking about caribou or moose and not watching for bears. The bears, however, will be aware of you and may take exception to your presence. In addition, some bears have learned that the sound of a gunshot means dinner, and all they have to do is run the humans off a carcass. If so, you have to stand your ground and shoot very fast at very close range.

In most of North America, what you'll encounter is going to be either a grizzly or a brown bear. These are essentially the same animal; however, brown bears are coastal, fish-fed for part of the year, and much bigger. A decent-sized grizzly bear will scale 600 pounds, but a well-fed male brown bear can double that weight.

Both animals share eyesight that ranges from mediocre to poor, excellent hearing, and a supernatural sense of smell. They have crushing bites, paws that can kill or

cripple a man with a single swat, and catlike quickness.

Hunting the bears on purpose puts the odds on your side. You locate them at long range with a spotting scope, figure out how you'll stalk them, get as close as possible, and pull the trigger. If all goes according to script, the bear's troubles are over, and so are yours, although in a more positive way.

157 GET LOADED FOR BEAR

If you're hunting bears, or if you're hunting in bear country, you'd better take something that will deal with a bear. Your .30/06 may kill moose just fine, but when you approach the carcass and see a grizzly already helping himself, you'll want a much bigger rifle.

Bear rifles are bolt-actions. Nothing else is as reliable or can handle the powerful cartridges that you need. The best cartridges are, starting at the low end of the power scale, the .338 Winchester Magnum, .340 Weatherby Magnum, .338 Remington Ultra Magnum, and .375 H&H. Of these, the .338 kicks the least and may be the best choice if bears are not your primary game. The .340 and .338 RUM also use .338 bullets, but at much higher velocity, and have a lot more recoil. The .375 H&H shoots even heavier bullets and is a huge favorite among Alaskan guides because it's a stopper.

To go with your rifle, you need strong bullets. The best of these, I believe, is the Swift A-Frame. I've used them in Alaska and Africa, on all sorts of large, tough beasts, and they deserve every bit of their peerless reputation.

You also want a good, low-powered scope. If you hunt bears you need a wide field of view combined with a heavy reticle that centers your eye instantly. I think that

the ideal scope is a 1X–4X, a 1.5X–5X, or something in that power range. And bring scope caps because it will rain on you. Heavily. I guarantee that.

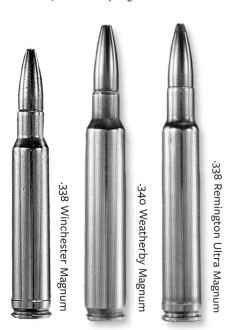

.338 Winchester Magnum

.340 Weatherby Magnum

.338 Remington Ultra Magnum

.375 H&H

158 PICK THE BEST ROUNDS FOR HUNTING IN AFRICA

African rifles have always been categorized as light, medium, and heavy, and the system makes so much sense that I feel compelled to follow it here, with two choices in each category.

LIGHT RIFLE

First Choice:
.30/06 Springfield
The '06 is as useful over there as it is here. Load it with strong 180-grain bullets.

Favorite Load:
Federal Premium Vital-Shok 180-grain Barnes TSX.

Second Choice:
.270 Winchester
In the 1950s, my friend Bob Lee used to kill lions with a .270. What more do you want?

Favorite Load:
Federal Premium Vital-Shok 140-grain Trophy Bonded Bear Claw.

.270

.30/06

MEDIUM RIFLE

First Choice:
.375 H&H
The .375 is to African hunts what the .30/06 is to North American—indispensable.

Favorite Load:
Remington Premier 300-grain Swift A-Frame.

Second Choice:
.338 Winchester Magnum
It's the near equal of the .375 H&H, but it's less available in Africa.

Favorite Load:
Remington Premier 225-grain Swift A-Frame.

.375

.338

HEAVY RIFLE

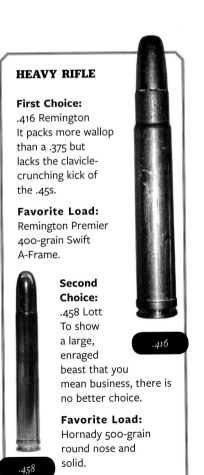

First Choice:
.416 Remington
It packs more wallop than a .375 but lacks the clavicle-crunching kick of the .45s.

Favorite Load:
Remington Premier 400-grain Swift A-Frame.

Second Choice:
.458 Lott
To show a large, enraged beast that you mean business, there is no better choice.

Favorite Load:
Hornady 500-grain round nose and solid.

.416

.458

159 TRIUMPH OVER CAPE BUFFALO

The Cape buffalo is, by far, the most commonly hunted dangerous game species on Earth. A good-sized bull weighs between 1,400 and 1,600 pounds. Ordinarily, they just want to stay as far from you as possible, but if you wound one, it will do its very best to even the score.

The beast's ability to take repeated hits from big rifles and keep coming is legendary. As a professional hunter with 60 years' experience put it, "It's like you're feeding them vitamin pills instead of shooting them." Also, this is one of two African animals—the other is the elephant— that will probably kill you if they get you down.

Hunting Cape buffalo is difficult because they're herd animals, very spooky, and have superb hearing, smell, and sight. If you get close, there will be lots of eyes, ears, and noses working to detect you. You'll almost always have to hunt them in heavy brush. I've killed a fair number of buffalo and have taken only one that was out in the open. Mostly, you go after them in places where the visibility ranges from a few feet to 50 yards.

You will also have to walk a lot, as well as run and crawl. I've done plenty of all three in a single day. Also: I've had a number of very bad scares in the course of 10 safaris, and every one has been caused by Cape buffalo. That's why you should hunt them.

160 LOAD UP FOR CAPE BUFFALO

Aside from the elephant, the Cape Buffalo is the only African species that justifies the use of a double rifle, so if you have the money and are willing to practice with the thing, why, have at it. But I still prefer a rifle that holds four or five shots instead.

The smallest legal rifle for Cape buffalo is a .375 H&H but, based on my own experience, I prefer something bigger. The first four Cape buffalo I killed were shot with a .375 and did not at first appear to be bothered much by it. Since then, I've used a .458 Winchester, .458 Lott, and .416 Remington and prefer them by a wide margin. I have also shot, but not hunted with, the .404 Jeffrey, an old cartridge that's enjoying a renaissance because it offers more power than the .375 but without recoil that will curdle your milk.

You'll need both solid and soft point bullets, and the soft points must be tough. A good solid should shoot clear through a buffalo, and a good softpoint should stop under the hide on the far side. Hornady solids work fine, and Swift A-Frames are the way to go for soft points.

One tip: When you load your magazine, have your soft point bullets on top and save the solids for finishing the animal off. Your first shot at a buffalo will almost always come while it's in the herd, and the one thing you don't want is that slug zipping through and wounding a second animal, who will, unbeknownst to you, run off and wait for a chance at payback.

Use a low-power scope. Picking out a gray animal in the half-light of heavy cover is more than I can do with open sights, and probably more than you can do, too. And remember to bring plenty of ammunition. Carry no fewer than 15 rounds on your person, in a place where you can reach it quickly. Sooner or later, you're going to need to use all of it.

162
SURVIVE YOUR ELEPHANT HUNT

How dangerous are elephants? They are sure as hell not Babar. The only professional hunter (PH) I hunted with who was killed by an animal was killed by an elephant. The only PH I ever hunted with who was openly terrified of a particular species was terrified of elephants because he was nearly killed by one as well.

In addition to their considerable intelligence, elephants have excellent hearing and smell, reasonably good eyesight, and six tons of muscle and bone (in the case of big bulls) to back up their opinions. They can't run; they can only walk fast, but that is still pretty fast. And they can move with absolute silence, without so much as cracking a twig.

Elephants, like Cape buffalo, are almost always found in dense cover, at least where they're hunted. Assuming you're after a trophy bull—one with good tusks—your problem lies in finding a herd, getting close to it without them getting your scent, picking out the pachyderm you want to pound, and then waiting until he's clear of all the other beasts.

Hunting elephants usually involves more walking than hunting any other type of African game. They move as they feed, and unless you have the good luck to catch a herd that's resting at midday, you'll need to be in good shape. You may also have to run, just as fast as you can, and hope it's fast enough.

161 CHOOSE THE RIGHT GUNS AND AMMO FOR ELEPHANTS

Elephant guns come in two varieties—bolt-actions and double rifles. Bolt-actions offer four or five shots, are highly reliable, and cost less than doubles, which cost a great deal. Doubles offer only two shots before you have to reload, but they are two very fast shots. I opt for the bolt-action.

It's not as hard to stop a charging elephant as, say, a Cape buffalo or a lion. The elephant is a big target, and it lacks both the lion's speed and the buffalo's adrenaline-fueled kamikaze tactics. The smallest ammunition you can use, by law, where elephants are hunted is the .375 H&H. This is one of the world's great hunting cartridges, because it combines excellent effectiveness without recoil that will detach your retinas.

The .416 Remington and the .416 Rigby are a cut above the .375 H&H, both in recoil and effectiveness. They throw considerably bigger bullets and can still be managed by shooters who are willing to practice with them.

Next up are the .458 Winchester, the .458 Lott, and the .470 Nitro Express. The first two use the same bullets, but the Lott is considerably more powerful and is about the limit of what even an experienced shooter can handle. The .470 is a superb cartridge but is available only in double rifles.

A low-power scope is a good idea, but not all scopes will withstand repeated recoil from cartridges in the .458 Lott class. For this reason, iron sights make sense, either as a backup or as a primary sight. You want a big ivory bead up front and an express rear sight that regulated for 50 yards.

You need both solid and soft-nosed bullets, depending on the kind of shot you are going to take. Ask your professional hunter, well in advance of the hunt, what he recommends. And when you see the price of a box of ammo that can slay an elephant, try not to swoon.

163 CHOOSE YOUR LION-HUNTING RIFLE

The lion is classed as dangerous game, and so in most places you're required to hunt it with a .375 H&H or bigger. You can, however, kill lions with a smaller cartridge. Lions lack thick hides, heavy bones, and massive muscles. What you want is a quick-expanding bullet that does a maximum amount of damage. Solid bullets or very tough soft points will get you into a world of trouble with lions because they'll punch right through, doing little damage. The bullets that work on big antelope are what you want for lions. I recommend the Nosler Partition, which is guaranteed to expand violently.

You can use a double rifle, but everyone I know who hunts lions uses a scoped bolt-action. Iron sights are useful, as they are on any dangerous-game rifle, but unless you can pick up your sight picture quickly—remember, it's a tan cat against a tan background—don't count on using them. Try a scope in the 1X–4X range instead.

Never try to head-shoot a lion. If you hit, you'll ruin the trophy, and a male lion has practically no skull above his eyes; there's nothing there but mane.

164 HUNT A LION CORRECTLY

A big male lion that's been eating regularly weighs in at 450 pounds or so, which is not especially big as dangerous animals go, but it has other gifts, foremost among them being blinding speed. An adult lion can run 100 yards in 3 to 6 seconds. You can't.

Lions' senses are not particularly acute compared to those of other predators—they're sight hunters and do their work in the open, depending on a combination of speed, teamwork, and numbers.

The best way to hunt a lion is to nail him when he has no idea that you're around. In Botswana, I saw a properly executed lion hunt. The trackers found his pugmarks in the sand, and we followed them for several miles. When we caught up to him, the cat was sound asleep, lying on his back, and a single bullet ended his life instantly.

Hunters get into trouble with lions because they lose their nerve and shoot from too far away (100 yards is about max). Hold your fire until you're so close you can't miss. If you wound the lion, he will come for you. Stand your ground and shoot; you're not going to outrun him.

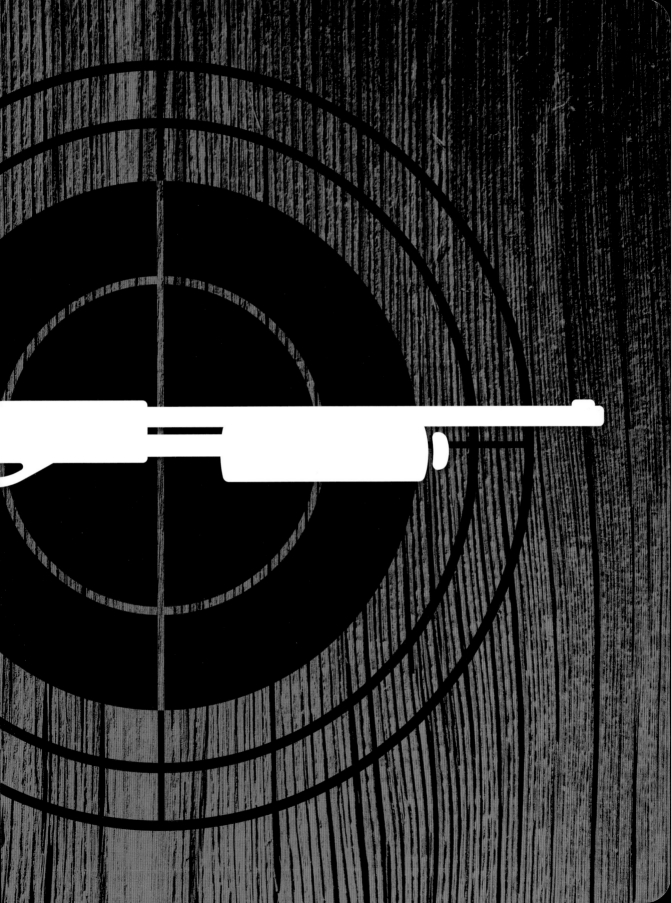

165 LEARN THE ANATOMY OF A SHOTGUN

Whole books have been written about the arcane terminology of shotguns (including "chopper lumps," "dolls heads," "water tables," and many more) but here is a quick guide to the important parts—which is to say, the ones that hold the guns together, help us hold onto them, and make them work.

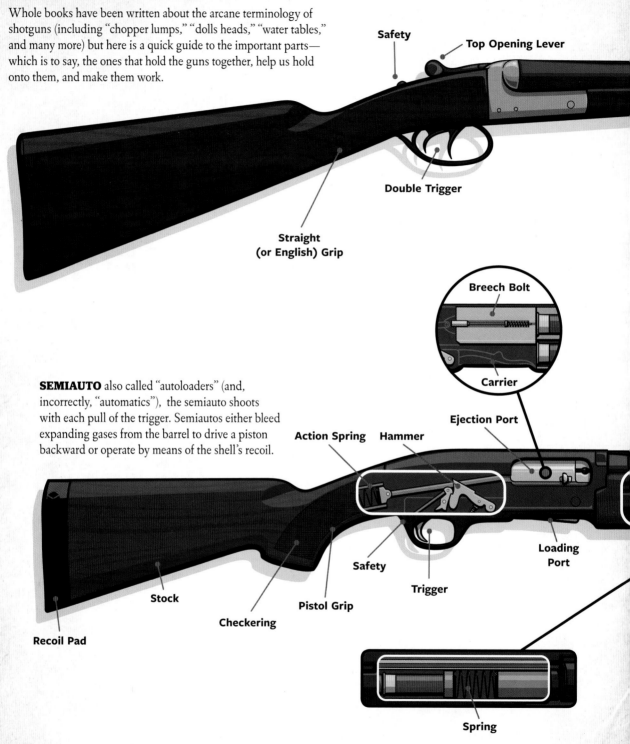

Safety

Top Opening Lever

Double Trigger

Straight
(or English) Grip

Breech Bolt

Carrier

SEMIAUTO also called "autoloaders" (and, incorrectly, "automatics"), the semiauto shoots with each pull of the trigger. Semiautos either bleed expanding gases from the barrel to drive a piston backward or operate by means of the shell's recoil.

Action Spring

Hammer

Ejection Port

Loading
Port

Safety

Trigger

Stock

Pistol Grip

Checkering

Recoil Pad

Spring

DOUBLE Commonly called "side by side," the double has two barrels joined horizontally. Twin triggers, one firing each barrel, are very common on double guns

Barrel

OVER/UNDER (O/U) The over/under has two barrels, one stacked atop the other. Most over/unders have a single trigger that can selected to fire either the top or bottom barrel first.

Breech Chamber

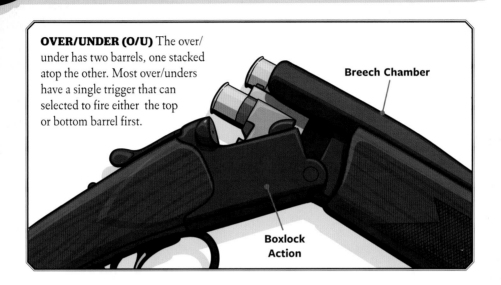

Boxlock Action

Gas Ports (inside)   **Middle Bead**   **Ventilated Rib**   **Front Bead**

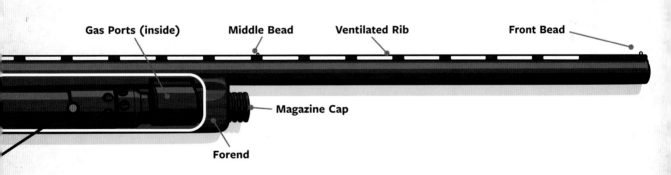

Magazine Cap

Forend

PUMP ACTION also called "slide action" the pump is a manually operated repeater. Pulling back on the forend back and pushing it forward cycles the action.

Magazine   **Action Bar**   **Fore-end**

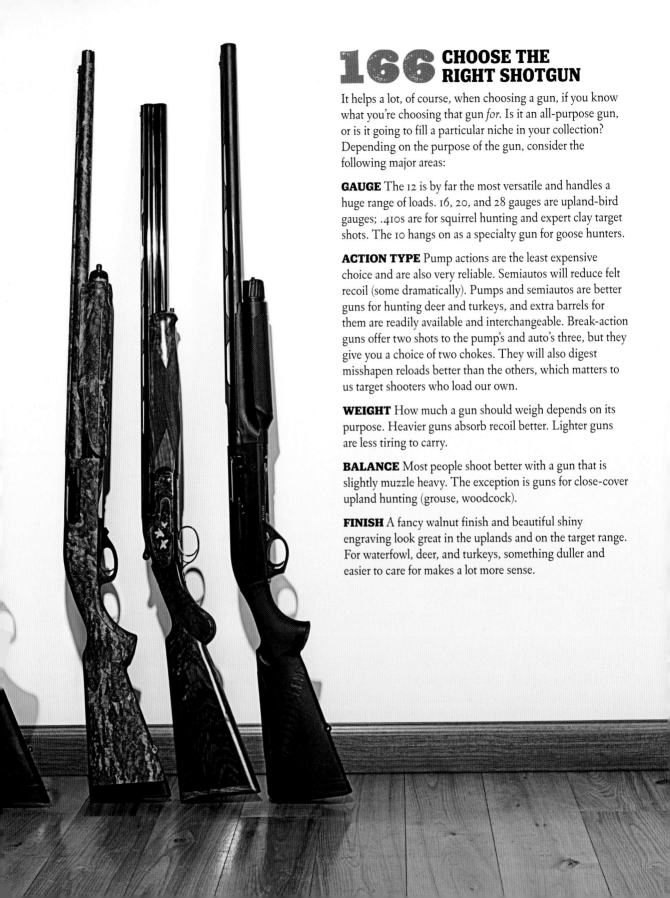

166 CHOOSE THE RIGHT SHOTGUN

It helps a lot, of course, when choosing a gun, if you know what you're choosing that gun *for*. Is it an all-purpose gun, or is it going to fill a particular niche in your collection? Depending on the purpose of the gun, consider the following major areas:

GAUGE The 12 is by far the most versatile and handles a huge range of loads. 16, 20, and 28 gauges are upland-bird gauges; .410s are for squirrel hunting and expert clay target shots. The 10 hangs on as a specialty gun for goose hunters.

ACTION TYPE Pump actions are the least expensive choice and are also very reliable. Semiautos will reduce felt recoil (some dramatically). Pumps and semiautos are better guns for hunting deer and turkeys, and extra barrels for them are readily available and interchangeable. Break-action guns offer two shots to the pump's and auto's three, but they give you a choice of two chokes. They will also digest misshapen reloads better than the others, which matters to us target shooters who load our own.

WEIGHT How much a gun should weigh depends on its purpose. Heavier guns absorb recoil better. Lighter guns are less tiring to carry.

BALANCE Most people shoot better with a gun that is slightly muzzle heavy. The exception is guns for close-cover upland hunting (grouse, woodcock).

FINISH A fancy walnut finish and beautiful shiny engraving look great in the uplands and on the target range. For waterfowl, deer, and turkeys, something duller and easier to care for makes a lot more sense.

167 UNDERSTAND BARREL LENGTH

You will hear that longer barrels "hit harder" than short barrels and that they have a longer sighting plane. Both statements contain an element of truth, but neither is a compelling reason to choose a gun with a longer barrel.

The main reason to choose one barrel length over another is balance. The longer the barrel, the more muzzle-heavy a shotgun feels. And, while we all instantly fall in love with the gun that jumps to our shoulder when we try it at the gun counter, slow and steady usually beats fast and flighty when you're in the field.

For most people, a pump or auto with a 26- or 28-inch barrel, or a double gun with 28-inch barrels, makes the best all-around field gun. Target guns—even guns for very fast games like international skeet—have 30- and 32-inch barrels, both because the extra weight combats kick and also because it helps smooth your swing on clays that won't change direction as real birds sometimes do.

Longer barrels deliver slightly more velocity than shorter barrels, and, in some cases, they'll give better patterns as they allow the shot charge time to stabilize in the barrel. The difference is minimal, however. And, while long barrels do offer a longer sighting plane, if you are sighting down your barrel, you're probably going to miss anyway, so it shouldn't be a determining factor.

168 GET BY WITH JUST ONE GUN

One of the first shotgun columns I ever wrote was "The One Gun That Does It All." A friend mentioned he had seen it. I was eager to hear his reaction until he said, "Thanks a lot. My wife read your column, then she asked me: 'Why do you need all these guns? It says here in *Field & Stream* you only need one.'"

While I have learned since then not to talk about it so much in print, it actually is true: you can easily get by with one gun if you must. The trick, of course, is to choose the right one.

The one gun that does everything is an alloy-receivered, 3-inch, 12-gauge, gas semiauto with a 26- or 28-inch barrel. Why? Let's break it down. The alloy receiver keeps the weight light enough to carry in the uplands, yet the gun will be long enough to be balanced to feel like a heavier gun when you shoot birds or clay targets.

Next, there's the gas action, which will reduce recoil despite the gun's overall light weight, making it a decent gun for skeet, sporting clays, and league trap. Choosing a 3-inch chamber in place of 3 ^{1}/$_2$-inch gives you better reliability with very light loads (even near-recoilless ^{7}/$_8$-ounce practice loads). On the other hand, 3-inch waterfowl magnums, turkey loads, and buckshot give up very little in effective range to 3 ^{1}/$_2$s.

So yes, you can get by with one shotgun. But if you thought that approach was a good idea, you wouldn't be reading this book.

Winchester Super X3 Composite

169 TAKE STOCK

A gun fits when it shoots where you look. The four main dimensions of concern are:

DROP The distance from the top of the comb to a line extending back from the rib, drop determines the elevation of your head and eye in relation to the barrel. Drop is usually measured at the heel (the top of the butt) and at the comb (the very front of the comb). Too little drop, and you'll shoot high; too much, and the gun shoots low.

LENGTH OF PULL (LOP) is the distance between the front of the trigger and the middle of the buttpad. To some extent, the right length of pull is whatever feels comfortable and maintains about two finger-widths between the back of your thumb and your nose. Changing LOP can alter drop slightly by shifting the spot at which your check meets the slope of the comb.

PITCH The angle or pitch of the butt determines how the gun fits against your shoulder pocket. Too little pitch, and the butt digs into your chest; too much, and the gun may slide up and slap your face.

CAST A slight lateral bend in the stock that puts the rib in line with the shooter's eye is called cast. Guns for right-handers have cast off; guns for lefties have cast on. In addition, shooters with thin faces need very little cast because their eyes sit above the cheekbone; shooters with round faces need more. Oliver Hardy, for instance, would need a ton of cast. Stan Laurel, not so much.

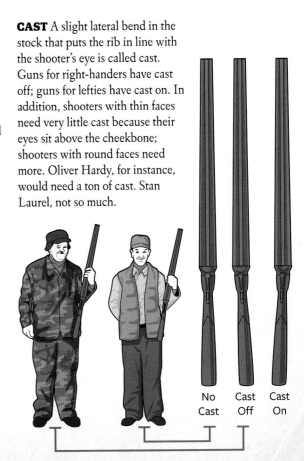

No Cast   Cast Off   Cast On

170 SHOOT A SHEET

Shooting a bedsheet is a quick and easy way to learn if your gun fits you properly.

Here's what you do: Hang it up, make an aiming mark on it, and measure off 16 yards. From there, start from a gun down position, mount the gun smoothly, and shoot without hesitation when the butt touches your shoulder. Don't correct if you perceive you're off target, just keep shooting at the mark. After five or six shots, a hole will appear, indicating the average center of all your shots. If the hole is centered over the mark or is an inch or so high, your gun fits you perfectly for field shooting. Every inch off the point of aim will require a 1/16 of an inch correction to your gunstock's drop or cast, according to gun-fitting theory.

If the point of impact and point of aim differ greatly, roll up the sheet and take it and your gun to a gunsmith.

171 CHECK FIT QUICKLY

Does a gun fit you? A very rough-and-ready way to check is simply to close your eyes, mount the gun, and see if you're looking down the rib. Don't squash your face down on the comb. No one cheeks the gun as hard in the field as they do when checking fit at the gun shop counter.

172 SPACE IT OUT

One more argument for the modern semiauto as the one gun that does everything is the growing inclusion of stock shim kits with most new autoloaders. The shims allow you to fiddle with fit without making permanent changes to the gun. Many guns now come with spacers allowing you to adjust length as well so you can easily experiment with different dimensions.

173 TREAT A LADY RIGHT

Just as many women have to struggle with scaled-down versions of men's hunting clothes instead of clothes designed for women, they also have to deal with most "youth and ladies" shotguns being just cut-down men's stocks that ignore the anatomical differences between men and women. Many women have longer necks than men, meaning that a Monte Carlo Stock (usually seen on trap guns) or a gun with an adjustable pad plate like the Jones Stock Adjuster can provide a better fit.

The toe of a shotgun's stock can dig painfully into a woman's chest as well, so a stock with slightly more pitch and the toe (bottom) of the pad angled outward can give a much more comfortable fit.

174 MAKE THE WORST MISTAKE IN SHOTGUNNING

Lord Ripon, the finest shot in Edwardian England, kept his eye sharp in the off-season by potting dragonflies with a .410. The .410 bore has been around since the late 19th century and outsells the 10, 16 and 28 gauges today. It is the only modern shotshell designated by bore diameter. To its haters, the .410 is a crippler and a ballistic disgrace. On the other hand, I know two waterfowling fanatics who shoot geese and swans with .410 handloads. So what is the .410: a toy, a tool, or the worst mistake in shotgunning?

Well, we can start by saying for sure that the .410 isn't a toy. It's a real shotgun, only smaller. That said, despite the light weight of the guns and minimal recoil, the .410 is a poor choice for kids because it is very hard to hit with. There simply isn't room for many pellets inside a shotshell the diameter of a Sharpie, so the pattern core (the part that smashes targets and folds birds) is smaller in diameter compared to the patterns shot by bigger gauges. There isn't much shot left over to fill out the pattern fringe either.

Twenty-five yards is the .410's effective range. In an unscientific but revealing test, I shot crossing targets with 3-inch hunting loads of 7 ½ shot. From skeet stations 3, 4, and 5, I could hammer targets at 21 to 22 yards. After I took 10 steps back, I could only crack targets in half or at best break them into three pieces.

Use a .410 within its narrow capabilities and it's a proven killer of everything from dragonflies to swans. Stretch that range, and you make the worst mistake in shotgunning: pretending a .410 can do everything a bigger gun can.

Browning Citori White Lightning

175 BE A PROUD GIRLIE MAN

A friend of mine came back from northwest Iowa, impressed by the numbers of birds but bemused at his reception by the locals. "They called me a girlie-man hunter because I shoot a 12 gauge," he reported. "They said real men shoot 20 gauges."

Me, I own guns of other gauges, but the half dozen I actually take out of the cabinet to hunt and shoot with are all 12s. No other gauge comes close to being as versatile as the 12. Mine range from a double weighing less than most 20 gauges to a near 9-pound target gun with 32-inch barrels, and I shoot loads from ¾ of an ounce (targets) up to 1 ¾ ounces (turkeys) out of them.

If you shoot steel shot, it takes a hull the size of a 12 gauge's to hold enough of the light pellets to kill a duck or a goose. And, as much fun as light, skinny small bores are to

handle, I believe it's easier to shoot well with a gun that's a little more substantial and hand-filling.

All of the above seem like logical reasons to shoot 12s to me. Still, the idea persists among some hunters that small gauge guns are somehow more sporting and more manly because they give the birds "a chance." (A chance to fly off and die crippled, maybe.) Me, I will stick to my 12 gauges because when I shoot birds with them, they fall dead. If that makes me a girlie-man, I'm okay with it.

176 SHOTGUN GAUGES

Unlike rifle shooters, who are faced with a bewildering number of calibers, shotgunners are limited to six: 10, 12, 16, 20, and 28 gauges and the .410 bore. Each has its niche, and each has its fans.

THE 10 (.775) The largest legal gauge in the United States, the 10 was an all-around gauge in blackpowder days. It hangs on for one purpose: goose hunting. It patterns well with BB and larger steel shot, and its massive 10-pound-plus weight absorbs the recoil of heavy loads.

THE 12 (.729) This is the standard and the most versatile gauge of all. The 12 shoots everything from nearly recoilless ¾-ounce practice loads to 2 ¼-ounce turkey stompers.

Ammunition is available everywhere, and the volume of 12 gauge sales keeps prices low. If you own only one gun, it should be a 12.

THE 16 (.662) The 16 is an upland classic squeezed ballistically into a tiny, overlapping niche between the 3-inch 20 gauge and the 12. A good 16, built on a true 16 or even 20 gauge frame, is an upland delight, living up to the 16's billing as "carrying like a 20, hitting like a 12."

THE 20 (.615) The 20 gauge is a capable upland performer with ⅞ to an ounce of shot. A 3-inch 20 shoots an ounce of steel, which is enough for ducks over decoys. Advances in slugs make 20s the equal of a 12 in a lower-recoil package. A gas-operated 20 gauge is the best starter gun.

THE 28 (.550) I have heard the 28 gauge called "the thinking man's 20" but really it's "the .410 for people who want to crush targets and kill birds." At ranges out to 30 to 35 yards, the light-kicking 28's ¾-ounce shot charge hits with authority. I've killed pheasants with 28s, but it's best for smaller birds and short range clays.

THE .410 (67 GAUGE) Although many kids start with a .410 because it is light and has little recoil, the .410's light payloads, poor patterns, and expensive ammo make it a poor choice for kids and better for expert target shooters. The best place for the .410 in the field, in my humble opinion, is in the squirrel woods.

10 Gauge
.775 inches
1-½ - 2-¼ OZS

12 Gauge
.729 inches
⅞ - 2-¼ OZS

16 Gauge
.662 inches
15⁄16 - 1-¼ OZS

20 Gauge
.615 inches
¾ - 1-5⁄16 OZS

28 Gauge
.550 inches
⅝ - 1 OZS

.410
.410 inches
⅜ - 11⁄16 OZS

177 KNOW YOUR SHOTGUN ACTIONS

What shotgun action do you want? Leaving single shots aside for the moment (great for deer, turkeys, and singles trap but not much else), your choices boil down to pump, semiauto, or break-action (over/under or side by side).

PUMP This is the least expensive, most popular action, in the United States at least. (The rest of the world shuns them.) The pump or slide action cycles a new shell with each pull/push of the forearm. Pumps keep shooting in dusty, dirty, or muddy conditions, and they're easy to clean. While a skilled hand with a pump gun can shoot them almost as fast as a semiauto, working the slide between shots can be distracting, which is one reason you hardly ever see them in the hands of serious target shooters.

SEMIAUTO Each pull of the trigger sends a shot downrange. The semiauto has become increasingly popular, although it ranges from slightly more expensive than a pump to four to five times the price of one. Semiautos have the huge advantage of noticeably reducing felt recoil. While modern semiautos are extremely reliable, they still come in third behind pumps and break actions on that count. Gas guns—which tend to reduce recoil more–can be somewhat involved to clean. Inertia guns, which kick slightly harder, are a breeze to maintain.

BREAK ACTIONS Two-barreled guns have the advantage of two chokes (and sometimes an instant choice of chokes), and many shotgunners prefer the balance of a break action. You can buy a decent break-action gun for less than the price of a high-end semiauto, but you can also spend the price of a house on one. Because you can clearly see when a gun is open and unloaded, some believe them to be safer than other designs. They are the best choice for reloaders, since they will handle almost any reload and won't fling valuable empty hulls into the long grass.

" Indeed, we no longer hand-crank automobiles, so why should we hand-crank shotguns?"

Famous late gun crank Don Zutz, in Shotgunning Trends in Transition, *explaining why the pump, in his opinion, was obsolete.*

178 CHOOSE YOUR CONFIGURATION

The classic British game gun and the great American doubles were all side by sides, yet today the O/U is the most popular break action. In the United States, the double hangs on only among tradition-minded upland hunters.

The O/U isn't better; it's just different.

The O/U has a more familiar feel in the hands of hunters familiar with pumps and semiautos. Its most-touted advantage is the "single sighting plane" of the O/U—the narrow profile of the top rib and barrels. It is probably true

that O/Us can be shot more precisely, especially when firing at crossing targets.

Side by sides tend to be stocked straighter and have lower ribs, which lets you see more barrel when you mount it. When I shoot a side by side, I always feel as though I'm looking up a two-lane road running uphill. I always think, "How can you miss with one of these?" They are great for upland hunting, where most birds you'll see are going to go straight away or quarter.

179 BEWARE THE BREAK ACTION

Break-action fans have a tendency to talk about the advantage of two chokes and of instant barrel selection (only true with double triggers, by the way).

And to that talk, despite the fact that I am in fact a double-gun shooter, I say, "Whatever."

Purely in terms of results, which is to say birds in the bag, the third shot of a pump or semiauto and, equally important, the speed of reloading are going to beat two shots and two chokes almost every time.

Granted, if you miss a flushing upland bird twice, your chances of hitting it with the third shot are slim. But if you miss twice and stop shooting with a pump or semiauto, when the second bird flushes at your feet, you aren't standing there with an empty, broken-open gun.

180 IDENTIFY 15 CLASSIC SHOTGUNS

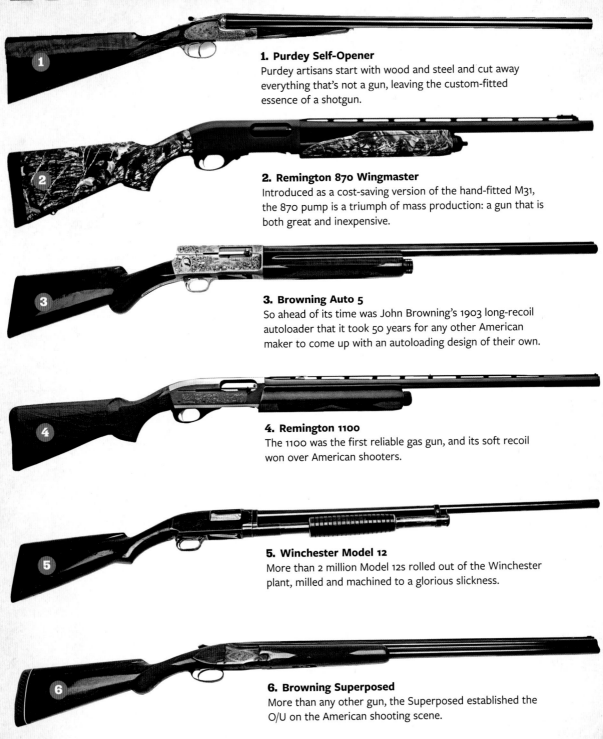

1. Purdey Self-Opener
Purdey artisans start with wood and steel and cut away everything that's not a gun, leaving the custom-fitted essence of a shotgun.

2. Remington 870 Wingmaster
Introduced as a cost-saving version of the hand-fitted M31, the 870 pump is a triumph of mass production: a gun that is both great and inexpensive.

3. Browning Auto 5
So ahead of its time was John Browning's 1903 long-recoil autoloader that it took 50 years for any other American maker to come up with an autoloading design of their own.

4. Remington 1100
The 1100 was the first reliable gas gun, and its soft recoil won over American shooters.

5. Winchester Model 12
More than 2 million Model 12s rolled out of the Winchester plant, milled and machined to a glorious slickness.

6. Browning Superposed
More than any other gun, the Superposed established the O/U on the American shooting scene.

7. Westley Richards & Co. Droplock
Westley Richards introduced the idea of internal hammers cocked by opening of barrels; doubles as we know them wouldn't be possible without that idea.

8. Beretta 390
Beretta's 300-series semiautos set the world standard for gas-gun reliability.

9. Perazzi M Series
Perazzis made their name grinding clay in competition, but their gorgeous O/U game guns work just as well on feathers.

10. Benelli Super Black Eagle
This is the first semiauto chambered for 3 ½-inch shells, and the flagship of Benelli's inertia line of guns famous for shooting every time, no matter what.

11. Beretta 680 Series
Along with Browning's Citori, the 680s set the standard of the affordable O/U excellence.

12. Parker Double
America's iconic double, "Old Reliable" came in more gauges, sizes, and grades than any other American gun.

13. A. H. Fox
Brilliantly simple in design, the American-made Fox was the choice of Teddy Roosevelt, among others.

14. Krieghoff K-80
Remington's Model 32 O/U failed in the Depression but was resurrected by Germany's Krieghoff to become one of the world's winningest target guns.

15. Tar Hunt
This fully rifled bolt action showed how accurate slug guns could be.

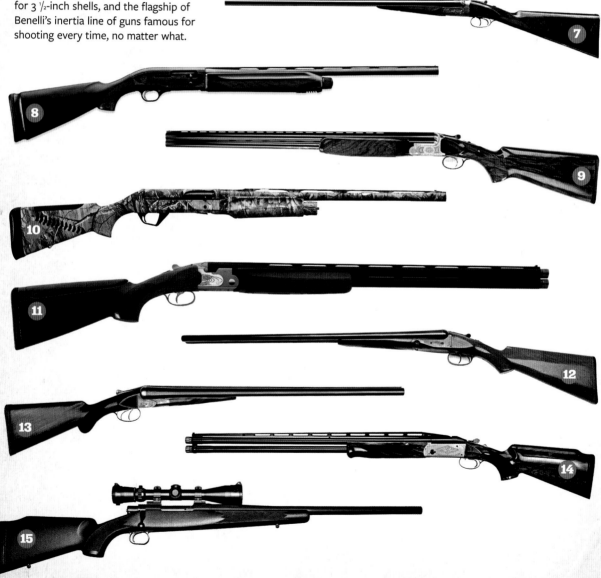

> " I have bought far more used shotguns than new and gotten a lot of good bargains. Buy from a reputable dealer and in the slim chance you get a lemon, they will make it right."

181 FIND A BARGAIN

Used shotguns are bargains. Let someone else take the depreciation hit, and you get a gun that will still last a lifetime. Some people shy away in the belief that there is something wrong with any used gun, but shooters get rid of perfectly good guns for all kinds of reasons. They trade up. They need money. (As someone who sold three perfectly good guns to pay for my German shorthair's emergency surgery, I know that's true.) They quit shooting, or they just want a different gun. Most of my favorite guns were bought used. The way I look at it, I'm not only saving money, but I'm also sparing myself the trauma of putting the first scratch on a pristine stock.

182 BUY LONG-DISTANCE

Many reputable dealers sell guns long-distance. If you're looking for a particular gun, it makes sense to widen your search by looking online. After you have the gun sent to a Federal Firearms License holder, traditionally there is a three-day inspection period. You should be able to test fire the gun unless it's an unfired collectible, but clarify this with the seller. Be sure the gun is exactly what you want. The gun may be exactly as represented, but if it doesn't feel right, or the wood looks different, or anything else feels off, don't buy it.

183
KNOW WHAT IT'S WORTH

Anyone interested in used guns should invest annually in a copy of S. P. Fjestad's *Blue Book of Gun Values*. It's the Bible of used-gun prices.

184 EVALUATE A USED SHOTGUN

Most reputable dealers will guarantee guns to be free of mechanical defects, but the fact is you still buy used guns "as is." Which means, of course, that you need to be an informed shopper. Here are some things to look for.

MAKE SURE CHOKE TUBES COME OUT Rusted-in or stuck chokes can cost a couple hundred dollars to remove and are a sign the gun has been neglected.

LOOK DOWN THE BORES FOR PITTING You might decide to live with very light pitting or have it polished out, but deep pits are deal breakers.

MAKE SURE THE BARRELS ARE FLUID STEEL, NOT DAMASCUS To identify Damascus steel, look for swirl patterns or the stamped words "twist," "laminated," or "Damascus." Unless you're an expert in metals, stay away.

LOOK FOR SAFE SCARS Check the toe of the stock, where it would bang into the bottom of a safe, and the sides of receivers, which can be marred by the bolt handle of the neighboring gun.

INSPECT BARRELS FOR DENTS Dents are dangerous but can be fixed. Bulges are very dangerous and also tend to be very expensive to repair.

LOOK WHERE WOOD MEETS METAL Wood that is flush with the metal or below its level means the gun has probably been refinished.

RING THE BARRELS Take the gun apart and hang the barrels on your finger from the underbolt or forearm hook. When you thwack them, you should hear a clear, bell-like tone. A "thunk" means side or top ribs need resoldering, a job necessitating the expense of rebluing.

LOOK FOR CRACKS IN THE STOCK Check around the tang, in the head of the stock, and in the wrist. Forearms can crack, too. Cracks should be repaired before you shoot the gun.

CHECK THE STOCK DIMENSIONS Many older guns, especially American doubles, have lots of drop, making them very difficult to shoot well. You're looking at a few thousand for a new stock to make the gun shootable.

TAKE PUMPS AND AUTOS APART If the magazine cap is rusted on, the insides have probably been neglected. Look for rust and missing rings on semiautos, underneath the fore-arm.

CHECK THE SCREWS Buggered slots mean an amateur has been poking around inside the gun. Also, engraved screws on higher-end guns are expensive to replace.

CHECK FOR WEAR BY LOOKING AT A DOUBLE GUN'S LEVER On new guns, the lever angles to the right and gradually moves to six o'clock. If it's past that point, it's time to tighten the action.

BRING SNAP CAPS AND TRY THE TRIGGER If the trigger's heavy, deduct the price of a trigger job (usually under $100) from your offer. If the gun is an older double, the price of trigger work goes up to a deal-breaking amount. Make sure the ejectors work, too.

WIGGLE THE BARRELS If the barrels wiggle with the fore-end off, the action needs tightening, which can run you a couple hundred bucks.

CHECK CHAMBER LENGTH Chamber length should be stamped on the barrel. Chambers may be shorter than standard, especially on older 16 gauges. On many guns, the chambers can be lengthened.

> " I'm mad at my husband, and I'm selling his guns."
>
> *Classified ad in the* Des Moines Register, *circa 1982. I was curious, but I didn't call. Good decision.*

185 BUILD A $10,000 SHOTGUN

A $10,000 target gun won't break four times as many birds as the garden-variety $2,500 Citori or Beretta 687. Serious target shooters gladly spend the extra money anyway, hoping it may buy them one or two targets on the margin, which is to say the difference between winning and losing.

An expert once explained the distinction between the 687 or Citori and a high-end gun: "It's the difference between a Corvette and a Ferrari. One is made to be a good car at a certain price; the other is made without cutting corners to be the best there is."

And, of course, a new gun won't automatically turn you into a champion shooter. "A good driver in a Corvette beats a bad driver in a Ferrari," he said "But, take two drivers of equal ability, and the Ferrari wins."

High-end guns also are built to withstand the pounding of shooting hundred of thousands of rounds. One expert I know has a Perazzi MX 8 that has over 1 million rounds through it. In the box below, an item-by-item accounting of where your money goes when you buy a base-model, high-end gun like this Krieghoff K-80 (MSRP $10,600).

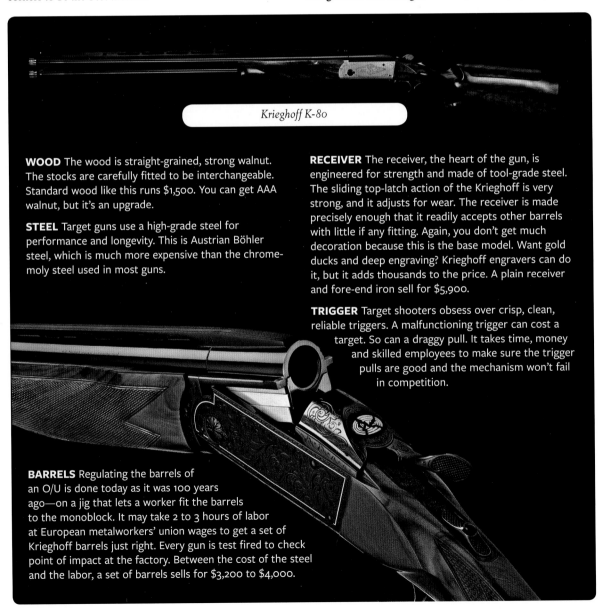

Krieghoff K-80

WOOD The wood is straight-grained, strong walnut. The stocks are carefully fitted to be interchangeable. Standard wood like this runs $1,500. You can get AAA walnut, but it's an upgrade.

STEEL Target guns use a high-grade steel for performance and longevity. This is Austrian Böhler steel, which is much more expensive than the chrome-moly steel used in most guns.

RECEIVER The receiver, the heart of the gun, is engineered for strength and made of tool-grade steel. The sliding top-latch action of the Krieghoff is very strong, and it adjusts for wear. The receiver is made precisely enough that it readily accepts other barrels with little if any fitting. Again, you don't get much decoration because this is the base model. Want gold ducks and deep engraving? Krieghoff engravers can do it, but it adds thousands to the price. A plain receiver and fore-end iron sell for $5,900.

TRIGGER Target shooters obsess over crisp, clean, reliable triggers. A malfunctioning trigger can cost a target. So can a draggy pull. It takes time, money and skilled employees to make sure the trigger pulls are good and the mechanism won't fail in competition.

BARRELS Regulating the barrels of an O/U is done today as it was 100 years ago—on a jig that lets a worker fit the barrels to the monoblock. It may take 2 to 3 hours of labor at European metalworkers' union wages to get a set of Krieghoff barrels just right. Every gun is test fired to check point of impact at the factory. Between the cost of the steel and the labor, a set of barrels sells for $3,200 to $4,000.

186
SPLURGE ON A CUSTOM SHOTGUN

The world's most famous custom shotguns—London's best guns like Purdey or Holland & Holland—cost upward of $100,000 and take more than a year to deliver. However, custom guns aren't only the toys of the rich. For a small fraction of the price of a Purdey, you can order a gun stocked to your measurements, with your choice of grip, barrel length, recoil pad and decoration. It will be one of a kind, and perfectly tailored to you and the type of shooting you do.

Several makers of hunting and target guns have custom shops. Most allow you to choose among a range of options, including stock dimensions, and your order is typically delivered within a couple of months. For instance, when I ordered a Caesar Geurni O/U, I had it stocked to my measurements and splurged on a classy leather-covered recoil pad. The extras added $1,400 to the base price but made a gun that is mine alone, and looks as good as it shoots.

187
ADD THE PERSONAL TOUCH

Personalizing a gun with engraving can cost as little as $400–$500 or as much as you want. The United States has a thriving cottage industry of skilled firearms engravers. The best place to see their work is at the annual Firearms Engravers Guild of America (FEGA) show held in Reno, Nevada, every January.

Some customers specify the design, others give the artist free rein. Engraver Lee Griffiths of Hyde Park, Utah, who has engraved spiders and dragons on shotguns at customers' requests, says the rule of thumb is to spend no more on engraving than a gun is worth, although that rule seems made to be broken. For instance, "optimizing" or upgrading old American doubles is a popular custom-gun trend. Says Griffiths: "Usually the gun is a lower grade to start with because the high grades have collector value in themselves."

Not every engraved gun winds up as a display piece. Griffiths recalls doing an elaborate and expensive engraving of a quail hunting scene on a shotgun for a man in Texas. Later Griffiths called and asked if he could borrow the gun back to display at the FEGA show. The man said no. Griffiths said: "I understand." The man said: "No you don't. I can't let you have it right now. It's quail season, and I'm hunting with that gun every weekend."

188 SHOTGUN OLD SCHOOL

The nostalgia, challenge, and allure of shooting and hunting with guns like the ones our great-grandfathers used attracts some people to black powder shotgunning. For these people, a shot at birds isn't complete unless a cloud of sulfurous white smoke billows out of the muzzle in the wake of the wad and pellets. Black powder shotgunning is satisfying, too, if you like playing with components, because every load with a muzzleloader is a handload, assembled in the barrel.

As a rule of thumb, start with equal volumes of powder and shot, meaning you use the same measure for both. By that formula, use 75 grains of FFg powder to 1 1/8 ounces of shot in a 12 gauge. Depending on barrel length, that load should generate about 1,000 fps of muzzle velocity. Go up or down from there. Consult your manual for maximum loads with modern guns. With old guns, proceed with caution, and the advice of a knowledgeable gunsmith.

189
LOAD THAT MUZZLELOADER

STEP ONE Measure the powder and pour it down the barrel.
STEP TWO Add an over-powder wad as a gas seal.
STEP THREE Pour in the shot.
STEP FOUR Top it with an overshot wad.
STEP FIVE Cap the gun.

With double guns, be very careful to load each barrel once, not one barrel twice!

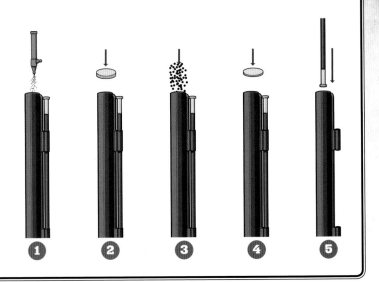

190 GO BIG OR GO HOME

Famous 19th-century English sportsman Col. Peter Hawker owned one of the largest muzzleloaders ever: a double-barreled punt gun with 1 1/2-inch bores (roughly a 0.65 gauge!). The gun weighed 193 pounds and was 8 feet 3 inches long. Mounted in the bow of Hawker's gunning punt, the double-barreled gun was used on flocks of sitting ducks and geese when Hawker and his puntsman were able to scull close enough across the tidal flats to make a shot. The gun had to be stood on end to load, and it fired 1 1/4-pound shot charges over four ounces of black powder. It had one percussion lock and one flintlock so the second shot would be slightly delayed when both barrels were fired.

Peter Hawker (mounted on Grey) talking to gunsmith Joseph Manton, September 1, 1827

Thompson/Center Muzzleloader Blued-Realtree

191 TAKE TURKEYS WITH A MUZZLELOADER

Suppose, like me, you find black powder shotguns intriguing, but you hate the idea of having to stop and reload your gun the old-fashioned way after every hit or miss in the field. Simple solution: hunt turkeys. You get all the fun of experimenting with components and working up a load, but you only have to actually shoot your gun in the field once or twice a year.

Blackpowder guns with choke tubes can deliver turkey patterns rivaling modern guns.

A choke-tubed muzzleloader not only puts XX Full chokes at your disposal, but because you can remove the choke, you can fit modern plastic shot cups into the muzzle. These cups act as a gas seal, protect the pellets from deformation, and keep the payload together in the barrel, making a huge difference in patterning. The gradual acceleration of slow burning black powder and the low velocity keep the pellets round in the barrel, and the turkey choke does the rest. I used to load 1 3/4 ounces of 5 shot over 90 grains of Pyrodex in my Knight shotgun and got 90-percent patterns with it. A friend cuts open HEVI-Shot and Winchester Xtended Range shells and loads them in his muzzleloader and gets even better results.

192 DISSECT A SHOTSHELL

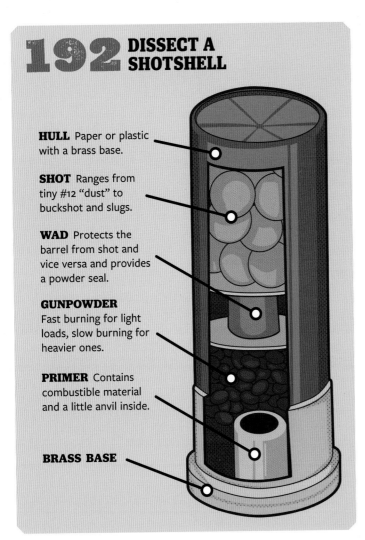

HULL Paper or plastic with a brass base.

SHOT Ranges from tiny #12 "dust" to buckshot and slugs.

WAD Protects the barrel from shot and vice versa and provides a powder seal.

GUNPOWDER Fast burning for light loads, slow burning for heavier ones.

PRIMER Contains combustible material and a little anvil inside.

BRASS BASE

193

GET THE BIG PICTURE

Pretty as these pictures are, they don't tell the whole story. Lead shot deforms easily (tungsten-iron and steel, not so much), and the pellets at the rear of a shot column are subject to deformation. Once squished out of round, they become less aerodynamic, and the added air resistance saps their velocity and sends them off-course to become "flyers," which are lost to the main pattern. The best ammunition remedies pellet deformation in three ways:

BUFFER Found in premium turkey and buckshot loads and made from ground plastic, the buffer protects the pellets from one another the way plastic peanuts protect fragile objects during shipping.

ANTIMONY This element is alloyed with lead to harden it. The very best pellets contain up to 6 percent antimony.

PLATING Nickel and copper plating doesn't harden pellets, but it does help them flow better through the constriction of the choke.

QUICK SHOT

194 SHOOT YOUR WAD

Most wads open to release the shot charge as it encounters air resistance. In this configuration, if the wad never released the pellets, they would all fly downrange together in the shotcup like a slug.

Federal's Flitecontrol shell, pictured below, is a notable exception to this standard. In this manufacturer's unique and proprietary shell design,
the shot stays in the wad for 15 feet or so out of the muzzle, resulting in noticeably tighter patterns downrange.

This patterning makes this design a great wad for buckshot or turkey loads. Instead of slits, the Flitecontrol wad has vanes that pop out of the sides and open at the rear, functioning as brakes.

195 EXPERIENCE THE BIG BANG

If you were to fire a shotgun in the vacuum of space, the pellets would stay nestled in their shot cup forever as they flew through the inky blackness. However, on Earth, atmospheric pressure affects your shot load as soon as it leaves the muzzle on its way to a clay target, a turkey, or a bird in flight.

Hot propellant gases expand suddenly as they exit the muzzle, creating the shock wave that we hear as muzzle blast. In the first 3 feet of travel, air resistance slows the load about 100 fps. The faster you drive pellets through the air, the faster they lose velocity. Increasing velocity by using fast loads does increase energy, but only somewhat. The best way to hit birds harder, is to shoot larger, heavier shot.

Air resistance pries open the petals of the shot cup, releasing the pellets. Shot cups protect barrels from hard pellets, such as HEVI-Shot or those made from steel or tungsten-iron. They also prevent soft lead pellets from being deformed by the barrel. A spent cup shows dimples caused by the inertia or "setback" forces that drive the pellets back into the plastic as it accelerates.

Some loads contain a ground-plastic buffer that protects lead pellets at the rear of the shot cup from being crushed by the weight of those at the front, enabling them to retain their round shape and fly truer.

Just 5 feet from the muzzle, the load will already have lost about 150 fps in velocity. As it encounters air resistance, the pattern begins to open up, with the pellets starting to veer off in different directions. The pellets at the back of the pattern are "drafting," like racing cars tucked in behind the leaders of the pack. These trailing pellets will eventually form the central core of the pattern—the dense part with which you hope to hit the target.

The tighter the choke you use, the longer and narrower the shot cluster will be as it leaves the barrel, and the more "drafting" pellets that will remain in the pattern core. The load will also pattern more tightly in thin air than in heavier air due to the lower air resistance. Air is not uniformly dense—it's denser at sea level than at high altitude, and cold air is denser than hot air. The difference may not be much, but it's no coincidence that the record target pattern (most pellets in a 3-inch circle) was shot in the thin air of a hot, dry day. Hedge your bets in the cold, dense air of late season by shooting high-velocity loads or by choosing one size larger shot than you ordinarily would and screwing in a slightly tighter choke.

196 CHOOSE SHOT SIZE

Picking a shot size requires you to choose between energy and density. Bigger pellets hit harder, but there are fewer of them in a given weight of shot. Smaller pellets promise multiple hits on the target, albeit with less punch per pellet.

For close-range shooting, smaller shot often proves more effective than larger pellets simply because there are more small pellets in a given shot weight. Out to 30 yards, most reasonably appropriate pellets carry enough energy to kill. The greater number of pellets increases the chances of an immediately lethal strike to the head or neck (a concept very clear to all turkey hunters and some goose hunters). In addition, smaller, more numerous pellets fill out the pattern fringes, adding margin for error if you mispoint the gun. That's why 7 $\frac{1}{2}$ shot compares poorly in terms of foot-pounds but, in my experience, hits pheasants hard in the real world at ranges of under 30 yards.

The standard advice on shot size, therefore, is to choose the smallest adequate pellet for the job. However, there are times when you don't know at what range the job will be done. Pheasants may hold tight or flush wild. Ducks may approach with their feet down or flare at the edge of the decoys. The corollary, contradictory advice to the "smallest adequate pellet" theory is: under hunting conditions, when ranges are unknown, err on the side of larger shot. Large shot also bucks wind better and plows through dense, cold, late-season air better. As a rule of thumb, a shell containing larger pellets will pattern 4 to 5 percentage points tighter than the next smaller size, too.

197 MATCH THE SHOT TO THE BIRD

The following chart gives a quick guideline to shot sizes. The larger sizes in each box should be matched to bigger birds; larger gauges. The smaller sizes are more appropriate for closer ranges; smaller gauges and open chokes.

Geese

● **Steel** T, BBB, BB, 1, 2

● **Lead** n/a*

● **Tungsten-Iron** BB, 1, 2, 3, 4

Ducks

● **Steel** BB, 1, 2, 3, 4

● **Lead** n/a*

● **Tungsten-Iron** 2, 3, 4

Small Ducks

● **Steel** 3, 4, 6

● **Lead** n/a*

● **Tungsten-Iron** 4, 6

Big Birds (Pheasants, etc.)

● **Steel** 2, 3, 4

● **Lead** 5, 6, 7 ½

● **Tungsten-Iron** 6

Medium Birds (Grouse, Partridge)

● **Steel** 4, 6

● **Lead** 6, 7 ½, 8

● **Tungsten-Iron** 7 ½

Small Birds (Quail, Woodcock, Doves)

● **Steel** 6, 7

● **Lead** 7 ½, 8

● **Tungsten-Iron** 7 ½

*Lead shot is banned from use on migratory waterfowl.

198 MAKE SIZE MATTER

Some hunters swear by a certain shot size. There's something to that, if only because confident shooters shoot well. So if you believe in a particular shot size, it does work better for you. A friend of mine who used to shoot on the high-stakes, high-pressure live pigeon circuit would deliberately mix up the 7 ½s and 8s in his pouch so he never knew which he was shooting when he practiced. That way, he didn't have a favorite size. "Otherwise," he said, "what if I got to a shoot, and they didn't have my favorite shot size?"

199 USE PHIL'S TOP LOADS

You have a lot of options when it comes to picking the best load for various types of game. Here's what I've found to be the best options, through years of experience.

	SHELL	GAUGE	LOAD
Pheasants	2 ¾-inch	12 gauge	1 ¼ ounces of 6 shot (lead), 1,300 fps 1 ⅛ ounces of 3 shot (steel), 1,500 fps
Ducks	3-inch	12 gauge	1 ¼ ounces of 2 shot (steel), 1,450 fps
Geese	3-inch	12 gauge	1 ½ ounces of 4 HEVI-Shot (tungsten-iron), 1,400 fps
Turkeys	3-inch	12 gauge	1 ¾ ounces of 6 HEVI-Shot (tungsten-iron)
	3-inch	20 gauge	1 ¼–1 ½ ounces of 6 Heavyweight or HEVI-Shot (tungsten-iron), 1,100 fps
Doves	2 ¾-inch	12 gauge	1 ounce of 7 shot (steel), 1,300 fps
	2 ¾-inch	12 gauge	1 ⅛ ounces of 7 ½ or 8 shot (lead), 1,180 fps
	2 ¾-inch	20 gauge	⅞ ounce of 8 shot (lead), 1,200 fps
Quails	2 ¾-inch	20 gauge	⅞ ounce of 8 shot (lead), 1,200 fps
Ruffed Grouse	2 ¾-inch	20 gauge	⅞ ounce of 7 ½ shot (lead), 1,200 fps
Woodcock	2 ¾-inch	28 gauge	¾ ounce of 8 shot (lead), 1,200 fps
Deer (rifled barrel)	2 ¾-inch	20 gauge	sabot slug with premium bullet, 1,500–1,600 fps
Deer (smoothbore)	2 ¾-inch	12 gauge	1-ounce slug, wad attached, 1,600 fps
Practice	2 ¾-inch	12 gauge reloads	⅞ ounce of 8 ½ shot (lead), 1,200 fps

200 SPEED IT UP (OR NOT)

The trend in shotshells is higher velocities, both because speed kills and because no one ever got rich selling "slow" to the American public. How important is velocity really?

Velocity improves shotshell performance in two ways: it increases pellet energy, so shot hits harder; and the faster time of flight reduces the amount of forward allowance (lead) needed to hit a target.

That's the good news. The downside is that increasing velocity increases recoil noticeably. Also, because pellets are round—a poor aerodynamic shape—the faster you drive them, the faster they slow down.

Because of that, you pay a price in much higher recoil for small gains in performance at longer ranges. You might have to endure 50 percent more recoil for a gain of 10 percent in energy and, say, 8 inches less lead needed to hit a crossing target at 40 yards.

The lighter the pellet material is, the more it benefits from high velocity to increase its downrange energy. Therefore steel, which is the lightest shot material, benefits the most from high launch speeds. Lead and denser tungsten-iron pellets, in my opinion, don't benefit nearly as much from added velocity.

201 STEEL YOURSELF

If I am often skeptical of the trend toward high velocity, I also believe there are instances where speed does kill. The less dense the pellet material, the more important velocity becomes. Steel shot, therefore, does perform better when you drive it faster, even though it sheds velocity faster than do lead and heavier-than-lead pellets.

Early steel loads were slow and the shells were poorly made. The 1990s saw steel improve, and, sometime around 1996, Winchester introduced their black-hulled Supreme loads, with a velocity measured at 1,450 fps. From the first time I shot Supremes, I quit complaining about steel shot and started killing ducks and geese. The combination of a slight increase in energy and a slight reduction in forward allowance really did lead to more birds being hit harder in the front end, thus resulting in quicker, cleaner kills.

I haven't felt the need to shoot faster steel, but I don't want to shoot anything slower, either.

QUICK SHOT

202 SHOOT BIGGER SHOT

The best way to increase pellet energy isn't to shoot faster shot. Instead, choose bigger shot. Larger pellets retain velocity better than smaller ones, and their greater mass hits targets harder. For instance, increasing the muzzle velocity of a steel 4 from 1,400 fps to 1,550 results in an increase in energy from 2.22 ft/lbs to 2.48 ft/lbs.

If you're switching from 4 shot to 3 shot at the same 1,400 fps velocity, you increase energy from 2.22 ft/lbs to 3.01 ft/lbs with no increase in recoil. No pain, no gain? Not always.

203 LEARN TO RELOAD

Years ago I was in a store with my mother-in-law, who looked at the flies, then the fly-tying materials, and asked, "Why would anyone make their own when they have such nice ones already done up?"

That was my attitude toward shotshell reloading when shells were cheap and my kids weren't old enough to shoot. Now, I roll my own shotshells so I can afford to go to the gun club. And I can make up 7/8- and even 3/4-ounce 12-gauge reloads that have very low recoil, both to soothe my wimpy shoulder and to serve as training loads for new shooters.

Be aware that reloading changes you in ways both good and bad. There's definite pride in shooting homemade ammunition, you can customize your hunting and target loads, there are savings, and looking for hulls adds an exciting little Easter egg hunt to every trip to the range. It's possible to get too fixed on the savings, though, to the point of self-delusion. I once shot with a $100-an-hour consultant who spent what could have been billable time at his reloading bench, putting together loads that saved him 75 cents a box. "Every time I pull the trigger, I'm making money," he bragged. Uh, no. But, you do feel like you're shooting for free when you can reach into a 5-gallon bucket of shells and take as many as you need.

204 RELOAD RIGHT

Here's what you need to get set up for reloading.

SOLID WORKBENCH Emphasis on "solid." Bolt your loader to it to make loading not only easier but also more consistent.

RELOADING PRESS A progressive or single-stage machine for the gauge you will be reloading.

ACCURATE SCALE You'll need a scale that measures up to two ounces in grains.

EXTRA POWDER AND SHOT BUSHING Most presses come set up to make a basic target load. You may want to make something else.

COMPONENTS Shot, powder, wads, primers, and hulls. Buy the first four; scavenge the hulls.

BROOM AND DUSTPAN You'll spill powder and shot. Vacuum cleaner sparks don't mix well with powder, and you will want to put any spilled shot back in the bottle.

205 CHOOSE YOUR PRESS

Reloading presses come in two basic kinds: the single stage and the progressive. With a single-stage reloader, it takes five pulls of the handle to load each shell.

The difference is in the number of shells produced. A progressive reloader works on 6 to 8 shells at once, with every pull of the handle producing a fully loaded shell.

Single stage reloaders, on the other hand, as the name implies, produce one shell at a time. They are best for beginners, because they're inexpensive, and by loading one shell at a time you can thoroughly learn all the steps of reloading ammunition.

Even so, you can still make a box of shells in 12 to 15 minutes with a single stage. If you only shoot two or three boxes of shells a week in summer trap league to tune up for hunting season, a single stage is all the reloader you'll ever need. A single stage is also best for making smaller batches of custom hunting loads.

Progressive loaders start at twice the price of a decent single stage. They work on several hulls at once, and you can load a box of shells in about three minutes. They cost more, and the potential to make bad reloads (no powder, for instance) increases if you don't pay attention. You will spill more powder and shot with a progressive machine and wreck more hulls. I do, anyway. But, once you get used to the speed of a progressive, especially if you're a target shooter, you'll never go back to a single stage.

206 SAVE YOUR PENNIES

Reloading can save you some serious money—up to 50 percent off the high price of factory loads in the small gauges. Here's how to maximize your savings.

BULK UP Once you find a load you like, buy components in bulk. A bag of 5,000 wads, a box of 1,000 primers, or an 8-pound bottle of powder offer significant savings over the same components bought in smaller amounts. Most gun clubs pool their buying power for annual buys.

SEND IN THE CLONES
Claybuster and Downrange produce "clones" of the big three wads that can be substituted for the originals and cost way less.

GO LIGHT You save lead when you use less. A 7/8-ounce load yields 102 more shells per 25-pound bag of shot over 1 1/8-ounce shells. Lighter payloads also use less powder.

SCROUNGE HULLS Spent hulls on the ground aren't litter; they're money. Look for Remington's Gun Clubs and Sport Loads. You're more likely to find them than the more desirable Winchester AA or Remington STS hulls. Also, when you find target loads with quality hulls on sale, buy them, shoot them up and reload the empties.

207 SEE THE ANATOMY OF A SHOT

Photographs of shot in flight are about as rare as credible photos of Bigfoot. I wrote about the photo that this drawing was made from. It was awesome—and it seems to have been lost to time. The drawing will just have to do.

THE PATTERN The duck was a scoter; the range 30 yards. 100 HEVI-Shot No. 2 pellets from a 3 ¹/₂-inch 12-gauge load containing 131 total hit in the 30-inch circle I drew around the densest part of this pattern. That's a 76 percent pattern. Ideally, your choke-and-load combination should print 70 to 75 percent in the 30-inch circle at the range where you expect to hit birds—15 pellets were about to hit the duck when the photo was taken. Five are usually enough to kill cleanly.

THE PATCHES All patterns have random gaps in them. This example has a couple of big gaps; even so, if you put the duck anywhere inside the circle, multiple pellets will hit it. What kills in the field doesn't always look good on paper.

THE FLYERS The uncropped photo showed several flyers that had veered out of the main pattern; one in the upper right-hand corner was 4 feet from the pattern's center. Deformed pellets encounter added air resistance that moves them out of the pattern.

THE SHOT STRING Some of the pellets look bigger and blurrier than others because they're out of focus. They're trailing behind the main swarm, and they will continue to fall farther behind. By the time this pattern gets out past 40 yards, it may be up to 6 to 8 feet long.

208 GET A GRIP ON CHOKE

My first gun was a 12-gauge Auto 5 with a Poly-Choke, an adjustable choke device permanently installed on a gun's muzzle. You twist a collar to open or tighten the choke. Unbeknownst to me, the collar on mine had been removed and put back on by my father, but not all the way, which meant all I was really doing was turning the loose collar and shooting cylinder bore at everything—no choke at all. I killed my first pheasants, ducks, rabbits, woodcocks, snipe, quail, doves, and deer with that gun, raising the question: Are you overchoked? For many, the answer is, "Yes."

Try patterning at 20 yards some time. Modified, which many regard as an "all-around" constriction, crams almost every pellet of a shot charge into a 16-inch circle at 20 yards. A Cylinder choke at 20 prints a pattern about 25 inches across. Do the math: a 16-inch circle covers 201 square inches; a 25-inch circle spreads pellets across 490 square inches. Which is easier to put on a bird? While a Cylinder choke is deadly at 20 yards, by 30 yards, its patterns spread thin. Since most gamebirds fall within 25 yards of the muzzle, no choke may be all the choke you need.

209 PLAY THE PERCENTAGES

Here are the specifications for 12-gauge chokes. Normally smaller gauges require slightly less constriction to achieve tighter patterns. Pattern percentage is for a 30-inch circle at 40 yards.

Choke	Constriction	Pattern Percentage
Cylinder	(.000–.004)	40%
Improved Cylinder	(.011)	50%
Modified	(.020)	60%
Improved Modified	(.027)	70%
Full	(.036–.040)	80%
XX-Full	(.050–.070)	90%

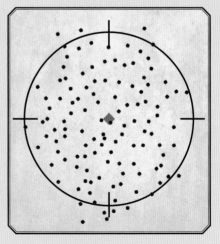

90% on a 30-inch circle at 40 yards

210 SIMPLIFY CHOKES

To simplify things almost criminally, a choke functions like the nozzle on a garden hose. When it's open, shot sprays widely; screwed down, the shell shoots tighter patterns.

Chokes come in thousandths-of-an-inch constrictions (from none at all to .060" or more) and have varying internal geometries. For what it's worth, I have found longer tubes bored with a parallel section before the taper work best. The advent of screw-in chokes in the 1960s means we have so many different choke offerings available that it's possible to become paralyzed by too much choice. Relax. You can get by with five tubes.

Here's what I'd use. If I had to limit my options, I'd replace Improved Cylinder and Modified with a Light Modified choke.

XX-FULL
Turkeys

IMPROVED MODIFED
Trap
Pass shooting with tungsten and large steel pellets

MODIFIED
Steel shot for waterfowl
Late, windy-day pheasants
High doves
Buckshot, predator loads

IMPROVED CYLINDER
Sporting clays
Most upland and dove hunting
Ducks over decoys

SKEET
Skeet shooting
Close-cover upland birds
Foster-style shotgun slugs

211 TO BEAD OR NOT TO BEAD

Look at the guns at a sporting-clays shoot, and you'll notice something's missing—beads. Many shooters now unscrew their shotgun's bead and throw it away. Removing the bead is a trend that comes and goes. Paradoxically, bright fiber-optic beads are also popular with shooters these days (also with manufacturers, who stick them on "sporting clays" models of other guns, in part to justify the huge price difference). Both types of shooters are trying to keep their eyes from wandering off the target and looking at the muzzle, which is a sure way to miss. When you look at the gun, it stops, and you shoot behind.

You have to know where the barrel is in relation to the bird, but you've got to keep your eye on the bird and the muzzle in your peripheral vision. For some shooters, removing the bead takes away a distraction. For others, it's easier to focus 100 percent on the target if there is a bright bead in their peripheral vision.

So, to bead or not to bead? That is the question. The answer is: whichever method makes it easier for you to not look at the barrel.

212 KEEP AN EYE ON YOUR TRIGGER

My trap gun, a Browning BT-100, has one of the niceties of a much more expensive gun: a removable trigger.

Theoretically, if you break a spring in competition you can easily fix it, or take your spare trigger out of the Crown Royal bag you keep it in and be back on the line in a couple of minutes. In reality, coil springs hardly ever break. The reason I like the 100's trigger is that it's jeweled and finely made. I can say, "Hey, check this out," and pop out the trigger and show it to them. I did that for a friend, who told me this story: he was at a gun club on Maryland's Eastern Shore, and one of the shooters in his party had driven a couple hours across the bay from northern Virginia, showing up with a brand new Krieghoff K-80. The guy took the gun out of its case, expecting to bask in the envy his friends. One of them looked at and said, "Nice gun. Where's the trigger?"

It was at home, in a velvet Crown Royal bag.

213 EXPLORE AFTER-MARKET CHOKES

The invention of screw-in chokes spawned a whole industry in aftermarket choke tubes. Where extended tubes once ruined the lines of a nice gun, now a turkey or target gun doesn't look "cool" without them. Extended choke tubes have three advantages: the longer tubes allow makers to put in a lengthened taper or longer parallel section inside, which can result in a big improvement in patterns over shorter tubes; a longer tube can move the stresses of shooting big, hard, nontoxic shot outside of the muzzle where it's better for your gun; finally, extended tubes are easier to check and change. Before you splurge, pattern the chokes that came with your gun. They might be fine. In my experience, you'll see the most improvement in patterns with aftermarket turkey chokes over factory models, and in general when you replace the shortest factory tubes (the old Winchoke style, still used by Mossberg and some others) with a longer tube. For the very best custom choke results, send your gun to a choke specialist who will measure the bores and make chokes to fit your barrels precisely.

214 PAD YOURSELF

Recoil pads are the in thing right now. As guns keep getting lighter, and therefore harder-kicking, recoil pads get higher-tech and softer. The new pads work much, much better than the hard rubber pads on some guns, and also better than the old honeycombed red and brown rubber pads. That said, manufacturers get a little carried away in the claims for them. Says one: "Our pad makes our pump gun kick less than the competition's semiauto." This statement is simply not true. Take those claims with a grain of salt but put a soft pad on your gun anyway. They are available in both grind-to-fit and pre-fit models for many popular guns.

215
GO WITH THE WIND

Dogs hunt with their noses. We all know that. And yet, it never fails to surprise me how many people don't think to take the wind into account when they hunt with a dog. Plan your route so you hit the likeliest cover with the wind in the dog's face. Running a dog downwind is almost like blindfolding him—he's much more likely to bump birds he doesn't smell until he's right on top of them.

216 BRING FIDO ALONG

A lot of people hunt birds without dogs. I used to. Not anymore. If there are no dogs on an upland hunt, I won't go. Why? Well, if you bring a dog, you'll see more birds on that hunt. You'll kill more, and you'll lose many, many fewer cripples. Beyond that, a dog tells you what's going on in the invisible world of grass and scent under your feet. Without dogs, you're just walking and hoping.

I do hunt waterfowl without a retriever. Many people won't, and they're probably right. Duck hunting without a dog means limiting the shots you take and always being aware of where a bird is going to fall when you make the decision to shoot. Hunting with a trained retriever means few cripples escape. More than once I've seen a lab dive underwater after submerged ducks and held my breath until the dog broke the surface with the duck in its mouth.

217 KEEP YOUR EYES UP

When you walk in to a point or approach a very excited flusher, lift your eyes off the ground in front of the dog's nose and up to, well, eye level. If you're looking down, you'll see the bird flush as a blur, and you'll be chasing after it, leading to panic and a rushed shot. When you have your eyes up where you want to shoot the bird, you'll be ready to make an unhurried shot.

218 POINT OR FLUSH

Pointing and flushing dog owners endlessly argue the relative merits of their relative favorites. Having hunted with both kinds of dog, I'll say it's not as different as either camp would have you believe. I like it when my dogs point birds, but half the pheasants I've killed over them didn't stick around to be pointed. Often, the dog will get birdy, and I'll go on the alert. When the bird flushes through no fault of the dog's, I'm ready, and I shoot it. Because I'm not a pointing-dog purist, I'm happy.

By the same token, flushing dogs don't immediately boost into range every bird they find. Often, when a bird sits tight, the flusher starts rooting around the cover, and you have plenty of time to get to it and get ready. It's almost like shooting a bird over a point.

219 BELIEVE THE DOG

"Always believe the dog" is one of the most important rules of bird hunting. My old setter, Ike, and I were once hunting with some friends and a few other dogs. We stopped to rest in the corner of a fence line after a long, birdless walk. Ike went to sleep with his head in my lap. We'd been there a little while when Ike opened his eyes, lifted his head, and sniffed the air. He got up, walked 15 yards, and pointed.

"Ike's got one," I said. No one else believed a pheasant would be stupid enough to stick around for several minutes while we sat and snacked and talked. I didn't really believe it either, but a rule is rule. I was the only one to stand up, load my gun, and walk over to Ike. A rooster flushed from under his nose. I shot it. Another flushed, and I shot that, too. Those were the only pheasants we saw all day.

220 MUZZLE UP

A while ago, I hunted grouse with a Marine, and after the first time he walked in on a point, I had to tell him that what he had clearly been taught as a safe carry (gun across the body, muzzle pointed at the ground) was all wrong for hunting with bird dogs. Carry that way, and your muzzle sweeps past the dog as you mount the gun. If your finger happens to hit the trigger too soon (I've seen it happen, although fortunately with no dog in the line of fire), you'll shoot your dog. When you hunt with dogs, the muzzle has to be level with the ground at the very least, and preferably angled up in the air. It calms dog owners considerably if you don't point a loaded gun at their best friends.

221

LINE UP YOUR CLEANING SUPPLIES

I keep the following cleaning and lubricating supplies on hand:

- Bore snakes for when I feel lazy
- Cleaning rods with brass brushes and wool mops in all gauges (10-gauge brushes make good 12-gauge chamber brushes)
- Old toothbrush
- Round brushes
- Plastic pick (looks like a dental tool)
- Shooter's Choice for greasing hinge pins and magazine cap threads
- Birchwood Casey Choke Tube grease
- Gun oil in spray cans and bottles (not WD-40)
- Gun scrubber or Liquid Wrench for thorough action cleanings
- Spray can of powder solvent for bore cleaning
- Cotton patches
- Rags
- Fine steel wool
- I am always out of: Spray cans of compressed air

222 DON'T BE THIS GUY

A friend who used to work for Remington's customer service told me about handling this call.

Caller: "My 1100 keeps jamming."

CSR: "Do you clean it?"

Caller: "Every time I shoot it I clean it just like my daddy taught me. I use a bronze brush and solvent and scrub out the fouling, then run cloth patches through the barrel until they come out clean."

CSR: "Do you take the forearm off and clean the gas system?"

Caller: "The forearm comes off?"

223 CLEAN A SHOTGUN

At a minimum, run a bore snake through the bore and wipe down the outside of the gun with a lightly oiled rag when you come in from the field or range. Use an old toothbrush to get the grit out from behind the ejectors and other hard-to-reach places. If you have shot a lot, clean your semiauto's gas piston with a brush and scrub fouling off the magazine tube. Very fine steel wool and a little oil works.

On break-action guns, clean the grime off the breech face and inside the receiver. Remove the fore-end and wipe the barrels.

224 GREASE IT WHERE IT NEEDS IT

A light oiling works best for most working parts of the gun, but three spots are better lubed with a dab of grease like the popular Shooter's Choice red grease that comes in a handy syringe applicator.

Grease stays put and does its job on surfaces where oil migrates. Use a dab of grease on the hinge pins and trunnions of a break-action gun. Grease choke-tube threads to keep chokes from sticking in the gun, especially if you shoot a lot of big steel shot. Grease the threads of your magazine cap, too, to keep it from rusting on when a gun gets wet. Use grease sparingly; clean it off and reapply it whenever you clean your gun.

225 DO IT QUICK AND DIRTY

I first saw this trick done with Liquid Wrench, and since then, several manufacturers have come up with their own spray-action cleaners. First, you'll need a couple of newspapers. Take the gun outside. Remove the barrel of a pump or semiauto and hold it by the grip pointing down over the papers. Spray the scrubber up into the action. Rivers of crud will run out onto your papers. When it finally runs clear, the action is clean. Oil it lightly and put the gun back together.

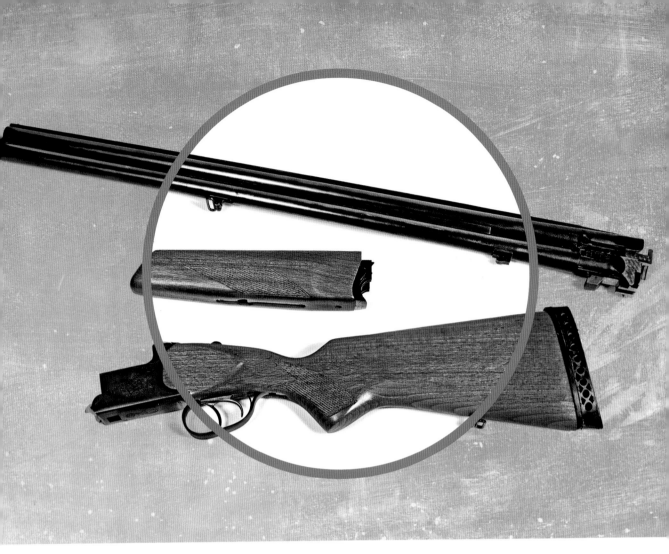

226 DEEP CLEAN

At the end of hunting season, and after every few thousands rounds shot with target guns, do a full deep-cleaning.

First, take your gun completely apart. Soak the piston and other gas system parts of a semiauto in solvent and clean them thoroughly.

Next, you'll want to remove the bolts of pumps and semiautos, and then clean all of the parts completely. Use a tiny amount of oil on the firing pin, so that it won't turn sluggish in cold weather.

Remove the trigger group, clean it with a nylon brush, then oil it lightly. Wipe out the inside of the receiver.

On pumps and autos—if it's possible with your particular gun— remove the magazine spring and retainer and clean the spring and the magazine tube with a 10-gauge brush.

You can also take the stock off a semiauto and remove the return spring for cleaning. It is a pain, but waterfowlers really do need to be sure they take this step.

Scrub bores with a bronze brush soaked in solvent, then patches, and then an oiled wool mop.

Use a chamber brush or a 10-gauge bronze brush and solvent on the chamber of 12 gauges to remove plastic

buildup. Use a tiny drill bit as a scraper to clean any built-up carbon out of gas ports.

Take the choke tubes out and clean them inside and out with a brush dipped in solvent. Brush out the threads in the barrel, too, then grease the threads and replace the barrel.

A toothbrush works well to clean those hard-to-reach spots beneath and around the vent rib posts.

Break-action guns can go many thousands of rounds before you have to pull the stock off and lube the locks. If you don't want to do it yourself, take it to a gunsmith.

227 BRING THE MOST BASIC REPAIR KIT

One time, I fell down a muddy creek bank on my way to a deer stand. As I flailed, my Browning pump flew like a javelin across the creek and stuck barrel first into the muck. Having no tools with me and several inches of mud packed in the muzzle, I removed the barrel and held it underwater in the icy creek until the current washed it clean. After my fingers thawed, I put the gun back together, loaded it, and shot a deer an hour later. Since then, I've always had with me, or nearby in the truck:

1. A bottle of Break Free CLP for freeing sticky firing pins.

2. A takedown cleaning rod for clearing obstructions or punching stuck shells from the chamber.

3. A mini Leatherman for punching trigger group pins out (the needle-nose pliers gets them started). I have used the flat-bladed file as an emergency extractor to pry stuck shells out of chambers, too.

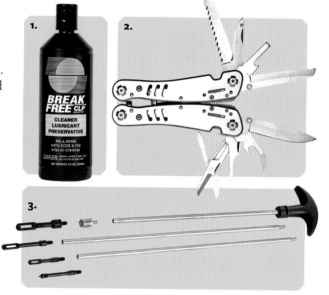

228 KNOW THE BEST REPAIR KIT

A friend of mine took a man he didn't know pheasant hunting. As they loaded their guns, the man realized his gun was plugged for ducks. He insisted they stop right there so he could take his gun apart and remove the plug to load five shells instead of three. The magazine spring—as magazine springs will—shot out, taking the spring retainer with it into the tall grass, where they were unable to find it. Fortunately, my friend had brought along an extra gun.

BOURJAILY ON: THE MORAL

" Don't hunt with people you don't know. If you can't hit a pheasant with three shells, two more won't help you. Take guns apart in a clean, well-lighted place where you can find anything you drop. The best repair kit in the field is a spare gun."

229 MASTER PRACTICAL PATTERNING

Does your gun shoot straight? Does it shoot too tightly to hit the game you're after? Are your patterns too sparse to kill cleanly? There's only one way to find out: blast holes in large pieces of paper. A tedious chore under ideal conditions and a paper chase on a gusty day, patterning is still essential homework that must be done. Fooling with flapping sheets of paper, taking aim, and punching holes is no fun; homework rarely is. But, when the final exam comes in the form of a greenhead over your decoys or a quail buzzing into the brush, it's good to know that your shotgun throws enough pellets to fill in the blanks.

STEP ONE: CHECK POINT OF IMPACT (POI) Screw in a tight choke and shoot two to three aimed shots from a rest (we want to take gun fit out of this equation) at the same sheet of paper from 25 yards. The center of your pattern should have obliterated the aiming point, or a spot 1 or 2 inches above it. Don't worry if you are off target by a couple of inches, but if the POI is far from the point of aim, try a few different choke tubes to see if you have a bad tube. If not, send the gun back to the factory.

STEP TWO: CHECK YOUR PATTERN Practical patterning takes place at whatever range you typically shoot your birds. Staple a 40-inch square sheet of paper to a backstop, retreat the appropriate distance, and shoot. Label the target with gun, choke, load, and distance, put up another piece of paper, trudge back to your gun and shoot at least two more.

At home, draw a 30-inch circle on your sheet with the densest cluster of pellets at the center. You don't have to count the holes; look for a pattern with enough pellets to put four or more hits on the vitals of the species you'll be hunting. Pay closer attention to the 20-inch center, which is the reliable killing and target-smashing part of any pattern. You can make life-size cardboard outlines of game birds and trace around them on the sheet or simply eyeball the pattern.

There will be gaps. There is no such thing as a perfectly even pattern with one pellet strike in every square inch of the circle; shot charges cluster pellets more tightly in the center and spatter them randomly around the edges. If the pattern has many, many gaps in it where only one or two pellets strike the bird, you'll need smaller shot, a heavier shot load, or a tighter choke. Patterns that are overly dense in the center and weak on the fringes indicate you're using too tight a choke.

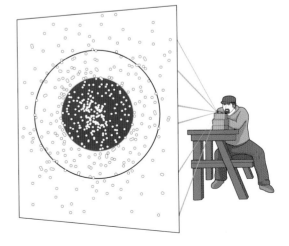

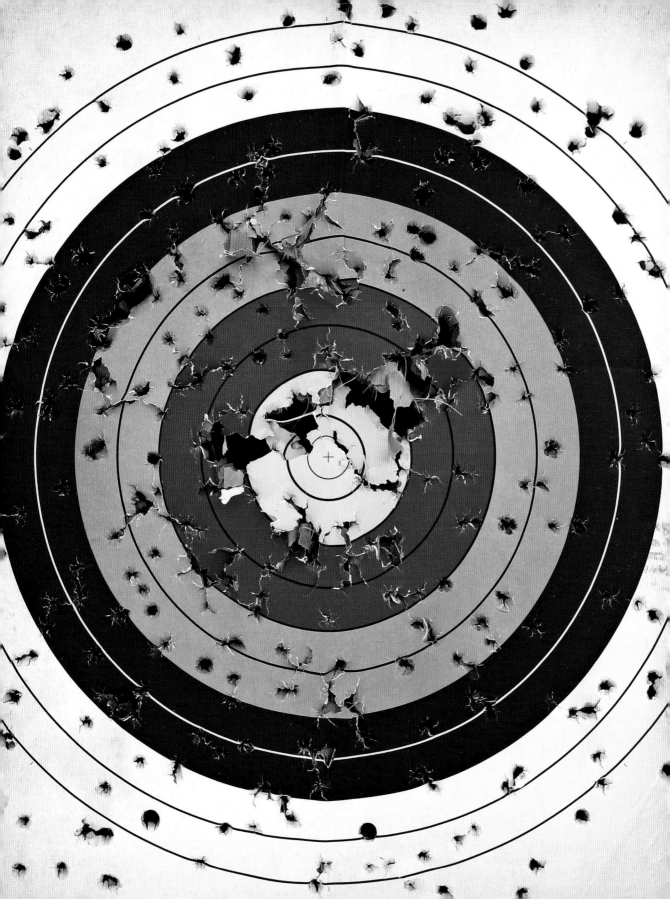

230 LEARN TO SWITCH

It's much better for a new shooter to learn to shoot from his dominant-eye side, even if it means shooting with their non-dominant hand. I taught my older cross-dominant son to shoot left-handed, and he does very well in the field. He's never handled a gun right-handed at all.

The reason to switch sides and be able to shoot with both eyes has nothing to do with depth perception or peripheral vision, in my opinion. It's simply that if you

shoot with one eye closed, you see the gun in sharp focus. And the better you see it, the more likely you are to aim it—which is the worst way to shoot a shotgun. Your eye-hand coordination and subconscious mind are much more effective at putting a gun on target than your conscious, aiming mind can ever be. With two eyes, you can "see through" the gun, and it appears as more of blur, allowing you to keep all your focus on the target, where it belongs.

231 FIND YOUR DOMINANT EYE

Most people have one eye stronger than the other, just as they're left- or right-handed. While many people have their strong eye and strong hand on the same side, not everyone does. Cross-dominance is especially common among women. It's very important that your dominant eye be the one looking down the barrel of a gun.

The first thing to do with any beginner is to give them an eye-dominance test. Have them hold their arms straight out, palms outward and overlapping so their thumb webs form a triangular hole.

Tell them to keep both eyes open and look at an object in the distance. Then, keeping that object in sight, have them bring their hands back until they wind up over one eye or the other with the object still in sight. The uncovered eye should be the dominant eye. To be sure, repeat the test, bringing their hands back so they cover the eye you think is dominant. The object they are looking at should be blocked from their view. Watch carefully when you give the test. Some young shooters will cheat in an effort not to appear cross-dominant. A rare few others will be center-dominant, able to see the object regardless of which eye they cover.

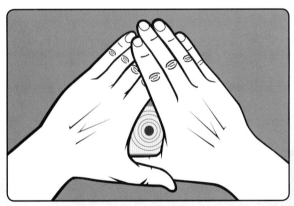

232 KNOW WHEN TO SHOOT ONE-EYED

It's not impossible to shoot one-eyed. The great trapshooting champion Nora Ross shoots with one eye shut tight. And, while there's no question that Nora would beat me in a shooting match, think of how much worse she'd beat me with both eyes open.

Nevertheless, some people who have shot on the wrong side for too long can't or won't switch no matter what. Some are center dominant, and if both eyes are equally strong, each eye will take over at different times. These shooters need either to learn to close one eye as they mount the gun or to put a piece of tape on the lens of their glasses to block their dominant eye.

The tape patch can be about the size of your thumbnail. If it's placed just right to block your vision when you mount the gun, it'll be high enough that it won't interfere with your vision when you have your head up normally.

233 READY YOUR POSITION

"Assume the position" in shotgun shooting means starting with proper foot placement and stance and then holding the gun in such a way that it can be brought quickly and smoothly to a firing position. The butt should be tucked very lightly under your arm. The barrel should be parallel to the ground or pointed slightly higher if there are bird dogs in the field.

Be sure to keep the muzzle below your line of sight. Your grip should be relaxed, and your finger should not be on the trigger or even inside the trigger guard.

Whenever possible in the field, I'll take a short step toward the target and bring the gun from whatever carry position I'm using into this ready position while my eyes find the bird. Then I'm ready to make the shot.

234 HIT THE RIGHT BALANCE

You see lots of people lean aggressively forward when shooting a shotgun, back knee locked, front knee bent, or else they lean back, usually a habit formed by trying to handle too long and heavy a gun when they started shooting.

The proper stance for shooting a shotgun is fairly upright. Your knees are neither bent nor locked, just relaxed. Lean forward slightly, with just over half your weight on your front foot. The easiest way to remember is to think "Nose over toes." When you're standing correctly, your nose should be directly above the toes of your front foot.

235 STAND UP FOR YOURSELF

Your feet should be no more than shoulder width apart when you shoot a shotgun. If you were to draw a line from your back heel through your front big toe, it would extend out to the point where you want to shoot the bird or target. Obviously you can set your feet at that angle before you call for a clay target. In the field, taking a short half step toward the spot where you plan to shoot the bird puts your feet in the right alignment.

Stand this way, and you'll put your body in proper relation to the target: halfway between sideways and squared up. Keeping your feet fairly close together allows you to pivot easily from the hips and swing in either direction.

236 COPE WITH A LONGER STOCK

Most shooters can handle a longer gun stock than they're used to if they adjust the placement of their hand on the fore-arm. It's a simple trick, but it really works. If a stock is too long for you, try taking a shorter grip on the forearm, holding it near the receiver. The shorter grip helps you push the stock out and away as you mount the gun so it doesn't hang up on your clothing. Conversely, if a stock feels too short, try taking a hold out near the end of the forearm, and the gun immediately seems longer. Theoretically, I (at 6 feet tall), Abe Lincoln (6'4"), or Granny Clampett (5' 2") all could shoot the same gun just by adjusting our grips.

237 MOUNT UP

Learning to mount a shotgun is the single most essential skill in field shooting. When you can bring the gun to your face, instead of putting the gun to your shoulder and lowering your face to it, you can look at a target and hit it without hesitation. The gun mount, done properly, combines the swing and the mount as one move, rather than the "mount, find the target, swing, then shoot" method of many American shotgunners weaned on rifle shooting.

Start from the ready position (see item 233). Before you move the gun, you have to see the target clearly so your eyes can tell your hands where the gun has to go, and your head has to come forward and incline slightly to accept the gun. Lock your eyes on the front edge of the target and then begin the mount by moving the muzzle toward the target as if you were going to hip shoot it. As the muzzle flows to the target, raise the stock to your face. The comb nestles under your cheekbone just before you settle the stock into the shoulder pocket below your collarbone. When the gun butt meets your shoulder, pull the trigger.

238 SHINE A LIGHT

Practice your gun mount with an unloaded gun and a Mini Maglite in the barrel (AAs fit 12 gauges; AAAs fit 20s; sometimes one or two wraps of clear tape make a snugger fit). Do this drill inside, standing in one corner of a darkened room with the beam of the flashlight cranked down to its tightest setting. Hold the gun in a ready position, butt down, with the beam shining into the corner where the opposite walls and ceiling meet.

Mount the gun, raising the stock to your cheek first, and concentrate on keeping the beam from bouncing out of the corner. You only have to do this for a few minutes a night to get results in the field.

239

MOVE THE MUZZLE BELOW THE TARGET

Never let the bird go below your muzzle. To hit a flying target, you have to keep your eye on the bird. If you let the bird dip below your muzzle, you lose sight of it for an instant. Without the target to look at, your eyes can flick back to the bead, the very last place you should be looking. If, on the other hand, you keep the barrel just below the target, the muzzle stays in your peripheral vision as a blurry reference point while you maintain a tight focus on the bird. You see where the muzzle has to go and connect the dots.

240

KEEP IN TIME

When I'm missing a target and don't know why, I try varying my gun speed, which usually means slowing down. A shotgun has to move in time with the target to be effective. I don't completely understand why it's so, but it is. Believe me.

241 SWING YOUR SHOOTER

A shotgun is not aimed; it is pointed or swung at the target. A proper swing starts before you begin the mount. The first step is to lock your eyes on the bird. There is no reason to move the gun until your eyes can tell it where to go.

When you can see the target clearly and read its path, move the muzzle toward it as if you're trying to hip shoot the bird. Keep moving—swinging—the muzzle along the line of flight as you raise the stock to your cheek.

The muzzle should stay below the bird so you always have a clear view of the target. Move the gun in time with the bird. I cannot emphasize those two tips enough.

Being too precise with lead will make you slow down or stop the gun and miss, which is why many engineers have trouble shooting shotguns: they want to be exact. Instead of feet and inches, think of lead in three increments: some, more, and a lot. "Some" is the amount of lead you see when you shoot a mid-range target. "More" is twice that, and "a lot" is twice as much as "more."

The spread of shot provides some margin for error. Trying to aim at the last second practically guarantees a miss. Trust your eye-hand coordination to put the gun in the right place and then just shoot without hesitation.

242 USE THE RIGHT METHOD

There are two main shooting methods that will get your muzzle in front of a flying target: swing-through and maintained-lead. Most good shooters can switch back and forth between the two as the situation demands.

Swing-Through The more intuitive style, swing-through, is excellent for upland shooting and short- to mid-range waterfowling. Trace the bird's line of flight, shooting as you pass the beak ("butt, belly, beak, bang" is how the British put it). You have to move the gun faster than the bird in order to catch and pass it. Because the gun keeps moving past the bird during the time it takes for you to pull the trigger and the gun to go off, you won't see much apparent lead but the bird will fall.

Maintained-Lead The staple method of skeet shooters, maintained-lead is the easiest way to hit long-crossing targets such as doves and waterfowl. Unlike swing-through, where you catch the bird from behind, in maintained-lead shooting, you never let the bird pass your gun barrels. Mount the gun ahead of the target, match the bird's speed for an instant, and shoot. Maintained-lead requires longer perceived leads than does swing-through.

243

BAYONET THE STRAIGHTAWAYS

The best way to hit birds that flush underfoot and fly straight away is to imagine a bayonet on your shotgun. When the bird flushes, take a ready position, with the gun held parallel to the ground just above waist level. Take a short step toward the bird and imagine jabbing it with a bayonet as you bring the stock to your face. Starting the gun low lets you see the bird clearly. Pushing the gun out toward the bird assures you won't catch the butt in your coat. Skip the part where you scream "Kill!"

244 HIT THE HIGH BIRDS

To make long shots on way-up-there birds, move the gun at about half the speed you think you should and shoot as the muzzle passes the beak. Slowing down doesn't seem as if it would work, but it does.

245 STAY FOCUSED

Ammunition companies will tell you that more velocity solves the problem of missing behind a flying target. Helpful kibitzers at the gun club will tell you that you need to lead the target more or to keep your gun moving. In truth, most misses behind result from the mistake of looking back at the bead to measure lead. It's a baffling miss to experience, because the last thing you saw before you looked at the bead was the gun ahead of the target.

However, the instant you look at the bead, the gun stops. You are going to end up shooting behind even though you think you're ahead of the bird. The answer to this problem isn't more feet per second, more feet of lead, or an exaggerated follow-through. It's more focus on the target. Relegate the barrel to your peripheral vision and keep your eye on the bird. Think "sharp target, fuzzy barrels," and your mystery misses will turn into hits.

Remington 870 ShurShot Synthetic Super Slug

246 GET AN ACCURATE SLUG GUN

BARREL Heavy barrel for rigidity and recoil reduction.

RIFLING One twist in 34 inches. Slower rates like 1 in 34 usually work best with 1,200–1,500 fps slugs. Faster rates (under 1 in 30) match up with 1,900–2,000 fps slugs.

PIN Barrel is fixed to the receiver to dampen vibration. This barrel was pinned at the factory, but a gunsmith can install a set screw in almost any gun to pin the barrel.

STOCK High comb suitable for use with optics.

RECEIVER Drilled and tapped for optics.

GAUGE 12 or 20. Twenty-gauge sabots give up little to 12s ballistically and have lower recoil.

PAD Soft recoil pad.

SCOPE Longer (4 to 6 inches) eye relief for mounting on a shotgun receiver. Low-medium power variable. Heavy reticle to stand out in thick cover.

TRIGGER Hard-kicking guns are easier to shoot if they have lighter (3 to 4 pounds), crisp triggers. Most factory guns can benefit from a trigger job by a qualified gunsmith.

Foster Slug

247 IDENTIFY SLUGS

FOSTER SLUG For smoothbores. The "vanes" don't make it spin, they help it swage down through a choke.

ATTACHED WAD SLUG For smoothbores and rifled barrels. The attached wad keeps the slug flying straight, like the feathers on a badminton shuttlecock.

SABOT SLUG The halves of the sabot separate and fly off after the round leaves the muzzle. Expensive and worth it in rifled barrels where they are accurate enough to take deer to 150 yards. Very inaccurate in smoothbores.

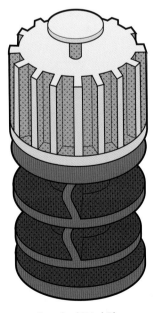

Attached Wad Slug

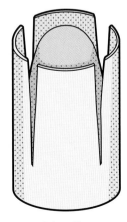

Sabot Slug

248 CHOKE IT RIGHT

One of the reader questions I get most often is "Will slugs hurt a full choke gun?" Probably not. The slugs are lead; the barrel is steel. A better question is "Will a full choke hurt my slugs?" and the answer is "Yes." For instance, a while ago I started with an Improved Cylinder, then switched to Modified and Full in a Mossberg 500 with Federal Truball slugs. IC shot around 3 ½ inches at 50 yards, Modifed did the same, but the Full choke group widened to 7 ½ inches.

249 GET A GRIP

We all know we're getting kicked when we shoot a slug from the bench. What we don't understand is that slug recoil can play a nasty trick on us. Slugs are so slow that they're still traveling down the barrel as the gun recoils upward and to the left, due to the torque of the heavy projectile as it spins out of the barrel's rifling. If you sight the gun in at the bench without holding the forend, you'll actually sight it in 5 to 6 inches high and to the left of where it will shoot when you hold the forend normally in the field.

Adjust your benchrest technique. Rather than using your left hand to plump up the sandbag as you would with a centerfire rifle, clutch your gun's forearm firmly or even put your hand on top of the barrel and press it down.

250 TRY A FULL-BORE SLUG

As long as sabot slugs cost $3 apiece, full-bore slugs selling for under $5 per box of five will always have a market. If your deer gun is a smoothbore, if you expect to empty your magazine several times during the course of a few deer drives, or if your shots occur well under 100 yards, then full-bore slugs are for you. As an added benefit, any slug measuring .729 puts a very large hole in whatever it hits and usually comes out the other side.

And full-bore slugs are much more accurate than they used to be. The best of them will shoot under 2 inches at 75 yards in a gun they like. Accuracy gets dicey after that, as the slugs slow and pass through the sound barrier between 75 and 100 yards. And they'll often group poorly and leave out-of-round or even sideways holes in the target.

251 DON'T DON'T STOP YOUR SWING

"Don't stop your swing," is the most common and the worst advice you'll hear at the gun club. It addresses a symptom (stopping the gun) not the cause (looking at the gun). People take it to heart and add a lurching follow-through to their swing-stop-shoot sequence that doesn't change a thing.

252 TEACH EACH OTHER

You and a friend can help each other learn to shoot better with only a hand trap and a few boxes of clays, if you learn how to teach. Telling someone where he or she missed doesn't help; you have to tell them why. The key is to watch the shooter's muzzle. The muzzle goes where the eyes send it. With a little practice, you can practically read a shooter's mind by watching where the gun goes.

If someone's gun stops short, it is not because the shooter consciously stopped his swing, it's because he looked from the target to the barrels to measure lead or to double check. When the muzzles pop over the top of a going away bird, it usually means the shooter didn't focus his eyes on the target hard enough. Missing high and behind a crossing or quartering target often means the shooter had the gun too high, and it actually blocked his view of the target for an instant.

Watch for head lifting, too, which is the other main cause of missing high.

253 READ A GOLF BOOK

There are only a couple of good books I know of about the how-to of shooting a shotgun. The *Orvis Wing-Shooting Handbook* teaches sound field style. Gil and Vicki Ash's *You've Got to Be Out of Your Mind* is an entertaining, useful look at the mental side of shooting. After you read those two, then what? Go to the golf section of your bookstore.

You'll find a long shelf of self-help golf books with touchy-feely titles like *The Inner Game of Golf, Fearless Golf, The Golf of Your Dreams, Mind Over Golf*, and *Deepak Chopra's Golf for Enlightenment*. Don't laugh. What these books teach you about the mental game of golf will help you become a better shotgunner.

Dr. Joe Parent, author of the excellent *Zen Putting* and *Zen Golf*, hasn't shot a gun himself since he was a Boy Scout, but he told me, "I coached a trapshooter for a year once. In 2003, she was browsing in a bookstore and found my book. We began consulting by phone. I helped her break her first 200 straight."

254 REDUCE RECOIL

The best way to reduce recoil is to shoot ammunition with lighter payloads and lower velocities. Shooting a gas semiuato runs a close second.

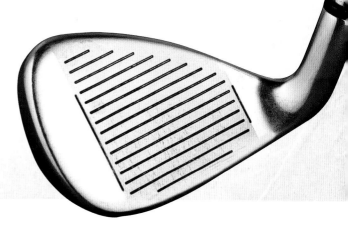

255 FILM YOURSELF

One of the surprise benefits of being on *The Gun Nuts* TV show has been the opportunity to see and correct mistakes in my shooting that I otherwise would never have noticed. For instance, I sometimes pull the gun off my face when I shoot right to left crossers.

You can achieve the same benefit by having someone film you with a video camera, or even your phone. You'll be surprised at what you learn, and it can only help you to improve.

256 USE THE FORCE

Like Luke Skywalker, you can use the Force to hit targets with your eyes closed. I stole this trick from instructors Gil and Vicki Ash. It's fun to try and a great way to learn what it means to have a feel for the target, as well as an excellent method for breaking yourself of the habit of looking back at the barrel to be sure (and by "to be sure" I mean "to guarantee a miss") before you shoot. Shooting with your eyes closed, you have to let go.

Call for the target with your eyes open. Focus on it, read its angle, and move the gun in time with the bird. Close both eyes as you start to pull the trigger. You'll crush the target. Once that becomes too easy, call for the bird and close both eyes a full second before you shoot. Stretch out, use your feelings—all that Jedi stuff—and you will be amazed at what you can do if you read the target's line and move the gun in sync with the clay.

After I showed this to two of our high school shooters who had bead-checking problems, I challenged one of them to shoot a whole round closing his eyes before pulling the trigger. He shot 22x25 and afterward admitted to opening his eyes twice during the round. He missed those two shots.

257 HIT FROM THE HIP

Learning to shoot clays from the hip is surprisingly easy once you learn the trick to practicing. With your gun unloaded, lay your trigger finger along the side of the receiver, so it points where the gun points.

Now, call for a few targets and pretend to shoot them. Think about pointing your trigger finger, not the gun. After years of trying and failing to shoot from the hip, it took me only a few practice points before I was able to hip shoot targets. After doing this exercise, I can hit them from the 27-yard line of the trap field . . . sometimes.

258 SHOOT A CHIP

Shooting target chips is fun. It's great practice. And while it's not difficult, it impresses the easily impressed. Chip shooting works best with outgoing targets. Shoot it, look for the biggest piece, and shoot it. You will be surprised at how small a piece you can rebreak. It teaches you to "stay in the gun": to keep the gun on your face after the first shot. And, to borrow a phrase from anglers: "A clay target is too valuable to shoot only once."

259 HAVE FUN WITH TARGETS

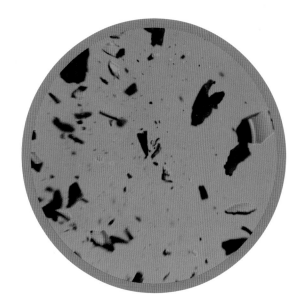

For more fun at the range, you can buy the flash targets we shoot on *The Gun Nuts* TV show or make your own. Buy some snap-line chalk, put some in the dome of a target, and glue paper over the top. An easier way is to find the right size plastic drink lids to hold the chalk on the underside of the clay, but then you have to clean those up after shooting

PUT A TAIL ON A TARGET Use 18 inches of surveyor's tape. Fix it to the bottom of the dome with clear packing

tape and roll the tail up inside the clay. When you throw it, the tail streams out behind.

PIGGYBACK A MINI Use some rubber cement to glue a mini target inside a standard clay. When you break the larger clay, the smaller one keeps going, "like an escape pod," as someone put it.

260 SHOOT A ROUND OF TRAP

A round of trap consists of 25 shots. You will shoot five in turn with the other shooters at each of five posts. You will need a pouch or deep pocket to hold your shells and, ideally, another pocket for your empty hulls.

Trap is shot in silence because a steady, uninterrupted rhythm helps everyone shoot their best. Load your gun as the person before you is shooting. If your semiauto ejects shells onto the ground, leave them until you change posts after five shots.

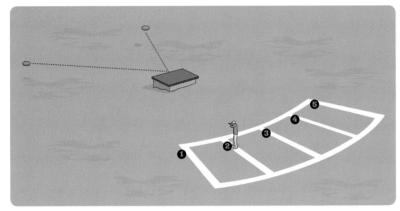

QUICK SHOT

261 KNOW YOUR HOLD POINTS

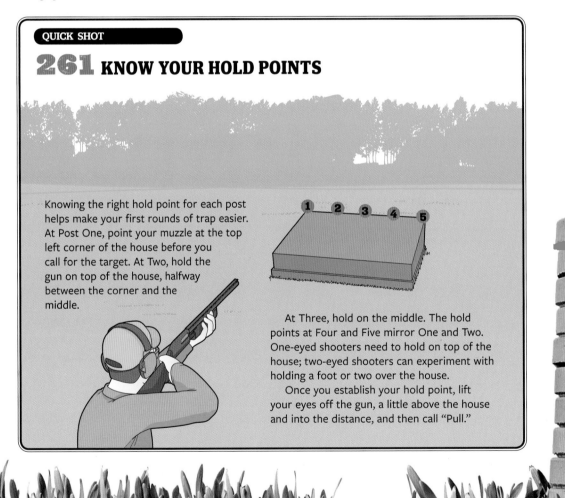

Knowing the right hold point for each post helps make your first rounds of trap easier. At Post One, point your muzzle at the top left corner of the house before you call for the target. At Two, hold the gun on top of the house, halfway between the corner and the middle.

At Three, hold on the middle. The hold points at Four and Five mirror One and Two. One-eyed shooters need to hold on top of the house; two-eyed shooters can experiment with holding a foot or two over the house.

Once you establish your hold point, lift your eyes off the gun, a little above the house and into the distance, and then call "Pull."

Browning Citori Trap XT

262 GET THE RIGHT TRAP GUN

Trap is a medium- to long-range game, with most targets shot at 35 yards away. Trap guns are 12 gauges with tight chokes. They have long barrels to point smoothly and are heavy to absorb recoil. Most trap guns have a high point of impact to deal with rising, going away targets. Many guns have weird, high ribs, recoil reducing stocks, and other features to help shooters deal with the repetitive pounding of hundreds of rounds in competition.

263 ADAPT A FIELD GUN FOR TRAP

A field gun will easily see you through many rounds of social or league trap and your first few 25 straights. Screw in a Modified, Improved Modified, or Full choke and shoot 1-ounce loads of 8 shot.

It is much easier to hit trap targets if you don't have to cover them with the barrel. Raising the comb of your field gun slightly either with shims or an aftermarket comb pad will adjust the stock to make the gun shoot higher, letting you "float" targets over the gun.

If you shoot a semiauto you will also want to be sure you have a shell catcher or at least a thick rubber band around the receiver to keep your empties from hitting the person to your right.

264

SHOOT A ROUND OF SKEET

A round of skeet consists of 25 shots. Stations run in an arc from the high house to the low, with the last station, 8, located between the houses in the middle of the field. You shoot a high house and low house target at each station, and doubles at stations 1, 2, 6, and 7. You repeat your first miss, called the "option" and if you don't miss, you shoot the last shot, Station 8 low, twice.

Besides following the normal rules of gun safety, be sure to wait until it's your turn to shoot and you are standing on the station—not walking up to it—before you drop shells in your gun.

265 CHOOSE A SKEET GUN

Skeet began as practice for grouse hunting, and a skeet field is the best place to hone all-around wingshooting skills. Any open-choked gun that shoots twice works. The short-range targets also make skeet a perfect fit for smallbores. The first 25 straight I ever shot at skeet was with a 28-gauge Browning Pump. The 28 is a great, low-recoil, hard-hitting skeet gauge, while the .410 is, let us say, "challenging."

Skeet shooters use tiny 9 shot. If you can't find it, 8s work almost as well.

> " Double triggers are the only true 'instant barrel selectors' but some people think they can't learn to use them. It only took a few rounds of skeet with two trigger guns and I could switch back and forth from one trigger to two without thinking about it. So can you."

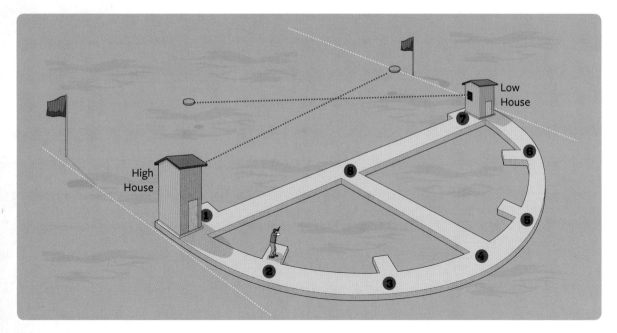

266 HIT YOUR CLAYS

Skeet targets fly on a known path when you call for them. You can set yourself up for every shot. Except for station 1 and High 8, right-handed shooters should point their belly button at the low house window (left-handers point at the high house window, except for 7 and Low 8). Start your gun roughly ⅓ of the way from the house you are shooting to the center of the field. Hold it low enough that you see the target over your gun.

Skeet targets at 3, 4 and 5 require lots of lead even though they are only 20 yards away. Remember you have a 30-inch wide pattern to put in front of the bird, so there is no need to be precise, just get the gun out in front of the target, focus on the bird, and pull the trigger.

Station 8, where the bird flies almost right at you, terrorizes beginners but is not so frightening once you know how to handle it. Start your gun at the bottom of the house window and a few feet to the side. Look into the window and concentrate on seeing the bird emerge. Shoot at the front edge, and it will turn into a black or white (depending on whether the target is pitch or biodegradable) cloud of smoke.

267 KNOW YOUR OPTIONS

American skeet competitions are held in 12, 20, 28, and .410. Most competitive shooters in American skeet use one O/U with sub gauge tube sets allowing them to shoot all four gauges with the same gun. Skeet guns have open chokes as targets are shot at close range. Most skeet guns have 28- or 30-inch barrels.

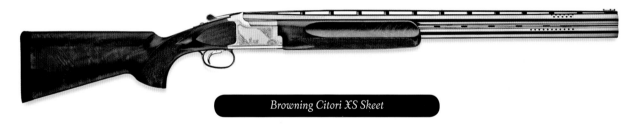

Browning Citori XS Skeet

Beretta A400 Xcel

268 USE WHAT YOU WANT

Sporting clay guns can be anything that fires two shots. You should never be afraid to show up with your hunting gun if all you want is target practice, but among competitors, guns tend to be O/U or semiautomatic. Twelve gauge shotguns predominate, and most guns have long barrels: 30-inches for semiautos, 30, 32, even 34 for O/Us. Extended choke tubes offer easy changes on the course. Because so many targets are shot falling, a gun that shoots fairly flat is best.

If you want to shoot one gun for all clay target games (and doves!), a dedicated sporting clays gun would be an excellent choice.

269 SHOOT A ROUND OF SPORTING CLAYS

A round of sporting clays consists of either 50 or 100 targets. Bring that many shells plus a few extras. Targets are shot as pairs, and you will take turns in the shooting cage shooting five pairs in succession. Never load more than two shells in your gun and do not load the gun before you're standing in the cage. The first shooter at each station can ask to see a pair of "show" targets. The shooting order rotates from one station to the next.

You will need a bag to carry your shells around the course, and you can bring chokes and change them between stations if you choose. I usually throw in a water bottle, too. Most sporting clays targets can be broken with an Improved Cylinder choke and 7 ½ or 8 shot.

Sporting clays is usually much more informal and sociable than trap (especially trap) and skeet. Behavior such as congratulations, fist bumps, and friendly heckling is usually allowed.

270 EXCEL AT SPORTING CLAYS

Sporting Clays shows you all the targets you will see on the trap and skeet fields, as well as specialty targets that make the game more fun, frustrating, and challenging. And, you shoot them as pairs. Here's how.

RABBITS Special hardened clays that bounce in front of the guns. The trick is to hold your muzzle below the path of the rabbit so you can see it. Then focus hard on the target, and your eye-hand coordination will cope with any bad bounces (hint: there will be bad bounces).

TEAL Teal go straight up, seem to hang for instant, and fall. Hold your gun to one side of the flight path so you can see the bird, and about ⅓ of the way to top of its flight. As it hangs, imagine it's a clock face, look at 6:00, and shoot.

CHANDELLES AND BATTUES Arcing and falling, chandelles and battues require lead both in front and below. Using the clock face analogy again, look at 5:00 on the right hand targets, 7:00 on the left, and give them more lead in front than you think they need.

271 PLAY THE HUNTER'S GAME

"Skrap" or "upland angles" uses a combination trap/skeet field and combines the best of trap and skeet for upland hunting practice. Skeet, although invented by grouse hunters and suitable for upland guns, is best as practice for doves and waterfowl with its incoming and crossing targets. Trap has going away targets that simulate the flight of flushing upland birds, but it allows a premounted gun, and dedicated trap guns have no place in the field.

Skrap is trap shot from the skeet stations. Rules vary, but the way I play it, you start with a low gun, get two shots at every target, and a hit with the second shot counts as much as a hit with the first shot. The puller is allowed to delay the pull by up to 3 seconds. You shoot three targets from stations 1 to 7 and four from station 8 to make a round of 25 birds. You'll have fun, and you'll be a better bird shot when the round is over.

272 TRY THE SMALLBORE VERSION

You can modify skrap to make it more smallbore-friendly and to better simulate typical upland shots by setting the stations closer to the house. Our local Ruffed Grouse Society chapter used to hold a fun shoot/competition and encouraged hunters to bring their open-choked, small-gauge grouse guns. They marked stations on the course with hula hoops (shooters have to have at least one foot in the hoop) 7 to 12 yards behind the house, with stations 1 and 7 directly on either side of the trap, and station 8 immediately behind it.

273 CHOOSE YOUR SKRAP GUN

Shots in skrap are long, with the exception of station 8. If your bird gun has choke tubes, go with Modified and Full from stations 1 to 7 and switch to Skeet or Improved Cylinder for the last four birds. Any gun of any gauge goes, but even in a clay game like this that attempts to simulate bird hunting, a dedicated sporting clays gun will win.

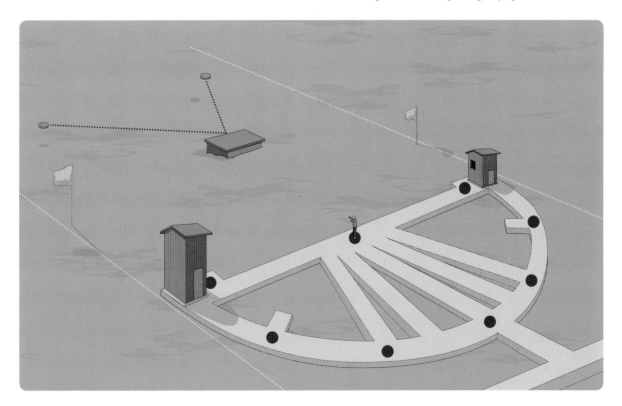

274 GET READY TO HUNT TURKEYS

I am old enough to remember the time before there were turkeys everywhere. Back then the off-season stretched for eight long, empty months. Then turkeys arrived, and I quickly learned turkey hunting was far more than a mere stepping-stone to help me get from one fall to the next.

Despite their feathers, turkeys are big game you hunt with a shotgun. You shoot them as they're standing flat-footed on the ground. That's the easy part. The real challenge of turkey hunting lies in getting into position to call, in remaining undetected, and in playing the part of another turkey. Do it right, and you're rewarded with a jolting, electrifying gobble. Then, perhaps, you'll find a tom puffed up in the mating display of the wild turkey: a sight

simultaneously majestic and slightly ridiculous.

Did I say shooting them was easy? It would be if it weren't for the pounding of your heart and the shortness of your breath when the bird you've been thinking about all year (yes, even during that other hunting time of year) finally steps into range.

While spring hunting gets most of the press, fall hunting for both sexes of turkey is legal in many states. It's a completely different style of hunt than spring. If you can find time among deer, birds, small game, and waterfowl, you can be one of the lucky few who get to shoot their own Thanksgiving dinner.

275 GEAR UP FOR GOBBLERS

Turkey hunting requires just the right amount of gear, somewhere between the minimalism of the upland hunter and the waterfowler's trailer-full of decoys. You need just enough stuff to keep yourself concealed, comfortable, and calling in the woods. Below, a breakdown of the basics you'll need.

Clothes You'll want to dress in head-to-toe camouflage, gloves and facemask included. Snakeproof boots are a good precaution in some regions.

Insect Repellent Either bug spray or a ThermaCELL helps keep the mosquitoes from chasing you out of the woods late in the season.

Vest Special turkey vests hold your gear and have a built-in seat for comfort in the woods.

Box Call The best style for getting loud, box calls are great for windy days and for reaching out and touching distant birds.

Mouth Call The diaphragm style mouth call takes time to learn. But once you can yelp and cluck with it, you can call hands-free and close.

Slate or Glass Call "Pot and peg" calls offer realistic sounds and a wide range of volume levels. Glass calls work when wet and have a higher-pitched sound birds like. Slates sound the most realistic and are easy to learn.

Owl Call An owl hooter, or the ability to hoot like an owl unassisted, is the best call for making turkeys gobble on the roost in the dark to give away their location.

Blinds Optional pop-up style turkey blinds are increasingly popular and an effective way to hide from turkeys. I personally can't stand sitting in a nylon cube looking out a window on a spring day, but some people won't hunt without them.

Other Calls You'll find lots of other styles of calls: tubes; wingbones, pushbuttons; gobble calls; and crow, hawk, and coyote howlers for locating. Experienced hunters often carry some of everything, since you never know what sound a turkey wants to hear on a given day.

Decoys Hen decoys attract gobblers eager to breed, except when they make the gobblers stand there waiting for the hen to come to them. Jake (yearling turkey) or gobbler decoys bring toms running to fight for territory, except when they scare them away.

BOURJAILY ON: TURKEY SHOTS

"They say you should write about what you know, and one thing I know way too much about is missing wild turkeys. One reason is that turkey chokes are so tight they throw patterns the size of a volleyball at 20 yards.

After my closest miss (5 yards) I shot a pattern at that range that made one hole you couldn't fit a golf ball through."

276 CHOOSE THE RIGHT TURKEY GUN

Turkey guns are their own animal in the world of shotguns, or they can be. They are aimed like rifles, so that you can achieve the goal of putting a tight swarm of shot onto your bird's head and neck, for an instant kill. Most turkey guns are either pumps or semiautomatics. Single shots are next in popularity, and doubles come last.

Dedicated turkey guns have short 18- to 24-inch barrels, very tight chokes, and often a dull or camo finish. Light weight and sling swivels are plusses for guns that are, after all, carried more than they're fired. Twelve gauge is the standard for a turkey gun. Tens were once the big guns of the turkey woods, but a 3 ½-inch 12 gauge does almost everything a 10 can in a much lighter package.

For 99 percent of turkey hunting, a 3 ½ inch 12 gauge is plenty of gun, and 20s make slim, easy-carrying, surprisingly effective guns.

277 SCOPE OUT YOUR TURKEY

You might not think optics are necessary on a gun made for shooting inside 50 yards, but it's easy to be off target just enough that the tight central core of the pattern misses the head and neck, and the bird runs away. Don't ask me how I know this, but I do. A low power (1 to 1.5x scope) is fast and easy to use. Put the crosshairs on the turkey and shoot. Red-dot sights are even faster to put on target and new models have battery lives measured in years, not hours.

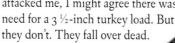

278 SAY NO TO 3 1/2-INCH TURKEY LOADS

I had a chance to shoot a Beretta O/U in .458 Win Mag a while ago. I'd never fired a big-bore rifle, and I was afraid it might kick hard, but I pulled the trigger, the steel plate target clanged, and honestly my first thought was: "That was nowhere near as bad as a turkey load." In fact, it was kind of fun, so I shot the plate about 20 more times.

Last time I fired that many 3 ½-inch turkey loads, my shoulder, neck, and head hurt when it was over. I was a bit punch-drunk afterward, and even simple tasks like casing guns and loading them in the car seemed very difficult.

A .458 shooting a 510-grain bullet at 2,100 fps out of a 10.5-pound double rifle generates a 53 foot-pound shove of recoil. A 3 ½-inch, 2-ounce turkey load at 1,300 fps in an 8-pound pump smacks you with 66 foot pounds. When a cartridge made to kill elephants before they kill you is more pleasant to shoot than a shotshell for 20-pound birds, something is wrong. If the turkeys I shot got up and ran away, or attacked me, I might agree there was a need for a 3 ½-inch turkey load. But they don't. They fall over dead.

279   DON'T GET CAUGHT WITH YOUR PANTS DOWN

This a story about my friend Phil. (This is not some cute way of writing about myself in the third person. My friend is a guy named Phil.) He says he was lucky. I say he followed hunting's Most Important Rule.

Walking into the turkey woods in the dark one morning, this guy named Phil bumped a roosted hen out of a tree. He figured a gobbler might be in the habit of meeting that hen, so he put out his decoy as a stand-in for the real bird and sat down against a tree 20 yards away.

As fly-down time approached, Phil began to feel intestinal rumblings that increased to the point he couldn't ignore them. He walked a prudent distance into the creek bottom, found an appropriate log and took care of business. Tiptoeing back to his spot, he saw a gobbler running full speed toward his decoy. When the bird reached his fake hen, he shot it. "I hadn't called or anything," he said.

That oh-so-important rule? Simple. No matter what you are doing in the woods, take your gun with you. If Phil had left it back at the tree, the gobbler would have caught him—metaphorically or maybe even literally—with his pants down. Instead, he got his bird. It may be better to be lucky than good when you go hunting, but it's most important to be armed.

280 PICK THE BEST WATERFOWL GUN

If upland shotguns resemble sports cars—sleek, fast, good-looking—waterfowl guns are like pickup trucks: built to deliver heavy loads through rain, mud, and snow. The following are the things I prefer in a duck and goose gun.

ACTION Go for a pump or semiauto. Repeaters hold 50 percent more shells than do break actions, and you can "top up" the magazine while the gun is in battery. It used to be a given that pumps were much more reliable than semiautos. If that's still true at all, the pump's edge is a slim one, and the recoil reduction of the semiauto more than makes up for the difference.

GAUGE A 3-inch 12 gauge is enough gun for nearly all waterfowling. Three-and-a-half-inch 12s and 10 gauges are best for shooting heavy loads of bulky steel BB and larger shot at passing geese. The 16s and 20s are fine for over-decoy shooting if you pay attention to range.

WEIGHT The gun should weigh in at 8 pounds or so. Guns below 7 pounds are in, but some heft helps a gun absorb recoil.

BARREL LENGTH A 28-inch barrel gives a gun a smooth, weight-forward feel.

FINISH A matte finish won't shine like a mirror in the sun. Camo is unnecessary, although dipped finishes add another layer of weather protection.

SLING SWIVELS A sling is a necessity for walk-in hunters and convenient on any waterfowl gun, as our hands are not always free to hold a gun.

281 EAT CROW, IF YOU MUST

To begin by digressing, two seasons ago I ate crow—literally, as in, I cooked one. A friend shot it on a duck hunt, and it bothered me to leave it in the field, so I breasted it and cooked it rare. It was very similar to duck in taste, but I had a hard time getting my mind past the fact that it was a crow, so I couldn't finish it.

However, having eaten real crow, it is now much easier for me to swallow the figurative kind.

My preference in waterfowl guns is a heavy, long-barreled gas gun. I have said so, expecting my word to be the last on the subject. When people asked me about inertia guns like Benellis I always said, "They are too light and kick too much. I don't like them."

I was wrong. There.

When a barely-used Benelli M2 showed up at my local store at a price too good to pass up, I bought it. A 12-gauge inertia gun, it weighs 6 pounds, 14 ounces (about the weight of many 20s) with a 26-inch barrel and slightly butt-heavy balance; everything I supposedly dislike in a waterfowl gun. And I love it. The M2 rides lightly slung over my shoulder when I'm burdened down with decoys; the shorter barrel and butt heavy balance haven't yet prevented me from killing nearly every duck I've shot at. With reasonable loads—1 ¼ ounces of shot at 1,450 fps—it doesn't kick too badly. A light, compact waterfowl gun can be a joy, and I was wrong ever to say otherwise, even though I also still shoot my long, heavy gas guns, too.

Benelli M2 Field

282 LAY DOWN ON THE JOB

The laydown blind has changed waterfowl hunting by letting hunters hide in plain sight. Laydown blinds are deadly—as long as you master the skill of sitting up and shooting. Just follow these basic hints.

ANGLE YOUR BLIND The easiest shot for right-handers from a sitting position is about 30 degrees to your left. Set your blind so your toes point to the right of where you expect to shoot.

DIG IN Older and/or heavier hunters who have trouble sitting up can dig a small depression under their seat or feet. Either makes sitting up much easier.

TAKE YOUR TIME Landing waterfowl have their eyes on the decoys. It takes them an instant to notice people popping up out of the ground. Don't rush. Keep your trigger hand on the gun. Use your other arm to sweep open the doors and grab the gun. Then sit up, mount, and shoot.

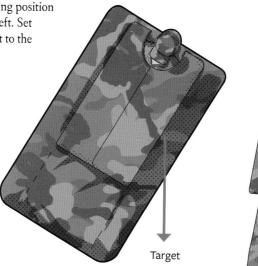

Target

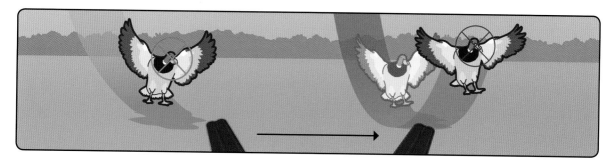

283 SHOOT A DOUBLE

Waterfowl fly in flocks, making doubles—even triples—possible, and even likely if you know a few helpful tricks. You can increase your chances of making a double by picking your first target wisely. Like a pool player, you want to make the first shot in such a way that it leaves you in a good position to make the second.

With crossing birds, it's often easiest to take the trailing bird first and swing through it to the leader.

If you miss with this tactic, however, stay with that bird until you hit it rather than switching targets.

When a flock comes in to the decoys, pick a low bird first so that after you make the shot, the others are above your gun where you can see them and see where you have to put the muzzle to finish the pair. I shot the only triple of my life by starting at the bottom of a bunch of teal and working my way up. Shooting doubles ethically means making sure the first bird is totally dead before you switch to a second. You should also consider where the birds will fall. It's much easier finding two downed birds in, say, a cut cornfield than it is in a thick stand of cattails.

BOURJAILY ON: SAY WHAT YOU WANT

" I was in North Dakota on a goose hunt on a very foggy day. I killed my limit and was hanging out when the guide told me I could shoot his limit, too.

I said, "No thanks." He insisted. We stood there arguing. Finally I said "This has been great. Three geese is enough for me. What I want now is to shoot a duck."

On cue we heard the quack of a mallard in the fog. I blew my duck call and the quacking got closer and closer as the duck homed in on us. It appeared out of the fog over our heads. I shot and it fell at our feet. I took one step, picked it up and said "There, I can go home now."

284 WORK HARD FOR DUCKS–AND LOVE IT

The coldest I have ever been in my life was on a duck hunt. We broke thick ice deep in the flooded timber of Arkansas' Bayou Meto Wildlife Management Area, then stood waist-deep in frigid water for an entire morning. We shot no birds that day, proving again that while duck hunting often involves suffering, enduring hardship does not guarantee waterfowling success. By and large, though, duck hunting involves worse hours, harder work, and colder, more dangerous conditions than any other wingshooting sport.

Duck hunting also involves the grown-up versions of childhood pleasures: You spy on ducks (we call it scouting).

You play in the mud and build a fort to hide in (we call it a "blind," but it's a fort). You arrange toy ducks on the water.

The reward of duck hunting comes on cupped wings, sometimes silent, sometimes with a whoosh that the old timers likened to the sound of a canvas sail tearing in a storm. As the ducks bank and circle the decoys, you bow your head to hide your face while simultaneously rolling your eyes up trying to look through the brim of your hat so as to not miss one second of the sight of ducks flying their tight, precise formations—a sight you've dreamed of since last season ended.

285 ADJUST YOUR CHOKE FOR DUCKS

The blind wasn't quite ankle deep in hulls, but the empties hitting the floorboards far outnumbered ducks hitting the water. Bunches of mallards made their final swing behind the blind, dropping suddenly into view at 15 to 20 yards, only to be scattered by another hasty volley.

The three shooters were experienced watefowlers and, like so many hunters, they were choked and loaded for the long shot. HEVI-Shot and Federal Black Cloud fired through Modified chokes are deadly at 40 to 45 yards, but they sling patterns the size of cantaloupes at close range. The mindset endures that the best choke/load combination for ducks is the one that throws the tightest pattern at 40 yards, even as the goal of waterfowling is to lure birds to half that distance.

Later, out of curiosity, I patterned the loads my blindmates used at 20 yards. At 20 yards, 3-inch Black Cloud 2s in a Modified choke put all its pellets into a 15- to 16-inch circle. HEVI-Shot 7 ½ patterned slightly tighter than the Black Cloud, printing a dense cluster of holes better suited to the turkey woods than to a timber hole.

To see a noticeable improvement in close-range patterns, I had to change loads and chokes. Winchester Xpert 1 ½ ounce loads of 3 steel shot through an Improved Cylinder filled a 23-inch circle at 20 yards. Compared to the Black Cloud and HEVI-Shot, the Xperts gave well over twice the pattern area: 415 square inches vs. 176 square inches. That's a huge difference when you are trying to hit a flying target.

Save your HEVI-Shot and Black Cloud for second and third shots, where they will give you tighter patterns from the same Improved Cylinder choke.

286 SET YOUR DECOYS FOR A GOOD SHOT

Decoys do attract more birds. Set correctly, decoys present ducks to the gun for a good, clean shot, steering them into the guns. Since ducks always land into the wind, you can predict their path on final approach. If possible, set your farthest decoy 30 to 35 yards from the blind and use it as a range marker.

Leave a gap in the decoys for a landing hole, and make that hole right where you want to take the shot. If you use a spinner, put it in the landing hole. I am a big fan of two blobs of decoys on either side of a landing zone about 10 yards wide. Do real ducks sit that way? Not often, but they don't seem to mind coming into my spread, either.

Finally, position yourself so you don't have to fight the low morning or afternoon sun. I'd rather have a good view of crossing ducks than have ducks coming right at me out of the sun where I can't tell the drakes from the hens.

287 MARK YOUR DUCK

Marking the exact spot where a bird falls and never taking your eyes off of it until you get there is an important part of hunting without a dog—and in fact, I make a point of marking birds even when the dogs are involved. If there are two of you, you can triangulate your mark. Keep your eye on the spot and walk straight to it. If you look away and look back, you lose your mark.

Years ago in North Dakota, another writer and I hunted a small pothole surrounded by thick cattails. We took turns and tried to shoot birds so they would fall in the water where we could retrieve them easily rather than dropping them into the heavy cover. Tom miscalculated and folded a mallard that fell dead on the far side. "We'll never find it," he said, and, although we walked around the pothole and looked and looked, we didn't. A while later, I shot a teal over the far bank. I marked its fall and kept my eye on one particular cattail. I waded straight across to it rather than walking around the edge, so I wouldn't lose my mark.

I found the duck right where I marked it. It was dead. I picked up Tom's mallard, too. Through pure coincidence, my duck had fallen right on top of it.

289 CALL YOUR SHOT

Calling the shot at the right time results in more birds in the bag and more shooting for everyone. Calling it at the wrong time, or not at all, leads to frustration and hard feelings.

Avoiding the latter situation is pretty easy. Start by picking a captain. Discuss beforehand whether you are shooting only birds in the decoys or if any bird in range is fair game. If you're the one calling the shot, keep up a running commentary as birds approach so everyone is

ready. Be patient, especially when birds come in from one side. Let them get all the way in to the decoys so the shooter at the far end of the line has a chance. Circling ducks are a tough call. As long as they get lower with each swing, wait. If they keep circling at the same height, shoot them on the third pass. If a single comes in, call one hunter's name to shoot the bird. If you don't know everyone in the group, have them number off and call out a number.

290 SHOOT SPORTING CLAYS TO PREP FOR DECOYING MALLARDS

Mallards with their wings cupped look too big and close to miss, but they are losing altitude and sometimes quartering as well, meaning they need lead both in front and below. Any low incoming shot on the sporting clays course can stand in for a decoying duck. As you wait for the bird to come to you, hold your gun to one side of it or the other so you don't block your view of the target.

You have to learn to lead below the bird. Often the easiest way to do that is to imagine the target as a clock face. If the duck is coming right at you, focus on 6:00. If the bird is a left-to-right, focus on 5:00; focus on 7:00 for a right-to-left. Keep the bird in sight over the top of the muzzle, while "staying in the gun"—that is, keeping your cheek on the stock.

291 DEAL WHEN DIVERS BUZZ THE DECOYS

Diving ducks often streak by the edge of the decoys without putting on the brakes. Station 4, in the middle of the skeet field, requires the longest leads, up to 4 feet, and makes great practice.

When you set up for a station 4 crosser, hold your gun halfway between the house and the middle of the field, and make sure it's below the target's line of flight. As the bird comes out, keep all your focus on the target, move the gun ahead of it while matching its speed, and shoot the instant you think the lead is right. For right-handed shooters, the high house (left) target presents the temptation to pull the gun off your face. The low house (right-hand) bird can be difficult, because they come out of the house low and get behind the gun and out of sight of a right-hander. When people miss 4, it's usually thanks to insufficient lead, or, more often, from shooters looking at the gun to double-check or measure lead.

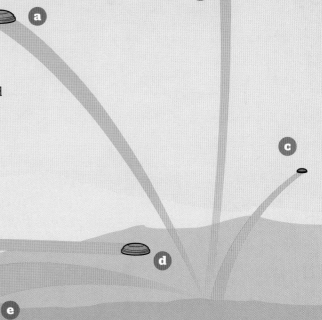

a High incomer for overhead geese

b Springing teal for flaring birds

c Going-away trap target for jump shooting

d Station 4 crosser for divers buzzing the decoys

e Low incoming shot for decoying duck

292 LEARN TO JUMP SHOOT DUCKS

When you jump shoot ducks, you get going-away shots similar to the kind upland hunters take all the time. Trap, with its rising, going-away targets at unknown angles, is great practice for jump shooting. You'll want to practice this with a 16-yard trap shot, from any station.

Start with an unmounted gun, as you would in the field. Call "Pull!" and take an instant to read the angle before you move the gun. Flushing ducks often take you by surprise, and learning not to move the gun until you know where it needs to go helps you avoid rushed, futile shots. See the target and then swing the gun through it and pull the trigger. Follow through by keeping your face on the stock and your eye on the target until after it breaks.

293 PRACTICE FOR FLARING BIRDS

Often your second shot in duck hunting is at birds flaring straight up out of the decoys. They appear to be hanging, but they're actually going back and up.

The practice clay you want to use for this is springing teal. Targets are launched straight up, rocketing into the air in a way no gamebird actually flies. Nevertheless, they make excellent practice if you shoot them as they near the top of their flight but are still on the way up. Hold your gun to one side of the flight path to get a clear look at the bird and then jab the muzzle over the bird's head, blotting it from view. Trust that you're on target and pull the trigger right away. Imagine trying to shoot the top of the target, just as you would think about trying to scalp a jumping mallard.

294 GET YOUR GOOSE

"What if there be no more goose music?" wrote Aldo Leopold in his 1949 classic *Sand County Almanac*. The threats to wild places today are bigger than they were in Leopold's time, but one problem we don't have is a shortage of goose music. To the contrary, Canada geese make themselves at home in the suburbs, while snow goose numbers have exploded to the point that they are a danger to themselves. From late August to the end of April, goose season is open somewhere.

A proper goose hunt has none of the hardship of a duck hunt. You drive into the field and dump out the blinds and decoys. You set up and then wait, hoping the birds will do today what you saw them do yesterday. On afternoon hunts, that hope edges toward desperation as the clock ticks toward the end of shooting time. But in truth, the last half hour of the day is the best, and the empty skies can suddenly fill with skeins of hungry geese coming your way.

Geese announce their arrival loudly and respond to both calling and motion. The first time I waved a goose-shaped flag at a flock of Canadas and saw it break up in the air, drop 20 feet, re-form, and turn in my direction, I was hooked. That hook was buried bone deep a few seconds later when I shot twice and 25 pounds of Canada geese crashed to the ground.

295 LOAD UP FOR GEESE

North America has 11 types of Canada goose, ranging in size from 3-pound cackling geese to giant Canadas weighing more than 15 pounds. Light geese range in size from the duck-sized 3-pound Ross goose to lesser snow geese at 5 to 6 pounds and greaters at 6 to 7 pounds. The white-fronted goose is about the same size as a lesser snow.

If I had to pick one load for all goose hunting, I might go with 1 1/4 ounces of steel BBs at 1,500 to 1,550 fps.

That load contains enough pellets to give you reasonable pattern density for small geese and enough oomph for big ones to 50 yards or so. For purely pass-shooting big 10-pound-plus Canadas, go up a size to BBBs.

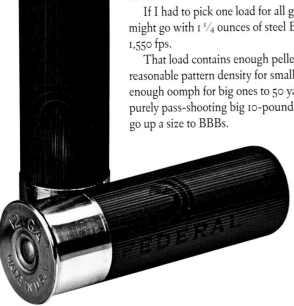

296 PRACTICE FOR GEESE ON THE RANGE

When geese come into a spread, then decide against landing and lift up over the blinds, you get the overhead shot. Any station on the sporting clays course that throws a high target passing over your head simulates this shot.

Keep your head on the stock when you shoot incoming birds. Swing through the target from behind—butt, belly, beak, bang. As soon as the muzzle blots out the head (or the front edge of the clays) pull the trigger without trying to double-check the lead. Many shooters lift their heads to try to look around the gun to see the bird. But to hit this target, you have to keep your head on the gun and trust that it will break, even though you can't see it.

I recently had an experience that served to remind me what I like and what I don't like about goose hunting. My friend M.D. called to say he had a field full of geese and did I want to hunt? I was leaning toward "Yes" when he delivered the clincher: "You can sleep in. They've been flying about 9:30, so we don't have to leave my house until 8:00."

The birds flew on schedule, and soon a flock swung close enough that I was able to kill a bird. A few minutes later three sailed in on M.D.'s side. I didn't want to shoot over his head, so I watched while he shot a double, and then swung on the third and lowered his gun. Our bag limit was two, and he wasn't going to shoot my second bird for me. I never did kill another goose, but I appreciated M.D.'s gesture, which is increasingly rare in waterfowling, where party shooting is prevalent.

First of all, party shooting is illegal: bag limits are meant for individuals and not to be combined among the group. Nevertheless, party shooting is widely practiced because shooting a group limit quickly is important for bragging rights and for posting impressive pictures on the Internet. Everyone shoots at everything, someone keeps a running body count, and when the group reaches their combined limit, the shooting stops.

Besides the whole legality thing, a hunt where everyone gets to try for his or her own limit is more fun. You can pick a bird and shoot it at your pace and timing without worrying that two or three other people will blast it before you do. Or, you can wait for the types of shot you like. If I do limit before everyone else, I either unload my gun or shoot backup on cripples. I don't shoot anyone else's birds, nor do I want my birds shot for me, and if I wind up shy of a limit at the end of a hunt, it's no tragedy.

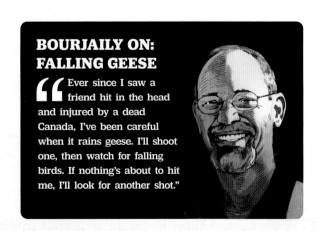

BOURJAILY ON: FALLING GEESE

"Ever since I saw a friend hit in the head and injured by a dead Canada, I've been careful when it rains geese. I'll shoot one, then watch for falling birds. If nothing's about to hit me, I'll look for another shot."

298 ENJOY A DOVE HUNT

It's 98 degrees in the shade, and the sweat running off your brow drips onto the gun in your lap. You swat at a mosquito and squint into the low sun, but there's no place you'd rather be. Shotguns pop around the field like champagne corks, celebrating September 1—New Year's Day on the hunter's calendar. From this day on, the whole of hunting season stretches out before you, and you're starting it quite literally with a bang—often three in rapid succession.

Ammunition companies love dove hunters. Limits run from 12 to 15 birds and the average shooter burns 5 to 8 shells per dove bagged. Even a dove loafing along makes a challenging target for hunters who have neglected their summer clay practice, but once the shooting starts, doves really show you "challenging," turning on the jets, dipping, weaving, and dodging.

Dove hunting mixes pass shooting with decoying, and it's sometimes possible to walk birds up, too, but the essential sport is sitting on a bucket, watching the sky—and shooting a lot. While most dove hunts take place around managed fields both public and private, it's entirely possible to scout doves like you would ducks and geese and find a hot field or a waterhole all to yourself.

The reward, besides the fun and camaraderie of a very social type of hunting, is a dinner of dark, delicious dove meat, and the knowledge that hunting season is here again and you've started it in the very best way possible.

299 SHOOT WHAT YOU WANT

A dove gun can be whatever you want it to be. Some shooters like to sit under a tree by a waterhole and plink doves with a .410. Years ago, I remember reading a magazine article about how to handload a 10 gauge for long-range doves. Both methods work. Neither is ideal.

A lot of people think because doves are small that a light, short, small gauge makes the best gun. I'll disagree here.

Last fall, I shot doves at home with a 12 gauge Beretta 391 with an Improved Cylinder choke and steel 7 shot. In South Dakota, I had a great hunt with a 32-inch barreled Citori 725 Sporting Clays gun with Improved Cylinder/Light Modified chokes. To me, those guns sum up what a dove gun should be: they are long enough to swing smoothly and have enough weight and/or a gas system in order to reduce recoil.

A 20-gauge version of either gun would be just fine, too, or even a 28, provided it was something like an 1100 with heft to it.

Browning Citori 725 Sporting

300
DO THE MATH FOR SMALLBORES

As a rule of thumb, figure you get 5 yards of clean-killing distance per $\frac{1}{8}$ ounce of shot payload, so a .410 is roughly a 20-yard gun, a 28 gauge is good to 30, and so on. I like 8 shot in smallbores for the increased pellet count over 7 $\frac{1}{2}$.

301 SHOOT A LIMIT "INSIDE A BOX"

It's a thing among dove hunters to shoot a limit "inside a box," meaning with 25 shells or fewer. While it is possible to accomplish the feat in a crowded field, most inside-a-box limits are shot by hunters who go alone, shooting cruising doves that don't know there's a hunt going on.

The best way to have an inside-the-box shoot is to find a pond with dirt banks and a dead tree nearby. That is the perfect place to spend the last hour of daylight. Typically, doves coming to water will light in the tree then drop down for a drink. You can set your bucket nearby and shoot them like decoying ducks.

Doves respond much better to decoys when they aren't dodging volleys. Set your fake doves up off the ground for visibility. If there is no fence or dead tree handy, make a tree of your own with PVC pipe.

It can be as simple as an eight-foot-tall T. Clip decoys onto the horizontal piece and stick it in the ground. Doves' reactions will vary, but you will usually get birds to at least swing by your decoys for easier shots.

Put your spinner in the dirt bank, simulating a dove landing for a drink, and pick your shots.

302 SHOOT LIKE AN ARGENTINE

South American dove shooting is the Daytona 500 to U.S. dove shooting's Sunday drive. The high volume tests shooter and gun alike. Argentine outfitter Zeke Hayes, whose clients average 1,250 rounds a day, says only two guns hold up: the Beretta 390 and the Benelli Montefeltro. Hayes keeps 20 gauges as house guns, both for lower recoil and because they're lighter than 12s; if you lift a gun several hundred times a day, you feel every ounce of its weight. Gas-operated and slightly heavier than the Benelli, the Beretta is the softer-shooting of the two, but Hayes says "Benellis are amazing guns with very few moving parts."

During dove season, the guns get a light cleaning at lunch, and the internal parts get a thorough bath with diesel fuel at night, which strips off fouling and leaves a lubricating residue. The Beretta's bolt and piston need careful attention; with Benellis, the hole in the bolt face around the firing pin can clog with powder fouling.

Hayes's gunsmith keeps spare parts for both guns, especially connecting rods for the Berettas and inertia bolt springs for the Benellis and the gun's recoil springs are changed every 30,000 to 40,000 rounds.

303 MAKE THE FIVE TOUGHEST SHOTS

As a nation of dove hunters, we average 5 to 8 shots for every bird bagged. With the price of shotshells, I can't afford to miss that much. I'm hoping to hit one out of three when the season starts; that's a good average if you try everything that comes into range. Although doves zipping randomly around a field present a wide variety of shots, most of those shots fall into the following five main categories.

Dove with the Jets On When you're in a crowded field, sometimes you have to root for a dove to get past other people so you can shoot it yourself. Problem is, when that bird reaches you, it's moving at top speed and juking all over the sky. This one is a no-brain reaction shot—you have to trust your hand-eye coordination and get your conscious mind out of the way. I like an aggressive swing-through system for these birds, which can duck out from under a maintained lead-style swing. Sweep the gun past the target from behind and shoot when the muzzle clears the beak. Because you are swinging the gun very quickly, you won't have to see much lead; just shoot as the gun clears the beak. Keep a tight focus on the target, and your eyes will magically send your hands to the right place if the dove pulls last-minute evasive maneuvers.

The Incomer You See Forever The bird that comes all the way across the field to you is surprisingly easy to screw up. It's even worse if you announce to the person next to you: "I'm going to shoot this dove." (I've done this.) Avoid the temptation to mount the gun early and track this bird all the way in. Inevitably, you'll look back at the bead to check your lead and stop the gun, or the dove will dip down below the muzzle, and you'll have to scramble to find it again. Instead, wait for it with the gun ready, butt tucked loosely under your arm. As the bird comes into range, look at the beak, make a smooth gun mount, and shoot the bird in the nostrils. This is not a fast-draw contest between you and the bird; mount the gun in time with the target's speed, keep a sharp eye on the beak, and pull the trigger when the gun meets your shoulder.

The Surprise Dove The bird that flies overhead from behind takes you by surprise and requires a little lead underneath. If you're a skeet shooter, you've made this shot a million times at High House 1. If not, here's what to do: resist the temptation to rush this shot. Before you start your mount, raise the muzzle, keeping it just to the right of the bird (if you're right-handed); that way, you won't lose sight of the bird behind the gun. Move the muzzle down through the bird while raising the stock to your face. Shoot when you see the dove above your barrel. Don't shoot right at this bird; instead, try to miss it underneath, or think "graze its belly" with your pellets.

The Long Crosser The dove that loafs along unalarmed, crossing at 35 yards, takes a lot of forward allowance. Keep your eye on the dove and mount the muzzle in front of the bird. Swing, matching the dove's speed. Trust your subconscious mind to tell you the instant the lead is right. If you try to measure the lead, analyze it, or double check it, your gun will either slow down or stop. You'll miss. Remember, lead doesn't have to be precise—you've got a wide pattern on your side. Focus on the bird, let the blur of the muzzle drift ahead of it, and shoot.

The High Overhead Dove Birds coming into a field over the treetops look impossibly high. In reality, they aren't as far up as they appear; it's a very tall oak or pine that measures 90 feet. That 30- to 35-yard shot is well within the capability of even an Improved Cylinder choke, and most trees are much shorter. And remember: a dove straight overhead is presenting all of its vitals to your shot. The higher the bird, the slower you have to move your gun. Start with the muzzle behind the bird as you raise the stock to your face and swing through the target. Keep your back leg straight with your weight on your back foot. When you can't see the dove behind the muzzle, consciously keep the gun moving and shoot. The dove will fall apparently from the stratosphere. I love this shot because it's much easier than it looks to impressed bystanders.

304 PATTERN YOUR DOVE GUN

Does your gun throw dove-killing patterns? The only way to find out is to put pellets to paper at the ranges you'll be shooting. Don't test a gun at the standard 40 yards if you take all your shots at half that distance over a waterhole.

The vitals of a dove are roughly the same size as a golf ball—a little less than 2 inches in diameter. To reliably put 1 to 2 pellets on such a small target, you will need to see a total of at least 225 to 250 holes in the 30-inch circle.

Don't worry about pattern percentages or about dividing the circle into quadrants; just count holes. If you're not coming up with enough, you'll need a heavier shot load, smaller shot, or more choke.

A great way to fill out a smallbore pattern is to use 9 shot, at least for short-range shooting. Even a puny 28-gauge skeet load of 9s totals 438 pellets, and 9s retain enough energy to kill doves at 20 to 25 yards. For shots out to 35 yards, stick with 8s and either shoot heavier loads or tighten your chokes if you need more pattern density. Long range, 40-yard-plus dove shooting calls for a 12 gauge with 7.5s and a Modified or tighter choke.

305 JUMP-SHOOT THOSE DOVES

When the doves don't come to you, you can go to the doves. If you can stand the heat, take a midday jump-shooting walk down an overgrown fence line, a tree-lined creek, or even through a stubble field. Keep your gun ready and be alert for the high-pitched twittering of dove wings. A word of warning: if you think doves are hard to hit when they fly at you, try shooting them on the jump. Flushed doves rise and twist evasively. You need to focus your eyes tightly on the top of their heads or their beak if you hope to make the shot. Bringing plenty of shells helps, too.

306 HUNT PHEASANTS LIKE A PRO

If I were paid by the head of roosters I killed, I would put aside my double guns and shoot my Benelli Montefeltro. Why? Consider the following.

It's a 12 gauge. The 12 gauge outperforms the 16 and 20 with lead and beats them by a wide margin with steel. The 12-gauge ammo costs less and is available everywhere.

It's a semiautomatic. While it's true I can only remember killing one bird with a third shot in 30 years of pheasant hunting, it's also true that when I hunt with a semiauto, the gun is never empty and broken open for reloading at exactly the time another bird flushes.

It's light. Although my Benelli is a 12 with a 28-inch barrel, it weighs only 6 pounds, 13 ounces—less than many 20 gauges on the market. It's light enough to be easy to carry all day, but it has enough weight forward that it moves smoothly to the target.

I definitely notice the Benelli kicks less than a double gun on those rare occasions I shoot heavy, high-velocity (1,500 fps) pheasant loads. As a side benefit, it's a handsome gun, and mine came with very nice wood. That matters, because even if I hunted pheasants for a living, I would still want to look good on the job.

Benelli Montefeltro

307 STOP MISSING PHEASANTS

There's no reason to miss pheasants, which come equipped by nature—as if by cruel practical joke—with both a target around their necks and a long tail streaming out behind to conveniently illustrate the bird's line of flight. All you have to do to hit one is run your gun along the tail, through the body, and pull the trigger when you get to the white neck ring.

Yet people do miss them. It has become a staple of outdoor writing to suggest that people miss because they are distracted by the tail. That is nonsense. If it were true, you would see pheasants' tails shot off, and I have not seen that happen once. Ever.

People miss pheasants because all the sound and noise of a flushing bird unnerves them, and most birds, I believe, are missed way over the top by hunters who mount their guns hastily and don't put their heads on the stock.

308 BELIEVE IN SECOND CHANCES

I'm a firm believer in following up flushed birds. If you can mark the bird, or, in heavy cover (where birds usually don't go far), mark the line of flight, you can follow the bird up for a reflush. Or, if need be, you can swing around the bird to get downwind of it so the dogs have a better chance of finding it.

Flying tires a bird's wings. Often wild flushing birds will sit for the second flush. My record is four flushes on the same bird on a Christmas Eve hunt a few years ago. The fourth time I marked him down, he'd flown almost to the edge of the property. When the dog locked onto him, he flushed and tried to fly back the way he came. I took that as proof that I had chased him to what he thought was the end of the earth. Whether or not that was the case, we had pheasant for Christmas dinner.

309 READ THE LINE

Shooting birds in heavy cover means often taking a shot at a bird as it disappears into the brush. Here's what you need to do.

ONE Absolutely know where you partners are at all times. Call out to them if you can't see them so you only take safe shots.

TWO When a bird flushes, don't worry about lead. Swing your gun along the line of flight ahead of it, ignore the brush and shoot.

THREE Send the dog whether you think you hit or not. Often, you won't even see the bird fall.

310 SHOOT SHARPTAILS

Although prairie grouse live in habitat practically devoid of trees, they are still grouse. And they also succumb to a few small pellets. They aren't particularly elusive cripples either; they tend to wander dazed in the short grass once they're downed.

Twelve-, 16-, and 20-gauge guns all work, loaded with good quality 7 ½ shot. Some days, 30-yard-plus shots may be all you get. Others will just sit obediently waiting for the dog. I would still shoot Improved or Modified choke in a break action, or Light Modified in a repeater.

A double gun is fine for sharptails, although a semiauto comes in handy should you run into a flock and what some call a "popcorn flush." It's not a covey rise so much as a staggered mass flush; one here, one there, all around you, making it possible to shoot a three-bird limit in seconds.

311 TRY MY GROUSE GUN BRACKETOLOGY

No hunters are nuttier about guns than ruffed-grouse hunters. They'll agree that a grouse gun should be light in weight and open-choked, but the consensus ends there. They'll argue forever about which grouse gun is best. The only way to settle that question is to draw up a bracket and let 16 great grouse guns fight it out to the Final Four.

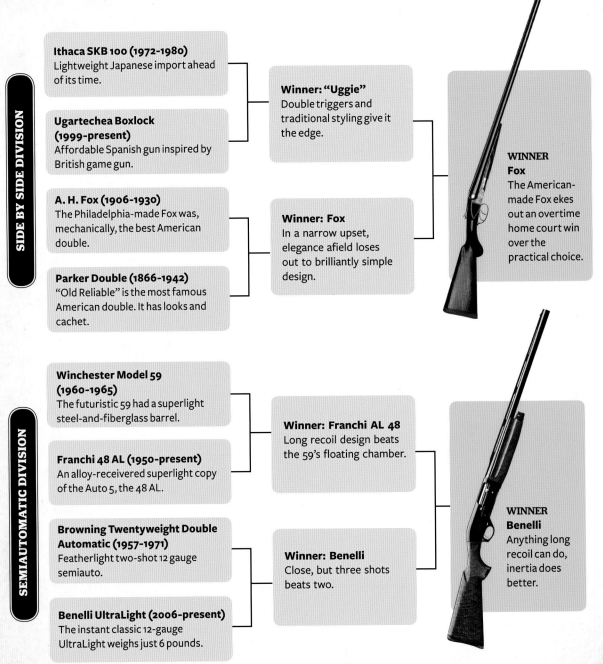

SIDE BY SIDE DIVISION

Ithaca SKB 100 (1972-1980)
Lightweight Japanese import ahead of its time.

Ugartechea Boxlock (1999-present)
Affordable Spanish gun inspired by British game gun.

Winner: "Uggie"
Double triggers and traditional styling give it the edge.

A. H. Fox (1906-1930)
The Philadelphia-made Fox was, mechanically, the best American double.

Parker Double (1866-1942)
"Old Reliable" is the most famous American double. It has looks and cachet.

Winner: Fox
In a narrow upset, elegance afield loses out to brilliantly simple design.

WINNER Fox
The American-made Fox ekes out an overtime home court win over the practical choice.

SEMIAUTOMATIC DIVISION

Winchester Model 59 (1960-1965)
The futuristic 59 had a superlight steel-and-fiberglass barrel.

Franchi 48 AL (1950-present)
An alloy-receivered superlight copy of the Auto 5, the 48 AL.

Winner: Franchi AL 48
Long recoil design beats the 59's floating chamber.

Browning Twentyweight Double Automatic (1957-1971)
Featherlight two-shot 12 gauge semiauto.

Benelli UltraLight (2006-present)
The instant classic 12-gauge UltraLight weighs just 6 pounds.

Winner: Benelli
Close, but three shots beats two.

WINNER Benelli
Anything long recoil can do, inertia does better.

**WINNER
Model 37**
Tradition and all steel parts narrowly top mass-produced excellence.

Winner: Model 37
The Ithaca edges out the Model 12, which is overpriced on the used market.

Ithaca Model 37 (1937-present)
The Ithaca is light, with bottom ejection.

Winchester Model 12 (1914-1964)
"The Perfect Repeater" has slick action and points beautifully.

Winner: 870
Through weight of numbers (over 10,000,000 made), the 870 wins.

Remington 870 Wingmaster (1950-present)
These old, fixed-choke, 20-gauge Wingmasters are light and lively.

Remington Model 31 (1931-1949)
The lightweight version is the best grouse gun you never heard of.

**WINNER
Beretta**
Winchester's notorious sticky safety hangs up at the buzzer.

Winner: 101
The 101's light weight beats a great, overweight O/U.

Browning Superposed (1931-1940; 1948-1976)
John Browning's last invention.

Winchester 101 (1963-1987)
Japanese-made classic.

Winner: Beretta BL 3
Better fit and finish at a lower price.

Ruger Red Label 28 Gauge (1994-2011)
The 28 gauge was a slim, wonderfully shootable smallbore.

Beretta BL 3 (1968-1976)
Low profile, light weight, affordable.

312 FIND THE RIGHT PLACE

Grouse always seem to flush at the wrong time, but this is actually not Murphy's Law at work says sporting clays shooter and grouse hunting nut Andy Duffy, who was never in the wrong place at the wrong time when I hunted with him in the Ruffed Grouse Society's National Hunt.

One reason Duffy was always in the right place when a bird flushed is because he never stopped in the wrong place.

Dogless hunters know the trick of stopping in order to unnerve birds and make them flush. Duffy says grouse hunters do it inadvertently, pausing on the way in to a point and making birds flush wild.

Duffy says: "When the dog goes on point, walk in a rhythmic steady cadence to the bird. Don't stop until you are in a place where you can shoot."

313
AVOID COVEY CONFUSION

Quail are not particularly fast flyers, but they reach top speed quickly, and they all go at once. By design, a covey rise overwhelms the senses of a predator, presenting an environment so target rich that the birds escape in the confusion. If you let a covey rise rattle you into shooting at the whole covey, you will hunt none of it. Pick a bird and focus on it before you move your gun. Watch that bird until it falls and then find another. If you want to shoot a double, start with a bird near the bottom of the flock so you will be able to easily find a second to shoot at without the gun blocking your view.

314 FOLLOW THE DOGS

Watching the dogs run is at the heart of quail hunting's appeal, regardless of whether the dogs are German shorthairs quartering to the honk of a pickup horn in Texas, pointers and setters ranging in front of mule-drawn wagons in Georgia, or Brittanies scouring the cover ahead of a hunter on foot in Kansas.

I saw the ultimate in Texas, where my host's four white setters strung out in a line, the first pointing the covey, the second and third on the ground, backing, and the fourth honoring the other three from the top seat of our quail buggy. Walking down a line of stock-still bird dogs knowing there's a covey somewhere in front of the last dog's nose is about as classically perfect as bird hunting gets.

Then, there is the payoff: the chaos of a covey rise. The first time I ever stepped into a covey, I thought for an instant that chunks of the earth all around me had sprouted wings. Then I realized what they were, and in the next instant I had emptied all five shots out of my semiauto without touching a feather.

315 SHOOT QUAIL LIKE A GENTLEMAN

If you find yourself invited to a southern plantation for bobwhites, the dress code will vary: you may be asked to wear a red vest or an orange one, depending on the region. However, anywhere you go (and that includes high-dollar Texas quail leases, too) you'll shoot a 20 gauge with two barrels. Period.

While tradition and snobbery are part of the reason for this, there's more to it than that. Quite simply, a pair of good shooters with 12-gauge semiautos can devastate a carefully tended and expensively raised covey of quail. Therefore, "gentlemen's guns" are required. Quail succumb easily to $7/8$ ounce of $7 \frac{1}{2}$ or 8 shot, and for shooting over pointing dogs, IC/M chokes work well.

For the rest of us, who take their quail when and where we can find them, a semiauto with an IC choke lets us make the most of our chances, not so much in shooting triples, but in having a shell left in the gun (after whiffing on the covey rise) for the "widow," the single bobwhite that often flushes after the rest of the covey has flown.

316 WAIT FOR YOUR WOODCOCK

Anticipation gives woodcock hunting its appeal. They are the one migratory upland bird, and their arrival is an event to watch for, calculate, and predict. There's not much downtime when the woodcock flights are in. Hit them on the right day, and another bird pops up every few minutes, bouncing off branches, changing direction in mid-air, ricocheting through the undergrowth like a feathery pinball. If you have to try a couple of shots tangled in the heavy cover, no matter: you'll have other chances soon enough.

Woodcock are small, not particularly tenacious, and live in thick cover where you often can't even see 30 yards, much less shoot that far. A 28 gauge, or even—used with restraint—a .410, packs enough 8 ½ or 9 shot to kill woodcock. Almost any choke is too much, and the gun with which I have killed most of my woodcock is a fixed Skeet/Skeet-choked 20-gauge O/U.

Although I am not usually a fan of short-barreled muzzle-light guns, I like them for woodcock. You often will be carrying your gun in your trigger hand while fending off branches with the other, and muzzle-light guns are the easiest to carry that way. Shots at woodcock tend to be quick points rather than full swings. You have to improvise in heavy cover, too. I once shot a woodcock one-handed with the forend of my 20 gauge resting on a stout branch.

317 DOWN THE DIFFICULT CHUKAR

In Idaho, I learned that it's very difficult to hit a chukar that flushes from an outcrop above you and curves down below you. Our guide on that hunt, fit and half my age, said he hunted public land every day of the season when he wasn't guiding. He also said there is so much public chukar cover that he never hunted the same place twice.

The catch is, none of that public ground is level. Chukars inhabit the deep and ancient rocky river valleys and ridges of the west. It is a physically demanding hunt. You will either have to climb up after them or get to their level and sidehill, which is more arduous than it sounds, since much of the hills seem to be composed of loose rock.

You will do a lot of your shooting while simultaneously sliding downhill.

A chukar gun, therefore, has to be tough because sooner or later you will drop it on the rocks; it has to be light, because every ounce matters in chukar hunting; and, it should shoot more than twice.

My pick would be a light-gauge semiauto with a synthetic stock (ordinarily I am loathe to hunt upland birds with a plastic-stocked gun, but chukar hunting is different in this regard). A 20-gauge Benelli M2 would meet my requirements perfectly. I would put in a Modified choke and shoot 6 or 7 ½ shot.

Benelli M2-MAX4 ComforTech

318 DO BUCKSHOT RIGHT

Buckshot is legal for deer in 30 states, and sales of it remain strong from Texas to Virginia—states in which dogs remain an important part of the deer hunting heritage. The hound hunter's preference for buckshot makes sense. After all, when you have to shoot a moving deer before it disappears into heavy brush, wouldn't you rather sling a spread of pellets than a single slug?

Buckshot is deadly within its limitations, and worse than worthless beyond them. Center a deer with buckshot at close range, and it will fall over dead. Stretch your barrel beyond the point where it puts five to six hits in the vitals and you'll wound deer you never find.

The best buckshot loads I have tested are premium ones that contain hard shot and buffer. You pay more for them and you get more in terms of pattern and range. A good 3-inch 00 12 gauge load shoots great patterns to 40 yards. I have had my best results with buckshot in Modified choke. At close range, standard loads of 1 buck have more pellets and give wider patterns. In very dense cover for shots of 25 yards or less, try 1 buck. Otherwise, 00 is the best all-around load. However, no matter how good your 40-yard patterns—or whatever you deem your maximum range to be—don't stretch beyond them. Buckshot patterns decay very quickly after a certain point, often within a few yards.

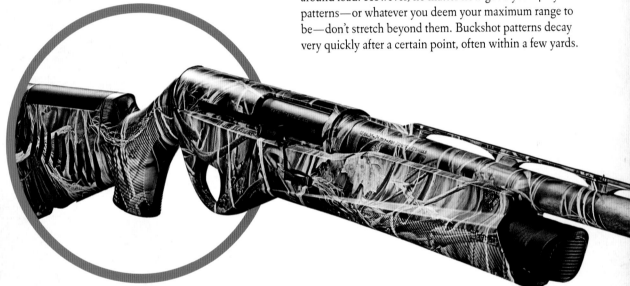

319 MATCH YOUR SLUG TO YOUR GUN

You will get your best performance from slugs if you match the ammunition to the type of barrel on your gun.

SMOOTHBORE Shoot full-bore slugs. Foster-style or attached wad slugs made for smoothbores (a few of this type are for rifled guns only) will perform best. Sabots require rifling to function properly and are a very inaccurate waste of money in a smoothbore.

RIFLED CHOKE TUBE You'll want to use lower-velocity (under 1,600 fps) sabots and attached wad slugs.

RIFLED BARREL Shoot sabots and attached wad slugs. You have to match the rifling twist to the slug. Barrels with slower rifling twists around 1 in 34 inches are most accurate with slugs in the 1,200 to 1,500 fps range. Barrels with a 1 in 30 or less twist are best with faster 1,900–2,000 fps slugs.

320 ACCURIZE YOUR SLUG GUN

Two easy, inexpensive gunsmithing jobs will improve your slug gun. Read on!

First, have the gunsmith smooth and lighten your trigger pull to 3 ½ pounds or so. A light, crisp trigger makes a gun much easier to shoot well.

Second, have the barrel pinned to the receiver. A set screw in the receiver will fix the barrel in place, eliminating the play and vibration that causes slug guns to sling the occasional shot far out of the group.

321 SIGHT IN AT 50 YARDS

Shooting slugs is like firing beer cans. The wind can move them all over the target. Therefore you should do your sighting-in at 50 yards. Sight in at 100, and all you have done is sight in for that particular day's wind conditions.

322 SLUG IT OUT WITH A DEER

People who haven't shot deer with slugs assume that if you shoot a deer with a giant chunk of lead, it will fly off its feet or "fall in its tracks." (If you think about it, actually, anywhere a deer falls is "in its tracks," because it makes tracks wherever it goes.) Usually, neither happens. Sometimes a mortally hit deer hunches or jumps, but often you will see no more reaction to a good shot with a slug than the deer running off with its tail clamped down instead of waving. It's dead on its feet but it can still run 100 yards.

Years ago I tracked a buck in fresh snow in a slow-motion chase that covered a few hundred yards in an hour. When I caught up to it, standing almost invisible behind a tiny bush at 40 yards, I shot with a full bore, 1-ounce 12 gauge slug and watched it bound away. I found no blood at all for the first 20 or 30 yards I followed its tracks in the snow. Finally I spotted a red fleck the size of a pinprick against the white. Ten yards after that, I saw where it had run against the side of a tree, leaving a bloody smear that looked painted on by a wide brush.

Shortly thereafter the deer's trail in the snow turned red. I found it piled up dead and shot through both lungs. Lesson? Any time you shoot at a deer, look hard for blood, even if you think you missed.

323 PLACE YOUR SLUG ACCURATELY

Several years ago in Texas, I met a man who worked for the county extension office; his job was to go into schools and teach kids how to shoot deer. I know. Texas is like a different country.

Anyway, his method was simple and effective: run the crosshairs up the leg and a little way up the body, and then pull the trigger. The goal was to make a clean heart shot. My son, who was along on the trip, did exactly that and killed his first deer, using a .243.

While that method works, slugs are huge chunks of lead that usually go all the way through a deer. Therefore, I prefer to shoot for the lungs. With a lung shot, you break a couple of ribs and puncture both lungs, killing the deer without losing meat. A slug through the shoulder will probably pass through the far shoulder as well, ruining both.

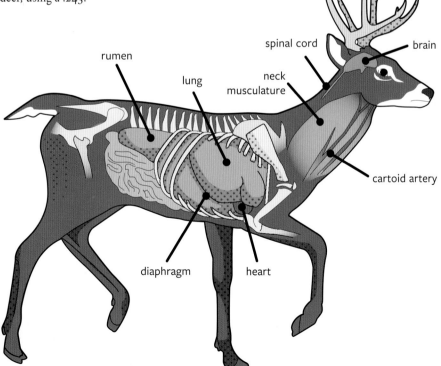

rumen

lung

spinal cord

neck musculature

brain

cartoid artery

diaphragm

heart

324 KEEP IT SMALL

"Small game" means small mammals. Traditionally, small game hunting is the portal through which kids enter the sport. Hunting small game teaches children of all ages patience and woodcraft, and there's the added benefit that small game animals live close to almost anyone's home.

Some smart hunters never outgrow small game. Indeed, you can easily find a lifetime of satisfaction in scanning the treetops for squirrels, or in hearing the sound of beagles running rabbits. If that's not reason enough, stewed squirrel and fried rabbit are.

Things have changed over the years, and many parents today skip squirrels and rabbits and go right to deer for their children's first hunts. Small game hunting is, if not a lost art, much less popular than it used to be.

This state of affairs is both a shame and an opportunity for those seeking uncrowded hunting grounds.

Rifle purists decry the use of a shotgun for small game, and they are, like most purists, annoying. Ignore them. Shotguns definitely have a place in the small-game fields.

325 GET THE SQUIRREL

Squirrel hunting with a shotgun resembles turkey hunting more than it does conventional wingshooting. You're in the woods, sitting, calling, and shooting at squirrels tightrope-walking through the branches, often aiming your shotgun as if it were a rifle. Here are a couple of things to consider.

GUNS AND GAUGES A 12, 16, or 20 gauge makes the most sense for squirrels, although you can shoot a Full-choked .410 if you limit your shots to 20 yards. Iron sights or a red dot on a 12 or 20 gauge turkey gun with Modified choke screwed into the barrel and a field load in the chamber might make the perfect squirrel shotgun.

CHOKES AND AMMO If you've skinned both rabbits and squirrels, you've found pellets stuck in the hide of a squirrel that would punch right through the fragile skin of a rabbit. Squirrels are tough, but not so tough you can't kill them with an ounce or so of 6s or 5s. Bear in mind that the very tallest oaks measure 100 feet (that's 33 yards) tall, in range of a modified barrel.

QUICK SHOT

327 THROW YOUR HAT IN

Hunting squirrels with a shotgun often means stalking right up to the tree underneath the squirrel. If it spots you and runs around the other side of the trunk, you can always try the old trick of throwing your hat to other side, in hopes of startling the squirrel back to your side of the tree.

326 SUCKER IN THOSE SQUIRRELS

The distress whistle of a young squirrel is the perfect call for shotgun hunters. It's a simple call to use: you blow (on some you suck air in) while thrashing a branch in the leaves to make a commotion. Squirrels come to the call, but in an extremely agitated manner—they think they are coming to rescue a juvenile from a predator—and they are ready to turn and run if they see the slightest movement. Your shots often come at moving or running squirrels, and they have to be taken quickly or not at all.

328 RUN DOWN THAT RABBIT

Rabbits running from beagles try to put distance between themselves and the dogs and then circle back to their hole, where you are lurking nearby. Be certain of where the dogs and the other hunters are, and don't shoot at a rabbit in front, as you might hit a beagle in the brush. Instead, take the rabbit as it goes by or is quartering away behind you, where it will be a close approximation to the bouncing rabbit on the sporting clays course.

As you turn to take the shot, keep the muzzle of your gun below the rabbit's line of flight (line of hop?), giving yourself a clear view of the target as you mount the gun. Otherwise, when the rabbit passes behind your gun your eye will go to the bead and the gun will stop. Remember, rabbits aren't as fast as they look: they can reach a brief top speed of 30 mph, which is 10 to 15 mph slower than the average game bird. Think about shooting it in the front toes —that's enough lead for all but the longest crossing shots.

330 BAG BRUSH BUSTING BUNNIES

Rabbits will sit tight until a dogless hunter pauses long enough (20 to 30 seconds) to unnerve them or kicks them out of the grass or a brushpile. When bunnies bolt from brush-busting hunters, they present a zig-zagging going-away shot. The best way to hit an erratic target is to focus on it tightly without trying to aim. Fix your eyes on the gap between the ears and resist the natural inclination to look at the tail (hint: it's there to distract predators) and back legs. Looking at the ears increases the chance of a head shot, decreases the chances of missing behind, and cuts down on the number of pellets you'll have to chew around when you eat the legs. As with ruffed grouse, don't be afraid to shoot as a rabbit disappears into brush. It only takes a few pellets.

329 EQUIP YOURSELF FOR RABBITS

Chances at rabbits come as quick snap shots at white tails and long ears bouncing through heavy cover or perhaps running or sneaking ahead of beagles. You will sometimes stalk sitting or slowly hopping rabbits and have time to shoot for the head.

GUNS AND GAUGE The ideal rabbit gun would be a 16 or 20 gauge that's light enough to carry in one hand while you fend off brush with the other. It should be capable of shooting two or more shots, although most rabbits are long gone before you can slap the trigger a third time. While iron sights don't belong on a rabbit gun, I might add a middle bead (about a $20 gunsmithing job) to help me aim the gun if I got a chance to head-shoot a sitting rabbit.

CHOKES AND LOADS Cottontails are nervous, thin-skinned, and fragile. Seven-eighths of an ounce to 1 ⅛ ounce of size 6 shot will suffice. The smaller the shot, the more pellets, and the greater the chance some will slip through holes in the underbrush. An Improved Cylinder choke works best in the briar patch.

331 CALL THE WILY COYOTE

Imagine trying to call a smart turkey that can smell you. Take away the feathers, add fur, and you've got coyote hunting, except that coyotes are coming to a call they think is a meal, giving you a little feeling for what it is like to be hunted. As coyotes have expanded their range to every state but Hawaii, so have hunters who enjoy the challenge, the easy access to hunting land (many landowners who won't let you hunt tastier animals welcome coyote hunters), and an extended season. Many coyote hunters pack shotguns along with their rifles, as coyotes sometimes come running to a call, presenting a fast-moving target better shot with a swarm of pellets than a single bullet. In fact, many prefer to just use a shotgun, both because shotgun pellets are easier on a pelt they may want to sell, and even more because calling coyotes inside of 50 yards for a good shot is far more exciting than plinking them at longer ranges with a rifle.

332 BARK AT THE BEAST

If a coyote comes in on the run, try to stop it with a bark for a standing shot. Some people use a call; others just make a guttural "woof." If this strategy doesn't work, and the coyote keeps running, be glad you brought a shotgun and not a rifle.

Remington Model 870

333 GET THE RIGHT COYOTE GUN

A coyote shotgun needs to shoot good patterns with big shot. It needs to be capable of quick follow-ups. And it should work equally well for running or standing targets. A 3-inch 12 gauge with the duck plug removed gives you five shots at a running coyote. Iron sights, a red dot, or a low-power scope help you make the shot. The gun should have a sling, for carrying in to your calling stands, and a choke that will give good patterns with BBs and buckshot. Test your factory modified choke first, then you might invest in an aftermarket model. Some of those will also run around modified constriction while others, for smaller shot, may be as tight as turkey chokes.

334 SHELL OUT FOR COYOTES

Coyotes are mostly made of fur. They look huge in the wild but even a very large coyote won't weigh 50 pounds, and its vital area (heart, lungs) is about the size of a volleyball. If you shoot premium tungsten-iron BBs and Ts or premium lead BB loads through the right choke, you can kill a coyote to 70 yards. To pattern your coyote gun and load, use an 8–9 inch circle or even a paper plate to simulate the vitals. Look for a load that will consistently put 2–3 pellets in it at your maximum range. While smaller shot puts more hits on target, some hunters prefer oo buck on the theory that one or two .33 caliber hits almost anywhere will kill or instantly disable a coyote.

335 STICK TO IT

Shooting sticks let you keep a gun at the ready as you sit or stand. Some hunters will put a rifle in the sticks and keep a shotgun in their hands to be prepared for a close-in shot or a long one. If you hunt with a shotgun only, sticks will steady it for a 70-plus yard shot and, just as important, keep the gun up and instantly ready as you wait.

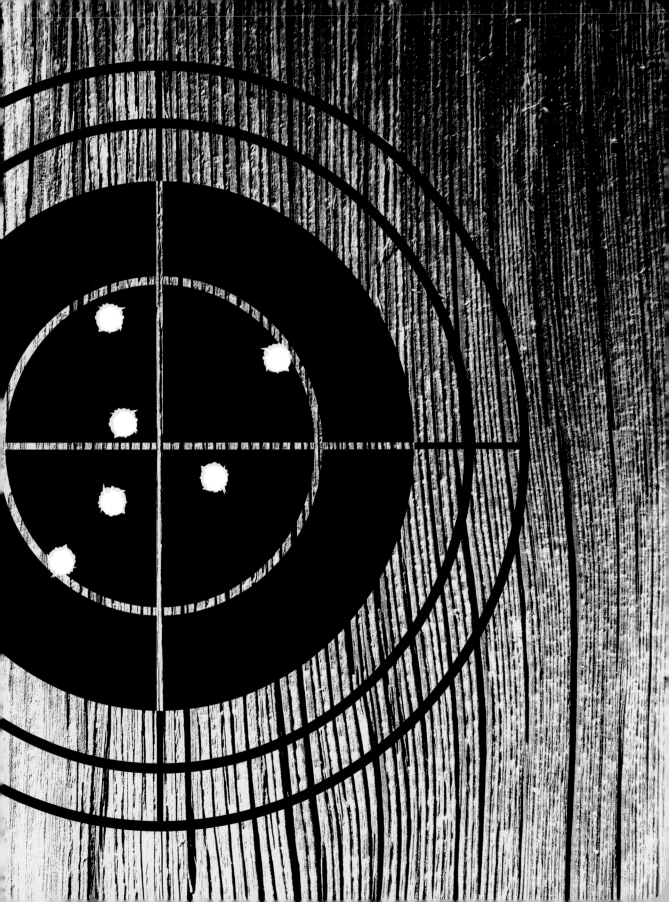

PETZAL SAYS

" The great pianist Ignace Paderewski famously said: 'If I do not practice for one day, I know it. If I miss the next day, the orchestra knows it. If I miss a third day, the audience knows it.'

Shooting, like playing the piano, is a perishable skill. The concentration and hand-eye coordination you acquire at the cost of much hard work can be lost very easily and very quickly.

A very few, very gifted people can simply pick up a rifle, shotgun, or handgun, and do well with it. I can't, and I doubt you can, either.

The really good shots I know are young and old, strong and weak, male and female, large and small. But the thing they all have in common is, they work at it all the time.

And so should you."

BOURJAILY SAYS

"When I was a kid, my dad threw a few clay targets for me. I hit them with a cut-down .410 and he pronounced me a 'natural shot'. Dad had little interest in target shooting and I didn't care much about hunting, so that was the end of my childhood shooting education.

Later, when I started hunting, I assumed was a natural shot because Dad told me I was and because I believed then, as many still do, that shooting is something you are born knowing how to do. I quickly learned how very untrue that is. I was not a good shot. At best I was no better than the average self-taught shotgunner and probably quite a bit worse since I never practiced.

It took me many years, thousands of rounds, several lessons and a lot of birds to become a good field shot. Believe me, if I can reach that point, anyone can, and I hope this book helps you get there."

GLOSSARY

ACTION The moving parts of a gun that allow it to be loaded, unloaded, and fired.

ADJUSTABLE COMB A comb that can be moved up and down, and side to side to fit a shooter; usually found on target guns.

AUTOMATIC SAFETY A safety found on some break-action shotguns that engages whenever the gun is opened.

BALLISTIC COEFFICIENT The mathematical expression of the relationship between a bullet's shape, weight, length, and diameter. A higher BC means a more streamlined bullet and better long-range performance.

BARREL SELECTOR A mechanism that allows the shooter of a single-trigger double to choose which barrel fires first.

BASE The bottom of the bullet. It can be either squared or boattail.

BEAVERTAIL FOREND A wide, hand-filling forend found on target guns and some doubles.

BEST GRADE A reference to the custom-built sidelock guns developed and refined by the British gun trade.

BONDED CORE A lead core that is joined permanently to the jacket. This is done chemically or by soldering. Bore The inside of a shotgun or rifle barrel. In England, "bore" is also used to refer to the gauge of a shotgun.

BOX LOCK The most popular style of double gun action. The Anson & Deeley box lock was the hammerless action developed in 1875 and is still in use today.

BREAK ACTION A gun that opens on a hinge at the breech to allow loading and unloading.

CANELLURE A circumferential groove in the bullet jacket into which the case mouth can be crimped.

CARRIER STOP BUTTON A button that must be pushed in order to lock the bolt in an open position. Found on many semiautomatic shotguns.

CAST A lateral bend of the stock right ("cast off") or left ("cast on") to put the shooter's eye directly over the barrel.

CHOKE An internal constriction at the end of the muzzle that controls the spread of shot to create more or less open patterns. Measured in thousandths of an inch (e.g. .010").

COMB The top side of a gun's buttstock, where the shooter's cheek rests while aiming and firing.

CORE The main mass of a bullet. Usually made of lead or a harder lead alloy, or occasionally other materials such as steel or tungsten.

DOUBLE Any gun with two barrels, although the term usually refers to a side-by-side. Also used for taking two birds or targets with two shots, or accidentally firing both barrels at once.

DROP The distance from the rib to the comb measured at the front of the comb ("drop at comb" and at the buttplate "drop at heel").

FORCING CONE The tapered section between the chamber and the bore. Most forcing cones are fairly short, around half an inch, but some factory guns have lengthened or "relieved" forcing cones to improve patterns and reduce felt recoil.

GAUGE "Caliber" of a shotgun; a measure based on the number of lead balls of the bore diameter equal to one pound. 10, 12, 16, 20, and 28 are the five popular gauges. The .410 is actually a bore diameter (it would be a 67-gauge).

HEADSPACE The distance between the bolt face and whatever part of the chamber stops the forward motion of a cartridge when the bolt is closed. All guns have headspace; too little, and a round won't feed; too much, and the case may rupture when firing the gun.

IMPROVED CARTRIDGE A cartridge with a case that has had most or all of its taper removed and its shoulder blown out to a sharper angle than it had originally. The increased power capacity may make a round more efficient by causing the powder to burn in the case rather than the barrel. Improved cartridges don't feed as well as rounds with more body taper and less acute shoulders.

INERTIA TRIGGER A trigger on a two-barreled gun that uses the recoil of the first shot to reset the mechanism for the second.

JACKET The casing enclosing the core. Made of pure copper, or a harder alloy called gilding metal.

LEAD The distance needed to shoot in front of a moving target to hit it. Also known as forward allowance.

LENGTH OF PULL The distance from the center of the butt pad to the front center of the trigger.

LOCK TIME The interval between the trigger's releasing the sear and the firing pin's striking the primer. Errors like flinching can move the muzzle between the time you squeeze the trigger and the time the rifle goes off, so quick lock time is highly desirable.

MECHANICAL TRIGGER A single-trigger mechanism that does require recoil to reset between shots.

MEPLAT Pronounced MEE-plat. The very tip of the bullet.

MIRAGE Image distortion caused by heat waves rising off a rifle barrel, usually causing the target to appear higher than it actually is.

MONTE CARLO STOCK A special stock with a raised comb, often seen on trap guns. It allows shooters to keep their heads upright, and is often a good fit for people with long necks.

MOUNT The act of raising the gun to a firing position.

OGIVE Pronounced OH-jive. The curved or rounded section of the bullet leading from the shank to the meplat.

OVERBORE To widen a shotgun's barrel to larger than nominal diameter to improve performance.

OVERBORE CAPACITY Used to describe a cartridge which holds more powder than it can burn efficiently. This is true of all magnum rounds that use disproportionately large powder charges in return for relatively small velocity gains over standard cases.

PATTERN The spread of shot downrange. As a verb, "to pattern" is the act of shooting a shotgun at paper to determine the size and effectiveness of the pattern. Results are usually expressed as the percentage of pellets striking a 30-inch circle at 40 yards.

PILLAR BEDDING The process of enlarging the bedding-screw holes in a wooden or synthetic stock, and reinforcing them with fiberglass, or by having aluminum tubes glued in them. Eliminates the stock's tendency to compress when tightening bedding screws, and often improves accuracy.

PISTOL GRIP A curved grip that gives the shooter's trigger hand added control of the gun.

PITCH The angle of the buttstock.

PLUG (aka "duck plug") A rod that fits into the magazine of a pump or semiauto shotgun, limiting the capacity of a magazine to two shells in compliance with federal migratory bird hunting regulations.

POINT OF IMPACT Where a gun shoots the center of its pattern relative to the point of aim if you were to sight down the rib. A gun that shoots exactly to point of aim is said to shoot 50/50—half the pattern above, half below. Many target shooters prefer a gun that shoots above POI.

PRINCE OF WALES GRIP A gently curved grip halfway between straight and full pistol.

RECOIL REDUCER A weight, spring, or hydraulic damper that reduces a gun's recoil. Usually fitted inside the buttstock, but barrel- and magazine cap-mounted models also exist.

RIB A flat-topped piece of metal running along the top of a shotgun's barrel; provides a flat sight plane and helps dissipate barrel heat.

SABOT A two-piece sleeve that encases a bullet or slug of less than bore diameter. The sabot engages the barrel's rifling as it travels down the bore, then separates as it exits the muzzle leaving the slug to travel downrange.

SEAR Part of the trigger that holds back a gun's hammer or firing pin until enough pressure is applied to the trigger.

SECTIONAL DENSITY The mathematical expression of a bullet's weight relative to its length. A 180-grain .30-caliber bullet has a higher SD than a 150-grain bullet of the same diameter, and will retain its velocity better at long range and shoot flatter despite the fact that the lighter bullet starts out faster.

SHANK The straight section of the bullet, between base and ogive.

SCHNABEL FOREND A thin forend used on O/Us that ends in a distinctive downward curve.

SHOT STRING The column of shot pellets strung out in a line after leaving the muzzle of a shotgun.

SIDE LOCK A double gun action in which all the parts of the lock are mounted on sideplates, usually removable for access and repair.

SLUG A single lead projectile used for hunting deer-sized game.

SPLINTER FOREND A very thin forend found on classic doubles.

STRAIGHT GRIP A shotgun grip without any curve. Also called an English stock.

TURKEY CHOKE An extra-full choke designed to shoot dense patterns for hitting turkeys in the head and neck.

WEIGHT OF PULL The amount of force required to cause a trigger to release the sear. Rifles operate within narrow weight ranges. For a big-game rifle, the acceptable range is 3 to 4 pounds. For varmint rifles, it can be much less. A heavy trigger pull reduces accuracy.

INDEX

ABOUT THE AUTHORS

DAVID E. PETZAL is the Rifles Field Editor of *Field & Stream*. He has been with the publication since 1972. A graduate of Colgate University, he served in the US Army from 1963 to 1969, and he began writing about rifles and rifle shooting in 1964, during his service. He is a Benefactor Member of the National Rifle Association and a Life Member of the Amateur Trapshooting Association. He has hunted all over the United States and Canada, as well as in Europe, Africa, and New Zealand. Petzal wrote *The .22 Rifle* and edited *The Encyclopedia of Sporting Firearms*. In 2002, he was awarded the Leupold Jack Slack Writer of the Year Award, and in 2005 he received the Zeiss Outdoor Writer of the Year Award, making him the first person to win both. His writing ability and knowledge of firearms are often referred to as "godlike."

PHIL BOURJAILY sold his first outdoor story—on snipe hunting—to *Field & Stream* in 1985. Today, he is the magazine's Shotguns columnist and co-writer, with David Petzal, of "The Gun Nuts" blog on Fieldandstream.com. He is the author of the *Field & Stream Turkey Hunting Handbook* and, as a turkey hunter, has renounced early mornings in favor of sleeping in and killing spring gobblers between the hours of 9 AM and 2 PM. A 1981 graduate of the University of Virginia, he makes his home today, with his wife and two sons, in his birthplace of Iowa City, Iowa. He has traveled widely in pursuit of upland birds, waterfowl, and turkeys, but his favorite hunts are for pheasants close to home with his German shorthaired pointer, Jed.

ABOUT THE MAGAZINE

In every issue of *Field & Stream* you'll find a lot of stuff: beautiful photography and artwork, adventure stories, wild game recipes, humor, commentary, reviews, and more. That mix is what makes the magazine so great, what's helped it remain relevant since 1895. But at the heart of every issue are the skills. The tips that explain how to improve your range accuracy, the tactics that help you shoot the deer of your life, the lessons that you'll pass on to your kids about the joy of shooting—those are the stories that readers have come to expect from *Field & Stream*.

You'll find a ton of those skills in *The Total Gun Manual*, but there's not a book big enough to hold them all in one volume. Besides, whether you're new to shooting or an old pro, there's always more to learn. You can continue to expect *Field & Stream* to teach you those essential skills in every issue. Plus, there's all that other stuff in the magazine, too, which is pretty great. To order a subscription, visit www.fieldandstream.com/subscription.

ABOUT THE WEBSITE

When *Field & Stream* readers aren't hunting or fishing, they kill hours (and hours) on www.fieldandstream.com. And once you visit the site, you'll understand why.

First, if you enjoy the skills and opinions in this book, there's plenty more online—both within our extensive archives of stories from the writers featured here, as well as our network of 50,000-plus experts who can answer all of your questions about the outdoors.

At Fieldandstream.com, you'll get to explore the world's largest online destination for hunters and anglers. Our blogs, written by the leading experts in the outdoors, cover every facet of hunting and fishing and provide constant content that instructs, enlightens, and always entertains.

Our collection of adventure videos contains footage that's almost as thrilling to watch as it is to experience for real. And our photo galleries include the best wildlife and outdoor photography you'll find anywhere.

Perhaps best of all is the community you'll find at Fieldandstream.com. It's where you can argue with other readers about the best whitetail cartridge or the perfect venison chili recipe. It's where you can share photos of the fish you catch and the game you shoot. It's where you can enter contests to win guns, gear, and other great prizes. And it's a place where you can spend a lot of time. Which is okay. Just make sure to reserve some hours for the outdoors, too.

ACKNOWLEDGMENTS

DAVID E. PETZAL: I would like to thank every one with whom I have ever hunted or shot, because I've learned from all of you.

PHIL BOURJAILY: Rob James and Mariah Bear of Weldon Owen held my hand every step of the way during this project, as did Dave Hurteau of *Field & Stream*. I would not be half of The Gun Nuts had Dave Petzal not made the blog a success before I joined it, and I would not be shotgun editor of *Field & Stream* had Deputy Editor Slaton White not taken an interest in a pheasant hunter from Iowa 20 years ago.

Thanks to everyone at *Field & Stream*, especially Editor-in-Chief Anthony Licata, Senior Editor Mike Toth, and Online Editor Dave Maccar. Finally, I'd like to give special thanks for the help and support of my wife Pam.

CREDITS

Illustrations Courtesy of: *Conor Buckley:* back cover (bullet), 43, 52, 59, 65, 189, 192, 207, 210, 257, 291 *Hayden Foell:* back cover (shot dynamics), 53, 102, 107, 125, 195, 229, 236, 237, 242, 243 247, 260, 266, 271 *Flyingchilli.com:* 303 *Raymond Larrett:* 123, 126, 169, 239, 283, 286, 335 *Joe McKendry:* author portraits throughout *Chris Philpot:* 261 *Robert L. Prince:* 12, 86, 165 *Mike Sudal:* 80, 94, 98, 112 *Bryon Thompson:* 283 *Lauren Towner:* back cover (man aiming rifle), 29, 40, 48, 61, 76, 83, 231, 234, 323

weldon**owen**

President, CEO Terry Newell
VP, Publisher Roger Shaw
Executive Editor Mariah Bear
Project Editor Rob James
Editorial Assistant Ian Cannon
Creative Director Kelly Booth
Art Director William Mack
Illustration Coordinator Conor Buckley
Production Director Chris Hemesath
Production Manager Michelle Duggan

Weldon Owen would also like to thank Amy Bauman,
Andrew Joron, Katie Schlossberg, and Jan Spauschus for
editorial assistance. Katie Cavenee, Sarah Edelstein, and
Jenna Rosenthal provided design and production help.

Library of Congress Control Number
on file with the publisher
Flexi Edition ISBN 978-1-61628-219-6
Hardcover Edition ISBN 978-1-61628-432-9
10
2014
Printed in China by 1010 Printing International

VP, Group Publisher Eric Zinczenko
Editorial Director, Anthony Licata
Executive Editor Mike Toth
Managing Editor Jean McKenna
Deputy Editors Dave Hurteau, Colin Kearns, Slaton L. White
Copy Chief Donna Ng
Senior Editor Joe Cermele
Assistant Editor Kristyn Brady
Design Director Sean Johnston
Photography Director John Toolan
Deputy Art Director Pete Sucheski
Associate Art Directors Kim Eddy, James A. Walsh
Production Manager Judith Webber
Digital Director Nate Matthews
Online Content Editor David Maccar
Online Producer Kurt Shulitz
Assistant Online Editor Sarah Smith Barnum

2 Park Avenue
New York, NY 10016
www.fieldandstream.com